Advance Praise for *Black Faces in White Places*

"*Black Faces in White Places* is both a thoughtful progress made by African Americans in the workplace and a sobering wake-up call for how much work remains to be done. This book will undoubtedly spark dialogue, but above all, it will help to spawn much needed action to ensure that we continue to make progress." —Dr. Johnnetta Betsch Cole, President Emerita, Spelman College and Bennett College for Women

"I have a great deal of respect for Dr. Randal Pinkett and the intelligent way he approaches individual and entrepreneurial achievement. His spirit and desire to help others is truly inspiring." —Hill Harper, Emmy-Nominated Actor, Author and Activist

"*Black Faces in White Places* is a timeless encapsulation of everything you wanted to know about being an African American professional in the 21st century. Your success today will largely depend upon your mindset and skill set. This book is a compass to lead you into getting out of your head and stepping into your greatness." —Les Brown, Speaker, Speech Coach, and Author

"I hope readers of any race or class find valuable insights and nuances in this book that will allow them to advance and help others in the process. Our differences are something to be thankful for, and there are great opportunities within those differences for everyone to excel." —Majora Carter, Environmental Activist

"Finally, a book that addresses what all African Americans talk about in private but rarely discuss in a public forum. *Black Faces in White Places* is bold, powerful, and inspiring. The content in this book confirms my approach to life: I am my best in every setting. Drs. Pinkett and Robinson not only show us how to be successful but also how to look beyond color to reach the goal of achieving success by the merit of our work without losing sight of our true authentic selves." —Ledisi, Grammy-Nominated Soul, R&B, and Jazz Artist

"With this book a new voice of clarity and leadership has emerged for African Americans. Dr. Pinkett and Dr. Robinson provide a direct and blunt assessment of what is required for Black professionals to succeed —a road map for success —along with the knowledge needed for liberation. Leveraging lessons and context from history —along with powerful and forthright advice, there is sustenance for both the career and the soul in this book. I have never read a better personal advice book and have never seen a book that imparted more knowledge with better efficiency. Phenomenal." —Luke Visconti, Chief Executive Officer, DiversityInc

"*Black Faces in White Places* deals directly with the contemporary role of race—its subtleties, its nuances, and its impact—in almost every professional arena. More importantly, the book offers ten proven and practical strategies to overcome the inevitable challenges." —Sean Covey, Bestselling Author of *The 7 Habits of Highly Effective Teens* and *The 6 Most Important Decisions You'll Ever Make: A Guide for Teens*

"*Black Faces in White Places* goes beyond how to be the only person of color in an institution to creating a strategy to own the institution." —Jeff Johnson, Journalist and Author

"This book is a must-read for anyone running to win in the race against racism." —Dr. Farrah Gray, Bestselling Author and Syndicated Columnist

"In the Age of Obama, African Americans are realizing an unprecedented potential to define ourselves beyond 'otherness.' *Black Faces in White Places* gives the individual a thoughtful guide to this cultural crossroad. This book needed to be written." —Tatyana Ali, Actress, Producer, and Activist, HazraH Entertainment

"Drs. Pinkett and Robinson choose to BE the message that they bring! They don't just enumerate the problems but offer solid solutions for navigating pathways to business ownership, and the halls and boardrooms of previously 'all white' corporate America. *Black Faces in White Places* is a necessary tool for anyone trying to make their own magic happen." —Malik Yoba, Actor/Musician/Entrepreneur

"From the time America met Randal Pinkett on *The Apprentice,* it was easy to see that he was an extraordinarily gifted person. He quickly showed, with his trademark intellect and style, why he has become one of the leading voices of the latest generation of business leaders. In *Black Faces in White Places,* Pinkett and Jeffrey Robinson share how to navigate the rough waters of the business world. They give a straightforward way for minorities to deal with the rigors and issues that can sometimes sidetrack a climb to the top of the corporate ladder or business ownership. Pinkett and Robinson give a new face on corporate America and entrepreneurship and share strategies that will allow others to become the best they can be no matter what hurdles they may face." —Ed Gordon, Broadcast Journalist and Executive Producer, *Ed Gordon*, Bounce TV

"We have all been there, we have all thought it; finally Drs. Randal Pinkett and Jeffrey Robinson have captured it in words—powerful words. *Black Faces in White Places* not only puts the issue of 'being the only one' in perspective, it gives us direction and skills to cope." —Herman "Skip" Mason, 33rd General President, Alpha Phi Alpha Fraternity, Inc.

"*Black Faces in White Places* takes an issue out of the recesses of the minds of people of color and puts it in words to which we can all relate. Thank you, Drs. Randal Pinkett and Jeffrey Robinson for giving voice, reason, and solutions to a problem as old as the ages." —Kevin Powell, Writer, Speaker, and Activist

"Randal Pinkett and Jeffrey Robinson have produced a tremendous resource for leadership development and community transformation. I would highly recommend anyone in the position of leadership to read Pinkett's book, or any student of leadership should have a copy of this book on their shelf." —Rev. Otis Moss III, Pastor, Trinity United Methodist Church

"Broad access to opportunity is the key to a truly equitable America. No matter who you are or where you grew up, *Black Faces in White Places* provides a blueprint to seizing opportunities at hand—and expanding opportunity for your entire community." —Angela Glover-Blackwell, Founder and CEO, PolicyLink

"Dr. King once asked the question, 'Will you be a thermometer or a thermostat?' *Black Faces in White Places* is both. It tells us the current temperature in business and corporate America for minorities—and how we can change it. For all minorities in the corporate world or looking to grow their own company, this is a must-read book!" —Warren Ballentine, Attorney and Nationally Syndicated Radio Host

"Forget about playing the game by existing rules. In *Black Faces in White Places,* Pinkett and Robinson provide the tools to redefine the game and create an entirely new set of rules. A timeless book in the Age of Obama that allows everyone to win!" —Kwame Jackson, Entrepreneur/Speaker/Author; CEO and Founder, "Krimson by Kwame" Executive Neckwear

"As someone who has been a Black face in a white place on the stage of Miss America to the halls of Georgetown Law School, on the gridiron as a sports and entertainment attorney, and even competing alongside my brother Randal on NBC's *The Apprentice,* I can attest that the formula outlined inside this book is a must-know for people of color. *Black Faces in White Places* shows that life is not about the challenges you face, which will be many. It is about how you face them. Bravo for cracking the code of conduct and challenging us all to take our talents to the next level." —Marshawn Evans, Attorney, TV Personality, Best-Selling Author , and President of ME Unlimited

"Regardless of whether you want to climb the corporate ladder and become an executive or create your own ladder and become an entrepreneur, *Black Faces in White Places* is an absolutely essential tool for your professional tool belt." —Stacie J, Entrepreneur, Jones Insurance Group and the "Stacie J Golden" Fragrance

"*Black Faces in White Places* is everything that business schools are too polite to teach. Whether you want to play by the rules or change the game, Drs. Pinkett and Robinson offer cutting-edge advice. Once I reached the last page, it became obvious that Randal and Jeffrey not only can see down the street, they can see around the corner." —Dennis Kimbro, Author of *What Makes the Great Great*

"The ten strategies found in *Black Faces in White Places* represent the complete roadmap for people of color to transform their careers, transform our communities, and transform this nation. This book could not have come at a better time." —The Three Doctors: Sampson Davis, MD; Rameck Hunt, MD; and George Jenkins, DMD

"WOW, this book is a game changer. Thank you so much Pinkett and Robinson for these insights, gems, and nuggets of brilliance. You and your team have put your heart and soul into this important masterwork. I was not only informed and inspired but also empowered by your impressive research and collection of thoughts, words, and ideas. This book is a prescription for our success, and everyone can benefit from reading *Black Faces in White Places*. My heartfelt thanks go out to each of you for giving us this important gem." —George C. Fraser, Author of *Success Runs in Our Race* and *Click*

"*Black Faces in White Places* is an indispensable resource for navigating personal and professional pathways not only to achieving success, but most importantly, achieving greatness. It is an absolute must for students, young adults and seasoned professionals alike." —Alonzo Adams, Award-Winning Artist

"There are written and unwritten rules for African Americans . . . and then there is *Black Faces in White Places*. This long overdue book offers the ten essential strategies that will redefine the rules and help level the playing field for people of all races, ethnicities, creeds, and colors." —David Steward, Founder and Chairman of the Board, World Wide Technology

"What distinguishes *Black Faces in White Places* from previous books geared toward African American professionals is that it speaks to a broad range of audiences: entrepreneurs, academics, lawyers, teachers, politicians, doctors, ministers, corporate executives, and far beyond. It addresses how to achieve greatness in almost any field while maintaining a critical sense of identity and purpose." —Zack Lemelle, Vice President, Information Technology, Johnson & Johnson; Chairman of the Board, Information Technology Senior Management Forum

"Much has been made, and rightfully so, of the need for America's institutions to embrace diversity and inclusion in anticipation of the 'browning' of America. However, not enough has been provided in the way of survival and success strategies for those brown pioneers, many of them African American, who must brave and conquer frontiers their parents could scarcely dream of. *Black Faces in White Places: 10 Game-Changing Strategies to Achieve Success and Find Greatness* is the much-needed playbook that will empower this intrepid generation with the confidence and courage to meet the challenge." —Alfred Edmond, Jr., Senior Vice President/Editor in Chief, BlackEnterprise.com

"*Black Faces in White Places* is insightful, compelling, and very smartly written. Pinkett and Robinson use a contemporary voice that speaks loudly to address critical issues that nearly every professional of color must face at different points in their careers." —Sheryl P. Underwood, International President, Zeta Phi Beta Sorority, Inc.; CEO, Pack Rat Productions, Incorporated

"*Black Faces in White Places* is required reading for African Americans at any stage of their career, including college students, young professionals entering the workplace, and even those who have reached the middle and upper levels of established organizations. Drs. Randal Pinkett and Jeffrey Robinson capture in words an issue that affects all people of color —and they offer viable solutions and coping skills to address the issue." —Dr. Charles E. Jones, Founding Chair, Department of African-American Studies, Georgia State University; President, National Council for Black Studies

"Dr. Randal Pinkett and Dr. Jeffrey Robinson's *Black Faces in White Places* should be required reading for all of us as the nation struggles to find its way to and through the much-heralded "post-racial" era. Pinkett and Robinson invite us into the heads and hearts and lives of professionals of color whose careers require in equal measure boundary-crossing, modern day passing, relentless advocacy and a keen sense of survival. Through it all, Pinkett and Robinson paint a portrait of those who bear the burden and pay the price to create more hopeful futures for those who follow." —Ralph R. Smith, Executive Vice President, Annie E. Casey Foundation

"Drs. Pinkett and Robinson are geniuses whose gifts and talents are contributing to the empowerment of many others. Their writing reflects the depth of academic preparation and the practicality of user friendliness. Anyone who is attempting to expand their capacity or increase their productivity can benefit from the wisdom found in *Black Faces in White Places*." —DeForest B. Soaries, Jr., Senior Pastor, First Baptist Church of Lincoln Gardens

"*Black Faces in White Places* is a deeply personal journey to find answers to the critical questions that almost every professional of color wrestles with at various stages of their career." —Rey Ramsey, Managing Partner, Centri Capital, and Founder and Chairman, One Economy Corporation

"*Black Faces in White Places* will usher in an entirely new wave of talented intrapreneurs who transform existing organizations ranging from corporations and schools to non-profit and faith-based organizations. It will also spawn a new cadre of entrepreneurs and social entrepreneurs who launch new ventures that generate wealth and empower communities." —Gwen Kelly, Multicultural Marketing Executive

"As people of color move from being 'minorities' to the majority of Americans, *Black Faces in White Places* tackles the challenges and the opportunities that emerge from this imminent reality." —Darryl Cobb, Chief Executive Officer, Academy of Communications and Technology Charter School

"*Black Faces in White Places* will spark an entirely new conversation about the role African Americans can play in leveling the playing field for people of all races, ethnicities, creeds, and colors." —Treena Livingston Arinzeh, Ph.D., Associate Professor, Biomedical Engineering, New Jersey Institute of Technology

"The combination of proven, practical strategies along with real-world stories from accomplished African Americans offers unique insight into the subtleties and nuances of exactly what it takes to succeed in any profession." —Dudley Benoit, Community Development Professional

Black Faces
in
White Places

10 Game-Changing Strategies to
Achieve Success and Find Greatness

RANDAL PINKETT AND
JEFFREY ROBINSON
WITH
PHILANA PATTERSON

Foreword by
Roland S. Martin

HARPERCOLLINS
LEADERSHIP

AN IMPRINT OF HARPERCOLLINS

Everything is Everything. Written by Lauryn N. Hill, Johari Jermone Newton, Tejumold Ramone Newton, and Vada J. Nobles, and performed by Lauryn Hill. © 1998 Sony/ATV Tunes LLC and Obverse Creation Music, Inc. All rights administered by Sony/ATV Music Publishing, 8 Music Square West, Nashville, TN 37203. All rights reserved. Used by permission.
Imagine Me. Words and Music by Kirk Franklin. Copyright © 2006 by Universal Music—Z Songs, Kerrion Publishing and Lilly Mack Publishing. All Rights for Kerrion Publishing Administered by Universal Music—Z Songs. All Rights for Lilly Mack Publishing Administered by EMI CMG Publishing. International Copyright Secured. All Rights Reserved. Reprinted by permission of Hal Leonard Corporation.
Imagine Me. Written and performed by Kirk Franklin. Copyright © 2005 Lilly Mack Publishing (BMI) (Administered by EMI Christian Music Group Publishing)/Kerrion Publishing (BMI) All rights reserved. Used by permission.

Published by HarperCollins Leadership, an imprint of HarperCollins.

Library of Congress Cataloging-in-Publication Data
Pinkett, Randal.
Black faces in white places : 10 game-changing strategies to achieve success and find greatness / Randal Pinkett and Jeffrey Robinson, with Philana Patterson.
    p. cm.
Includes bibliographical references and index.
ISBN-13: 978-0-8144-3997-5
ISBN-10: 0-8144-3997-7
1. African American businesspeople—Psychology. 2. African Americans—Race identity. 3. Discrimination in employment—United States. 4. Success in business—United States. I. Robinson, Jeffrey, 1971– II. Patterson, Philana. III. Title.
E185.625.P52 2011
650.1—dc22

2010020878

978-0-8144-3997-5

Printed in the United States of America
18 19 20 21 22 LSC 10 9 8 7 6 5 4 3 2 1

To my daughter, Amira Leslie. I pray that our generation will indeed "redefine the game" and create a better world for your generation and those who follow.

—Randal

To my children: Gabriella Imani, Michael Jeffrey, and Zachary Mason. May this book be a guide for you in your life journey.

——J.R.

CONTENTS

Foreword XV

Acknowledgments XIX

Introduction 1

Not Getting Trumped: Randal's Nationally Televised
"Black Faces in White Places" Moment 1

The Four Dimensions of Black Faces in White Places 9

A Roadmap for Redefining the Game and Reshaping America 14

The 10 Game-Changing Strategies to Achieve Success and Find Greatness 16

PART I: LEARNING THE GAME **21**

America's Story: The United States and Race 21

Learning What the Game Is All About 23

Strategy 1: Establish a Strong Identity and Purpose **28**

Identity 29

Purpose 35

Identity and Purpose for African Americans 37

Self-Determination: Your Identity as an Asset
and Your Purpose as a Source of Power 45

The Interdependence of Strategies 1 and 2 47

Strategy 2: Obtain Broad Exposure **48**

Your Comfort Zone and Growth Zone 50

Why Moving Beyond Your Comfort Zone Is Important 51

Pursuing Broad Exposure and Diverse Experiences 54

Looking Back, Looking Ahead 56

Strategy 3: Demonstrate Excellence **58**

One Playing Field, Two Sets of Rules 60

Defining Excellence 62

Why You Must Be Excellent 79

Game-Changing Strategies for Demonstrating Excellence 80

From Independence to Interdependence 86

PART II: PLAYING THE GAME **87**

Three Trends in a More Interconnected World 87

Relationship Building: The Power of Connectedness 89

Playing the Game: Relationships, Relationships, Relationships 91

Strategy 4: Build Diverse and Solid Relationships **92**

Personal Diversity 93

Relationship Building 96

Three Compelling Ideas about Relationships 98

The Strength of Weak Ties 99

Bridging Network Gaps 102

Game-Changing Strategies for
Networking and Relationship Building 107

Strategy 5: Seek the Wisdom of Others **110**

What Is Wisdom? 110

The Five Tenets of Seeking Wisdom 112

Developmental Relationships 114

Mentors and Protégés 117

Game-Changing Strategies for Mentors and Protégés 121

Strategy 6: Find Strength in Numbers **126**

The Power of Strength in Numbers: Don Imus Gets Taken Down 126

Group Relationships 131

Strength in Smaller Numbers: Inner Circles, Teams, and Partnerships 134

Strength in Smaller Numbers Leads to Strength in Larger Numbers 143

Strength in Larger Numbers: Organizations 144

Game-Changing Strategies for Organizational Involvement. 150

Strength in Numbers Sets the Stage 155

PART III: MASTERING THE GAME. **157**

The Entrepreneurial Mindset 157

Intrapreneurship and Entrepreneurship 158

Five Ways to Master the Game 161

A Two-Pronged Approach for Redefining the Game 163

Strategy 7: Think and Act Intrapreneurially **165**

African-American Intrapreneurship 166

Game-Changing Strategies for Intrapreneurship 168

Social Intrapreneurship and Community
Investment as a Competitive Advantage 178

The Cycle Continues 182

Strategy 8: Think and Act Entrepreneurially **183**

African-American Wealth Creation 185

Applying the Entrepreneurial Mindset 191

Game-Changing Strategies for Entrepreneurship for a Profit. 194

Social Entrepreneurship 200

Game-Changing Strategies for Entrepreneurship for a Purpose. 203

Institution Building 210

PART IV: REDEFINING THE GAME **213**

Prerequisites to Redefining the Game 213

What We Mean by "Redefining the Game" 215

Changing the Game vs. Redefining the Game. 216

Strategy 9: Synergize and Reach Scale **219**

Creating Synergy 219

Reaching Scale and Expanding Scope 222

Profiles of Synergy, Scale, and Scope 224

The Critical Importance of Synergy
and Scale to African Americans 228

Strategy 10: Give Back Generously **233**

Leaving a Positive Legacy 234

America's Shape and Reshaping America 239

The African-American Tradition of Giving. 240

The Four Foundations of Giving 244

Strategy 10 to Strategy 1: Identity and Purpose Revisited 249

Final Quotations and Final Questions on Giving Back 251

What Does Redefining the Game
and Reshaping America Mean to You?. 251

Epilogue: Is Success the Standard or Is Greatness the Goal? **253**

Success vs. Greatness 254

Notes 259

Index 261

About the Authors 267

F O R E W O R D

It is an arduous road to get there. Its path is laced with obstacles and dangers and pitfalls and traps. Those who make it will find that when they finally arrive—they will likely be alone and will be left to their own devices with only grains of guidance, no direction, and little advice. The euphoria of success is tempered with the reality that in this place, their degrees will mean little, their past accomplishments even less, and the experience and talents that brought them here will be put to the test—a new test, never before given—and one whose rules are ever-changing. It is not a reality show, but it is real. It is all part of "the game"—a very serious competition.

Drs. Randal Pinkett and Jeffrey Robinson have opened the door to a place that few have talked about but many have experienced—that phenomenon of being "a Black face in a white place." It is a life that many have had to confront, especially from the end of the 1960s to present day. This book captures in words the essence of the lives of thousands of Americans who dove headfirst into the exclusive waters of corporate America's most guarded pool. They invaded education's most honored institutions, and they had the audacity to proclaim their place as business owners, elected officials, and community leaders. They emerged as significant figures in the philanthropic, nonprofit, and religious sectors. The places they were are places few of "us" had ever been or seen. Some struggled, some floated, and a few actually swam against the tide and survived to give birth to others.

It is sobering that in 2010, African Americans are still underrepresented in several fields and in some cases grossly absent at the highest levels. Yet most successful people of color can tell you a story of being the only one in the group of their particular race or ethnic group. The money doesn't matter. The prestige of the title on their business card is irrelevant. The fear of having to be a company's Jackie Robinson—the only one shouldering the burden of an entire race—is difficult to bear unless you have been heavily fortified by your upbringing and have a strong core group of friends and family to lean on in the difficult times.

These modern day warriors can tell you the stories of the loneliness and the fear, the apprehension and the challenges. Now, this book captures that, and perhaps most importantly, offers solutions to make it easier for those who will follow in their footsteps. This is not just about corporate America—it is applicable to almost every professional endeavor you can imagine, from scientist and entertainer to pastor and entrepreneur to student and educator, and beyond. The areas of discipline are many, the issues are real, and from this the readers will be entertained, enlightened, and informed.

I have interviewed people from around the world, including leaders of major industrialized nations, corporate magnates, and celebrities. In far too many instances, I have heard stories of how people become successful—how to *get there.* This book gives sound advice on how to be the most effective while you *are there*—and how you can *stay there.* Drs. Robinson and Pinkett are well researched and thorough in this regard. However, they reach beyond the statistics to offer ten simple strategies for a wide range of circumstances. Their "10 Game-Changing Strategies" should be for people of color what Stephen Covey's "7 Habits" were for highly effective people.

In addition to giving tools of survival, *Black Faces in White Places* encourages the reader to pursue greatness. Far too many of us are content with being successful, but not enough of us venture on that divine quest for greatness. Drs. Pinkett and Robinson admonish each of us to find our greatness by using our God-given gifts, individually and collectively, to "Give Back Generously." This is a concept that has sustained us as a people for generations. Were it not for those who crowned themselves as guardians and keepers in our community, there could not have been the kinds of accomplishments we celebrate today. These were people who reached beyond their grasp to pull others ahead, thus creating scores of individuals who would perform in like fashion. They weren't in it to win it for themselves; it was always about the next brother or sister, the next generation, the next millennium.

Another great thing about this work is that it stresses the importance of building bridges to other races, genders, and ethnicities, and reinforces the need to create coalitions that can address the issues affecting us all. Ultimately, this book draws upon our cultural and spiritual foundation as a source of strength and a means to transform America.

I am inspired when I read this work. I am empowered to share it with others and I know that you will too. This is not something we can afford to keep to ourselves. There are so many more who will follow and we must encourage them to lead with the ten measured strategies given to us in this book. We must, as Drs. Pinkett and Robinson put it, "redefine the game."

Your greatness awaits you. The question that only you can answer is, "What are you prepared to do?"

Roland S. Martin
Host and Managing Editor, TV One Cable Network,
and Senior Analyst, *The Tom Joyner Morning Show*

ACKNOWLEDGMENTS

Black Faces in White Places has truly been a team effort. This five-year project has embodied the core principles of Strategy 4: Build Diverse and Solid Relationships and Strategy 6: Find Strength in Numbers by involving the coordinated and dedicated efforts of many different people. Without their assistance, support, and guidance this book would never have been possible. First and foremost, we commend the outstanding work of Philana Patterson, a friend and talented journalist who brilliantly helped transform our prose into words and concepts that will hopefully inspire the Black faces in white places who read this book.

Our public relations and strategic efforts have been capably led by April Peters, senior public relations and business affairs manager for Randal, as she has done anything and everything necessary to shape this project in a way that will resonate with its intended audience. Sakina Spruell-Cole from Cole Media, Renau Daniels, and Renee Warren from Noelle-Elaine Media have been instrumental in orchestrating the book's national tour. Sakina also provided valuable input to the book's first incarnation, which significantly shaped this final published work. We would also like to recognize our colleagues at BCT Partners, especially Darlene Harris, Lawrence Hibbert, and Vasya Dostoinov, for their ongoing administrative, editorial, and moral support.

We are grateful to our literary team, including David Vigliano from Vigliano and Associates, and Adam Korn, who represented us; Regina Brooks from Serendipity Literary Agency, who represented Philana; and the entire team at AMACOM books, including Ellen Kadin, James Bessent, William Helms, Alice Northover, Irene Majuk, and Lauren Johnson, all of whom signed-on to bring this book to the market when several agents and dozens of publishers rejected it. Thank you also to our graphics and website design team, which included our former creative director at BCT Partners, Rodney Frederickson; our interns, Quaison Carter, from New Jersey Institute of Technology, and Robert Dambreville, from Christ the King High School; and Frankie Gonzalez and Rob Monroe at 3rd Edge Communications, who helped design the iconic "10 Strategies" diagram.

We are eternally thankful to the dozens of prominent African Americans who agreed to interviews for this project, including the following: Roland Martin, Hill Harper, Jeff Johnson, Cory Booker, Benjamin Jealous, Angela Glover-Blackwell, Kevin Powell, Don Thompson, Deborah Elam, Gabriella Morris, Dudley Benoit, Anthony Jerome Smalls, Gwen Kelly, Lawrence Jackson, Majora Carter, Dr. Cheryl Dorsey, Rey Ramsey, David Steward, Zackarie Lemelle, Rev. Otis Moss, III, Marnie McKoy, Darryl Cobb, Dr. Treena Arinzeh, Alonzo Adams, Wayne Winborne, and Ralph Smith.

Nikki Hopewell was invaluable in helping conduct, transcribe, and edit the hours of interviews conducted for this book. Brittany Alston, a Rutgers University student, Clifford Joseph, a Rowan University student, and Vic Carter from Lee-Com Media Services, provided editorial and research assistance at various points in the development of this book. Roland Martin was gracious in agreeing to furnish a superb foreword.

We owe a great debt to our wives, Zahara Wadud-Pinkett and Valerie Mason-Robinson, who not only encouraged us but also carried the extra weight of family life when we were sequestered away researching and writing this book during evenings and even entire weekends. Without their love and support, it would have been impossible to find the time and space needed to bring this project to fruition.

We would like to thank our parents, the late Leslie and Eleanor Pinkett and the late Ronald and Doreen Robinson, for the foundational lessons that they gave us when we were growing up. Their unconditional love and support has made us the men we are today and the "game changers" we endeavor to be tomorrow. And last, but certainly not least, we thank our entire families, friends, and above all, God, with whom *all things* are possible.

Randal Pinkett, *www.randalpinkett.com*
Jeffrey Robinson, *www.jeffreyrobinsonphd.com*
Black Faces in White Places website, *www.redefinethegame.com*

Introduction

I wrote these words for everyone who struggles in their youth.
Who won't accept deception instead of what is truth.
It seems we lose the game, before we even start to play.
Who made these rules? We're so confused. Easily led astray.

—Lauryn Hill, "Everything Is Everything"

Not Getting Trumped: Randal's Nationally Televised "Black Faces in White Places" Moment

It had all come down to this moment: Onstage at New York's Lincoln Center, on live television with millions of people watching the possibility of me, Randal Pinkett, being chosen as real estate mogul Donald Trump's next Apprentice.

It was the fourth season of the NBC hit reality show *The Apprentice*, and Trump would ultimately choose one person, out of eighteen candidates—selected from more than one million applicants—to work for The Trump Organization. At stake: the $250,000 prize and the opportunity to be part of a renowned company that runs—in addition to real estate—gaming, entertainment, media, and educational enterprises.

The competition was whittled down to Rebecca Jarvis—a financial journalist who had previously worked for a short time in investment banking and trading—and me.

I believe Trump's choice should have been clear. Each week on *The Apprentice*, teams were charged with tasks under the direction of the team member selected as project manager. As project manager, I was undefeated, while Rebecca had a record of one win and two losses. When other project managers had a chance to choose team members, I was picked far more often. Rebecca was twenty-three years old at the time, and just beginning a career in business journalism. Ten years her senior, I was running BCT Partners, a multimillion-dollar consulting firm, and had already founded four other companies. Rebecca did have great education credentials, having earned an undergraduate degree from the prestigious University of Chicago. Still, my academic experience included five degrees, including an MBA and PhD from MIT, and a Rhodes Scholarship to attend Oxford University.

But this was reality television, and things turned on the unpredictable, so I was prepared for *almost* anything to happen. The final show of the season was a two-hour live event. Our final tasks, the outcome, the boardroom evaluations, and the debriefing of our team members had been taped and aired. It was time for Trump's choice.

For those of you who missed it, or need a refresher, here's how those final seconds went down:

Trump said, "Randal you're an amazing leader. Amazing. Rarely on this . . . (Applause) Rarely have I seen a leader as good as you, and you lead through niceness. I mean, you really lead through example, and I think you'd be the first to admit that, Rebecca. People follow Randal whenever there's a choice—we want Randal—I mean it just happened four or five times. I've never seen anything quite like it."

Then he declared, "Rebecca, you're outstanding. Randal, you're hired."

I leaped out of my chair, did a bit of an end-zone-esque celebratory move, and was embraced by several of the previously "fired" Apprentice candidates. My family and friends in the Lincoln Center audience and a group at a party in Newark, New Jersey, cheered my victory.

Then, the "moment."

My celebration was stopped short when Trump's voice called over the applause and well-wishes.

"Randal. Randal. Randal. Randal. Randal," Trump said. "Sit down for a second. I want to ask your opinion."

I took a seat at the "boardroom" table next to Rebecca.

Trump continued: "You two were so good, I have to ask your opinion. What do you think of Rebecca? If you were me, would you hire Rebecca also?"

I thought, *Is he serious?* Apparently he was, and I was insulted and angered. No previous winner had ever been asked that question before. That marked my nationally televised "Black Faces in White Places" moment.

—Randal Pinkett

▸ ▸ ▸

Your "moment" may not have been viewed on-air by millions of people, but if you're Black, it's likely you've had one. Perhaps you are the only Black in your predominantly white high school and have been asked to speak to the student body, as if you represent the entire Black community. Perhaps you serve as the founder and CEO of a Black-owned business that constantly has to prove and re-prove itself to the marketplace while larger firms are allowed to fail without any repercussions. Perhaps you work for a corporation with little to no minority representation and, for some reason, your opinion seems to fall on deaf ears, while the opinions of your colleagues somehow always carry weight. Perhaps you are one of the few, if not the only person of color in your department, division, or even company, and feel the weight of your race with regard to basic performance. You're worried that if you're late, all Black people are considered tardy. If you fail, all Black people are considered failures. But if you succeed, you're the exception!

The range of such moments is as varied as we are as a people. While the larger society often views Blacks as a monolithic group, we know better. We are liberals and conservatives. We are rich, poor, working, and middle class. We are laborers, blue-collar and white-collar workers. We are Protestants, Catholics, Muslims, Buddhists, atheists, and agnostics. Though small in number, there are even Black Jews. Some of us have dropped out of school and some of us have earned multiple degrees. We are diverse— but at the beginning of the day, in the middle of the day, and at the end of the day, we are Black. And at some point—whether it's early in life or late, we all will have our "moment" when we are confronted with a challenge related to our race.

Coach C. Vivian Stringer and the women of the Rutgers University women's basketball team had their moment when radio personality Don Imus decided to refer to them as "nappy-headed hos" the morning after they played in the championship game of the NCAA Tournament. But they spoke back with dignity and held their heads high as they graced the cover of *Newsweek* magazine and received the Wilma Rudolph Courage Award from the Women's Sports Foundation—awarded to female athletes who exhibit extraordinary courage and surmount adversity. Coach Stringer and her team "redefined the game."

Olympic speed skater Shani Davis had a moment when he was unfairly criticized by a white skater (who had previously lost a race to Davis) for not being a "team player" when he chose to participate in an individual competition over the team event: an educated decision that was actually as much (if not more) for the benefit of the team than for himself, since Davis had never practiced or participated in the team event. But rather than submit, Davis stood by his decision and redefined the game when he became the first Black athlete to win a gold medal in an individual sport at the Winter Olympics.

Cathy Hughes had her moment when she realized the inherent limitations of remaining at a white-owned radio station, WYCB. Though she had faced thirty-two rejections before a bank granted her husband and her a loan, she persevered and redefined the game by creating Radio One, the largest radio broadcasting company targeting African American and urban listeners.

And perhaps the most stunning "Black Faces in White Places" moment of our time: Barack Obama making the bold decision to run for the presidency of the United States when many, including prominent Civil Rights leaders, said America wasn't ready. But not only did he win the Democratic nomination, he redefined the game by becoming the first African-American president of the United States in the face of millions of naysayers—a Black man in the White House.

What all these people have in common is that they learned the game, played the game, mastered the game, and, at that "Black Faces in White Places" moment, found themselves in a position to redefine the game.

So how did Randal perform in his moment? Read on . . .

▶ ▶ ▶

Randal: Mr. Trump, Mr. Trump, Mr. Trump. I firmly believe that this is *The Apprentice*—that there is one and only one Apprentice, and if you're going to hire someone tonight it should be one.

Trump: Okay.

Randal: It's not "The Apprenti"!

Trump: Okay.

Randal: It's "The Apprentice."

Trump: All right, I'm going to leave it at that, then. I think I could have been convinced, but if you feel that's the way it should be.

Randal: I think that's the way it should be.

Trump: I'm going to leave it that way, then. Congratulations.

Randal earned the right to be named the *sole* Apprentice and refused to be one of two apprentices. (The plural form is, of course, "apprentices," not "apprenti"—but, hey, it made for a great one-liner!) He asserted himself and did not allow the rules of the game to change at the last minute. In front of millions of Americans, in his own modest way, he redefined the game. And Trump never asked that question of any winner on *The Apprentice* again.

But you don't have to be a college basketball player, a world-class Olympic athlete, a radio titan, a presidential candidate, or a reality TV star to have such a moment. Many others have overcome their moments, too. This book is designed to help you transcend your own "Black Faces in White Places" moments, redefine the game, and make it easier for the next generation to do the same.

FROM "THE GLASS CEILING" TO "THE EVER-CHANGING GAME"

The long-standing metaphor to describe the barriers to advancement for minorities and women is the "glass ceiling," a term that was originally applied to white women who had the abilities to advance and sought to follow the pathway men had taken to run organizations, but found they could only get so far in corporate America. Since then, the term has also been used to describe the phenomenon of African Americans and other underrepresented groups being denied access to higher-level positions. African Americans represent 12 percent of the U.S. workforce. Yet, according to some sources, African Americans only hold between 3 percent and 4 percent of senior-level positions in Fortune 1000 companies today, a scant increase from 2.5 percent in 1995.[1]

As a metaphor for the challenges facing minorities, we believe the glass ceiling is outdated. To be clear, we are not suggesting that the impediments suggested by the term "glass ceiling" don't exist. Undoubtedly, several barriers for African Americans still remain. We are suggesting that "the glass ceiling" is no longer an appropriate metaphor or symbol in the new millennium.

As a metaphor, the phrase suggests unseen and impenetrable barriers (hence the adjective "glass" and the noun "ceiling"), and it applied when we were still new to professional environments, had yet to understand their inner workings, and when minorities were not represented at all at the executive levels. But those days are now gone. Today, it's time for a new metaphor. So we are officially retiring the glass ceiling and suggesting as a replacement a new metaphor that we call "the ever-changing game."

The word "game" is subject to multiple interpretations:

▶ It can be a noun meaning "ability," as in "He's got game."

▶ It can be a verb meaning to "cheat," as in "Don't try to game me."

▶ It can be an adjective meaning "ready and able," as in "I'm game," or "She's game."

A common definition of the word game, "activity engaged in for diversion or amusement," is perhaps the furthest from our use of the word, as we in no way intend to trivialize the very serious issues raised in this book. To the contrary, we use "game" to refer to a very specific phenomenon. The closest definition of our usage of the word game comes from the Merriam-Webster dictionary, which defines game as "any activity undertaken or regarded as a contest involving rivalry, strategy, or struggle."

In the context of this book, we define "the game" as any activity undertaken to pursue personal and professional pathways to success involving rivalry, strategy, or struggle, and that are governed by a collection of spoken and, more often, unspoken rules.

Along these lines, there is a "game of politics." There are activities in the political realm that must be undertaken to achieve success, whether it is to get yourself elected or reelected or to work to help someone else get elected or reelected. There is a "game of corporate America," where success can be defined as becoming a highly paid executive. There is a "game of entrepreneurship," where success can be defined as generating millions, if not billions, of dollars in revenue. And there is even a "game of education," where success can be defined as achieving good grades and being accepted to an institution of higher learning.

Each of these games is governed by a collection of rules; some are spoken and others are unspoken. As times and conditions change, so do the rules. We therefore propose using the adjective "ever-changing" to elaborate on the game metaphor. The ever-changing game applies to any competitive environment where the rules are differentially applied and subject to change. Unlike the glass ceiling, the ever-changing game is something we encounter from grade school to graduate school and from the classroom to the boardroom. It applies to employees and entrepreneurs, high school students and graduate students, as well as professionals, politicians, and professors.

The twentieth-century glass ceiling conjured the associated metaphor of *the ladder*. This focused our attention on individuals who "climb" the ladder in an attempt to "break through" the glass ceiling and ultimately "reach the C-suite" once they get the title of CEO, CFO, or COO, etc. But today's ever-changing game conjures the metaphor of *the playing field*. By comparison, this focuses our attention on teams or groups of people who "work together" to "change the game" and "level the playing field" for everyone. The *game* and the *playing field* are appropriate metaphors for anyone aspiring to reach the top of their field, not only those who aspire to reach the C-suite, but also those who aspire to become school principals, head nurses, nonprofit executive directors, or reach other career heights, since they too are in the midst of a competition (whether they realize it or not).

So we are not concerned with breaking through a glass ceiling. Rather, the strategies you'll find in this book are those we have found to be most effective for African Americans to compete, win, and ultimately change for the better an ever-changing game.

WHY THE GAME MUST BE REDEFINED NOW

Since the Civil Rights movement, African Americans have made great progress in the United States. In 2006, 19 percent of Black adults, age 25 and older, had completed college; it was only 4 percent in 1970. We are represented at every level of business, academia, corporate America, non-profit organizations, and government, including the presidency. The growth of new African-American businesses at 6.4 percent is almost five times the rate of new companies overall. African Americans' buying power is more than $913 billion today, and is expected to grow to $1.2 trillion by 2013. Yet these and other statistics reflect a persistent "illusion of full inclusion."

As a group, we still lag far behind whites. In 2002, the Black poverty rate was three times greater than the white poverty rate, according to a study from the Pew Research Center. Based on the rate of change since 1968, it will take 150 years to close the gap. Black homeownership rose from 42 percent in 1970 to 48 percent in 2002, while white homeownership climbed from 65 percent to 75 percent in the same period (Pew study again). At that rate, it would take a staggering 1,661 years or fifty-five generations to eliminate this gulf.

For years, African Americans have passed down conventional wisdom that they must work twice as hard as their white counterparts and they must go to school—preferably to a good college—and make good grades. The advice isn't completely off the mark, but if that's all it takes, certainly many of us should be much further along.

Working hard and getting an education or training are cornerstones of success for any race of people. But the world is changing, and today these strategies simply aren't enough. African Americans who cling to strategies that worked in the past, without taking into account how the world is shifting, will likely feel frustrated as they progress at a snail's pace or, worse, lose ground in the future.

We must redefine the game now because while we have made tremendous progress, we still face tremendous challenges, and tremendous work remains to be done. Our communities and our country cannot afford to wait.

The Four Dimensions of Black Faces in White Places

So what do we mean by "Black Faces in White Places"? It is more than just a numbers game and being the only person of color in a predominantly white environment. It is more than being subjected to racism and discrimination based on the color of your skin. It is even more than being a "Black first."

It is, in fact, about pursuing greatness in ways that leverage your culture and ethnicity as *assets,* not as liabilities.

The experience of being Black while pursuing such a path may raise issues along four dimensions (see Figure I–1): *identity, meritocracy, society,* and *opportunity.*

IDENTITY: WHO AM I?

The foundation of personal identity is often your ethnic and cultural background. Are you African American or Caribbean American? Were you, or your parents, born in Africa? Is one of your parents white, Latino, or Asian?

Then there's professional identity. Are you working toward becoming (or already working as) a lawyer, doctor, professor, graphic artist, or software developer? Often our career aspirations shape our interests and social groups—even how we dress. Do you wear a suit most days—or maybe it's a lab coat. Perhaps you find yourself in environments where jeans and polo shirts are the norm, even at the highest levels of your profession.

Another element is how you think of yourself. Are you a founder of, say, a business or a community group? You could be an activist—working to organize people in communities to fight for social change. Or perhaps you think of yourself as a trailblazer. Maybe you are the first Caribbean American to have earned a degree in a particular field or to develop a technical process.

Why Is Identity So Important for African Americans? According to Patricia Hewlin, PhD, a professor of organizational behavior at McGill University, African Americans are particularly aware of the issue of

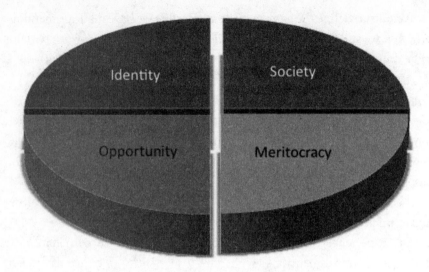

Figure I–1. The four dimensions of Black faces in white places.

identity because we often make choices between our own personal and cultural identity and the identity and culture of our surroundings, especially if we are in predominantly white institutions and workplaces. And, Hewlin noted in an interview, "Since race has been such a prominent issue in American history, it is often the most salient when we ask people to define who they are."

This complicates the internal and external conversation that African Americans have with themselves and others. Is race important to me because it is central to who I am or because I am defined by it in society?

There are many examples of these questions of identity. Am I the manager who happens to be Black or the Black manager? Am I the Black professor or the professor who happens to be Black? Who do I want to be and how do I want to be treated by others? This is where the first dimension of being a Black face in a white place, identity, intersects with questions about meritocracy, society, and opportunity.

MERITOCRACY: CAN I BE JUDGED ON MY MERITS?

When you are the Black person in a white institution or workplace, you won't be alone if you wonder, "Can I be judged on my merits, or will race always be a factor?"

The idea of *meritocracy* (a society that is based solely upon merit) is illusive in America. Instead, we ask ourselves: How do people view me? Are the decision makers evaluating me based on my education, skills, character, and performance, or on the color of my skin?

Let's recall the play-by-play of Randal's final seconds before being named Donald Trump's season four Apprentice, and then right after his victory, when he was reminded that he was a Black face in a "white place." Here's some of what the TV viewers that night didn't see . . .

In the days leading up to *The Apprentice* finale, there were hints that Trump might throw a curveball. Reality TV message boards were lighting up and cast members were abuzz with rumors that Trump was considering a double hiring—which would have been the first in the show's history. However, it was also clear that Randal still faced an uphill battle despite his standout performance on the show. One week before the finale Trump was quoted as saying, "He can be lazy" with respect to Randal, while referring to Jarvis as "smart" and "beautiful." The article not only identified Jarvis as the "front-runner," but also included separate pictures of her and Trump while conspicuously omitting a picture of Randal.[2]

Was it a coincidence that Randal was set to be the first-ever African-American Apprentice? This is the kind of question we're talking about here; many people have concluded that Trump's curveball was based on race. It certainly couldn't have been based on performance—Randal won every time he was a project manager and had a winning team record, while Jarvis had a losing project manager and team record. During the final task—a charity fund-raiser—Randal raised $15,000 for his assigned charity while Jarvis raised zero dollars for hers. At the second to last episode, when it was clear that Randal and Rebecca Jarvis were the finalists, an NBC poll showed that 81 percent of respondents thought Randal should win. And many of his competitors—about nine of them—joined Randal for dinner the day before the live finale. Much of the conversation that evening centered on how unacceptable it would be if Trump decided on a double hiring.

We jumped into action, meeting with several friends to strategize how Randal should respond to Trump in the event of a double hiring—or if he hired Randal and then consulted him on how to handle Jarvis. We didn't play out that second scenario with any great level of detail because it seemed so implausible, but the response we decided on was essentially the same as if there had been a double hiring. If Trump insisted, Randal would stick to his guns and settle for nothing less than being the sole winner, or else he would quit!

In the end, Trump accepted Randal's argument and named him the sole winner. But even then, Randal was only able to enjoy his victory for so long. Randal's response resulted in a firestorm of media controversy and hundreds of blog posts from people who thought he should have allowed Rebecca to be hired. One website, RealityTV.com, registered 582 comments, many of them negative, about Randal's response. Hackers took down his personal website. Hate messages were left on the voicemail at his company. A "Fire Randal" website popped up within hours.

Conversely, Randal still gets kudos from people—particularly African Americans, but also some whites, who think he did the right thing.

Even still, when Randal travels the country, a similar scenario often plays out: A Black person will approach, congratulate Randal on his success, and then whisper, "I'm glad you did what you did, but I wouldn't have done it."

We have two questions for all those folks who say they wouldn't have made the same choice. Why not? *And why are you whispering?*

There's no need to whisper when you are confident about what you bring to the table. (In Randal's case—it was his winning record.) There's no need to whisper when you know the facts. (In Randal's case, this was a competition billed from the very beginning as having one winner.) Instead, you should be willing to stand up and speak out for what you believe in and what you have worked for and earned. That's what Randal did, and that's your responsibility as well.

SOCIETY: IS AMERICA COLOR-BLIND?

No, America is not color-blind.

Okay, we said it, and if you're reading this book, our guess is that there's a 99.9 percent chance you agree. Minorities represent about 28 percent of the U.S. population; however, our collective businesses only represent 2.7 percent of all U.S. gross revenue. In 2001, the typical Black household had a net worth of $19,000—including home equity—compared with $121,000 for whites. The median net worth for whites is $88,000, while for Hispanics and Blacks, median net worth is only $8,000 and $7,000, respectively. And the number-one company on the Black Enterprise 100, World Wide Technology, doesn't make the Fortune 100, or even the Fortune 500.

Power, wealth, and influence continue to be concentrated outside of Black America, and the institutions of influence have not changed sufficiently to allow for a color-blind ideal.

So where does that leave Black people? There are three key things you must understand before moving forward.

1. *Relationships to people and organizations have importance.* We must identify and connect with influential institutions. Whether it's a university, a workplace, or a professional or volunteer organization, we must determine (and follow) the patterns that will enable us to successfully navigate those structures. Additionally, we must recognize and link to social and professional networks that help people progress. That means building meaningful relationships both inside and outside of predominantly white institutions.

2. *Disparities exist, but there is progress.* It's easy to get mired in the negative statistics. But there are more highly educated, well-compensated Blacks than ever before. We can learn from those who have made it to the C-suite, opened high-growth firms, built wealth, wielded influence, and risen to the top of their professions.

3. *As a Black person, the rules, though often subtle, are different for you,* and the same strategies—good or bad—employed by your white counterparts will often yield a different result for you.

OPPORTUNITY: DO I HAVE EQUAL OPPORTUNITY TO FULFILL MY DESTINY?
The question that defines the final dimension of Black faces in white places is one that weighs on the heart of every American. Can I achieve my dreams in this country? Can I have life, liberty, and the pursuit of happiness just as anyone else in this nation? Can I achieve my American dream?

African Americans want what everyone in the United States wants. We want a level playing field. We want good schools for our children, good jobs and businesses that flourish, safe places to live, and fulfillment in what we do. But often, African Americans do not believe they have equal opportunity to achieve their highest potential and fulfill their dreams. Many believe that there still are many obstacles to fairness and equality in the workforce, in our schools, and throughout society.

African-American professionals wonder why the "pursuit of happiness" looks so white, given the lack of African Americans at the executive level. We wonder why the boardroom doesn't reflect the diversity of America. We wonder why the number of Black professors at the nation's top-fifty institutions is so low. And we wonder why all institutions of power are not proportionately filled with people that look like us.

Consider your own access to opportunity, and try to answer the following questions:

▸ How can I reach my highest potential in the organization or field I am in right now?

▸ How can I find fulfillment in my personal and professional life?

▸ How can I give back to others to help them fulfill their potential?

When we asked these questions of ourselves, we did some soul-searching and sought the advice of others. Finding answers to these key questions propelled us to a higher purpose, and ultimately, this book will challenge you to do the same.

Table I–1 provides a summary of the four dimensions and how they will relate to the ten strategies on which we'll be elaborating.

A Roadmap for Redefining the Game and Reshaping America

For centuries, African Americans have been learning the game, playing the game, and mastering the game, based on rules traditionally defined by others. Overcoming barriers to advancement for African Americans has generally meant developing effective strategies to learn, play, and master *their* game. The roots of these barriers are found in historical, overt, and legal restrictions in voting, housing, employment, and education. Modern-day manifestations take the form of subtler yet observable obstacles that make it difficult to advance in corporate America, establish businesses, create wealth, and pursue one's dreams.

Dimension	Description	Questions	Strategies
Identity	Who am I?	▸ How do I leverage my culture and ethnicity as assets? ▸ How do I maintain a strong sense of self and direction?	1. Establish a strong identity and purpose 2. Obtain broad exposure
Meritocracy	Can I be judged on my merits?	▸ Does racism still exist? ▸ How can I be judged on my merits? ▸ How can my performance be evaluated objectively?	3. Demonstrate excellence
Society	Is society color-blind?	▸ Does equity truly exist in our society? ▸ How do I build relationships in an increasingly diverse society? ▸ How do I learn from the experiences of others? From people like me? From people different from me? ▸ How do I find common ground with others?	4. Build diverse and solid relationships 5. Seek the wisdom of others 6. Find strength in numbers
Opportunity	Do I have equal opportunity to fulfill my destiny?	▸ How do I reach my full potential? ▸ How do I achieve fulfillment in my personal and professional life? ▸ How do I give back and help others to reach their full potential?	7. Think and act intrapreneurially 8. Think and act entrepreneurially 9. Synergize and reach scale 10. Give back generously

Table I–1. Four dimensions and 10 strategies for Black faces in white places

The rules of the game for Blacks have evolved and changed significantly over time. As a result, some strategies that worked in the past are now less effective, while others are simply outdated.

Additionally, the rules of the game have been, and continue to be, applied differently to Blacks: Greater penalties are often levied on African Americans for failure; higher expectations are often set for African Americans in order to achieve; and in response to those African Americans who reach a certain level of success, circumstances can often change in ways that make it difficult to attain even greater accomplishments.

Generally speaking, these dynamics are no secret to Black people. However, what is not as widely acknowledged is that the rules of the game for African Americans are becoming more complex, and therefore the strategies needed to win the game and succeed in life now require greater and greater levels of sophistication.

To thrive today, it is no longer adequate to be the smartest student in class, the top employee on the job, or the highest-scoring athlete on the field. Whether the landscape involves the cutthroat milieu of business and politics, the hallowed halls of academia and the church, or the popular fields of sports and entertainment, African Americans need to know and apply a new set of lessons for the twenty-first century.

In this book, then, we present to you a roadmap to help you apply those lessons so that you can learn the game, play the game, master the game, change the game, and, in the process, ultimately reshape America.

The 10 Game-Changing Strategies to Achieve Success and Find Greatness

First, we'll be guiding you through the ten strategies we have determined to be most effective for African Americans to navigate today's rapidly changing professional landscape. Along with our stories, we'll share the stories of the dozens of accomplished African Americans we interviewed while completing this book. Excerpts from these interviews, which can be found throughout the book, clearly demonstrate how the ten strategies have unfolded in their lives. We interviewed a broad spectrum of people, ranging from prominent elected officials, corporate executives, nonprofit and community leaders, entrepreneurs, and educators to foundation executives, pastors, entertainers, artists, and scientists, such that the ten strategies we've identified reflect a wide range of paths. Our objective is not that you emulate their paths or even our paths, but that we help you to find your own path. Like any good roadmap, ours will provide a range of options and pathways that can lead you to the same destination of learning, playing, mastering, and redefining the game *your way.*

As you read on, you'll see that we are following the roadmap illustrated in Figure I–2. The first three strategies are the seeds of Part I: Learning the Game. A firm grasp of these principles is necessary to move forward in your

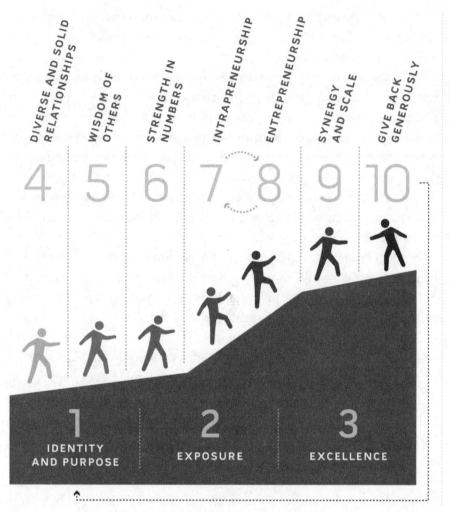

DIVERSE AND SOLID RELATIONSHIPS

WISDOM OF OTHERS

STRENGTH IN NUMBERS

INTRAPRENEURSHIP

ENTREPRENEURSHIP

SYNERGY AND SCALE

GIVE BACK GENEROUSLY

4 5 6 7 8 9 10

1
IDENTITY
AND PURPOSE

2
EXPOSURE

3
EXCELLENCE

Figure I-2. The "10 strategies" roadmap: the path to greatness

journey, since these strategies provide the foundation upon which all the other strategies are built.

The stories we present for Strategy 1 explore the complexities and importance of establishing a strong *identity* as an African American, with strategies that will help you determine your *purpose*.

In Strategy 2, we stress the importance of obtaining broad *exposure* and diverse experiences and moving beyond your comfort zone—and we show you how you can do so in your own life.

Strategy 3 illustrates the concept of demonstrating *excellence* through the application of discipline and empowering beliefs to your individual passion and God-given gifts.

With the first three strategies as a foundation, you will be ready to move on to Part II: Playing the Game, which will bolster your playbook with additional strategies that are all about relationships.

Strategy 4 shows the benefit of building *solid and diverse relationships* with all kinds of people as you move through your education and career.

Strategy 5 emphasizes the importance of *developmental relationships* with coaches, sponsors, counselors, and mentors, and helps you unlock the mysteries of finding and utilizing them. Tapping the "wisdom of others" is a vital aspect of playing the game.

Strategy 6 discusses informal and formal group relationships and the benefits of joining with like-minded people, within your organization or in outside groups, not only to boost your own success but to work for collective gain (the "strength in numbers" concept).

At this point, you are prepared to make a steady climb to the next set of strategies, so you can take the game to a higher level in Part III: Mastering the Game. Strategies 7 and 8 encourage you to tap into a mindset of *thinking and acting intrapreneurially* and *entrepreneurially.* Intrapreneurship and entrepreneurship are part of an ongoing cycle; they are different sides of the same coin. They represent an inside game and an outside game, depending on whether you find yourself working inside an established organization as an *intrapreneur* or working outside to create an entirely new entity as an *entrepreneur.* You'll notice in Figure I–2 that the transition from Part II to Part III represents an inflection point—the incline becomes steeper moving ahead. That's no accident. We regard this transition as the most difficult one because the entrepreneurial mindset is not a traditional way of thinking and acting.

Strategy 7 applies the principles you added to your repertoire to strategic career management, networking, mentoring, and organizational involvement, so that you can become an intrapreneur who not only effectively navigates your organization, but also exerts your influence to help the community.

Strategy 8 orients what you've learned so far toward starting your own company or organization—and understanding your responsibility as an entrepreneur to launch ventures for a profit and for a purpose.

Once you've mastered the game, you are ready to move on to Part IV: Redefining the Game. Here, everything you've learned from Strategies 1 through 8 comes together in harmony to bear fruit, while we introduce two new strategies for how you can work with others to effect large-scale change in your industry, in the community, and in society.

Strategy 9 describes how to achieve *synergy* by creating connections between people and organizations, and then *reach scale* by amplifying their collective efforts to have the broadest or deepest possible impact. We harness the capabilities, relationships, and organizations discussed throughout the previous strategies and show how to apply them to leveling the playing field. As you can again see in Figure I–2, the transition from Part III to Part IV represents the final inflection point—the incline becomes less steep as you continue forward because, like a lever, you are able to multiply your efforts by working with others who share a common agenda.

Strategy 10 reveals how *being generous* with your time, talent, treasure, and touch throughout your life and career not only benefits others, but solidifies your sense of identity and purpose. It enables you to create a powerful and lasting legacy that makes America a better place and levels the playing field for everyone.

To guide you in applying the ten strategies to your daily life, throughout the book we will provide Game-Changing Strategies or strategic considerations, most of which are geared specifically to African Americans. Be sure to also visit the website *www.redefinethegame.com* to browse or contribute to the wide range of resources available there. You can also download additional materials that supplement this book and learn more about us.

So, with great joy and excitement we invite you into our lives and the lives of the intrapreneurs and entrepreneurs profiled in these pages. Learning, playing, mastering, and redefining the game is an uphill climb, but as we have found in our own lives, when you are armed with the right set of strategies, reaching for the top is that much easier. And the opportunity to put oneself in a position to reshape America is simply awesome.

P A R T   I

LEARNING THE GAME

Whatever you choose to do, you will end up playing in one game or another. You may play a corporate game, you may play an education game, you may play a health game. You can play any game, but if you want to be successful, you need to understand the rules and the subtleties of that game. Take it seriously. It's a serious game.

—Bruce Gordon

America is commonly described as the "land of the free," "home of the brave," and "the Land of Opportunity." America has also been described by a series of alternative phrases that speak to its orientation toward race. Expressions such as "segregated" and "integrated," "multicultural" and "multiethnic," "pluralist" and "post-racial"—are a reflection of America's prevailing, yet evolving, laws, customs, norms, and attitudes regarding race during a given period. But it is important to understand how these notions have changed over time, because it helps paint a historical picture of why being a Black face in a white place can be a challenging experience, while at the same time an empowering one.

America's Story: The United States and Race

Looking beyond the era of African enslavement, the years of reconstruction and Jim Crow (1876–1965) were a period of "separate but unequal." Legal segregation of public facilities was in effect in many places in the southern United States, including public schools, restaurants, restrooms, and transportation systems—leading not only to substandard facilities but also poor treatment of non-whites based on the notion that they were inferior to whites.

As European immigrants came to the United States in the early twentieth century, the term *melting pot* emerged to describe the American experience. The idea behind it was one of assimilation: To get ahead in America one must shed his distinct ethnic identity and become something new. While this may have been useful for Europeans coming to a new country in search of opportunity, clearly this metaphor overlooked the history of African Americans who were brought to this country against their will (and Native Americans, who were displaced or decimated by European colonialists).

The Civil Rights Era (1955–1968) challenged American society to give all of its citizens equal rights and live up to its motto of "liberty and justice for all." This was a period of desegregation during which America came to be regarded as a more "integrated" society. In putting an end to legal restrictions in housing, voting, education, and the like, the Civil Rights movement marked a period of significant progress in terms of granting rights to people of color—rights we were previously denied.

In the 1980s, the "multiculturalism" movement gained prominence as a way to recognize the history, perspective, and contribution of all cultures to the development of America. *Culture* is defined as the history, norms, and values embodied in the people, organizations, and institutions of an ethnic group. Multiculturalism led to proactive measures such as accepting different types of clothing in educational and professional environments; organizing cultural celebrations and festivals; and providing government services in multiple languages, to name just a few. For example, this movement embraced Black History Month and created month-long celebrations for other underrepresented groups (e.g., Hispanics, Native Americans, women, etc.).

Building upon the tenets of multiculturalism, voices also emerged in the 1990s to challenge the age-old metaphor of America as a "melting pot"—a country where cultures mix and combine to form a multiethnic society that is homogeneous and reflects a general combination of the ingredients in the pot (i.e., the various cultures). Instead, these voices argued that we actually live in a *pluralist* society, and they described America more accurately as "a salad bowl"—a collection of distinct cultures that, like ingredients in a salad, coexist while maintaining their individual uniqueness. As a result of both multicultural and pluralist advocates, we have a much greater recognition of the various, distinct cultures that comprise American society.

Finally, here in the new millennium the phrase "post-racial" has begun to receive attention. We see this expression as referring to two phenomena. The first phenomenon is the increasing number of people who are perhaps more naturally inclined to see beyond race. This includes members of Generation Y, also known as the Millennial Generation, who neither grew up nor were born during the years (or the years immediately following) the Civil Rights Era. Generally speaking, this generation fully reflects the changing demographics of American society and, as a result, has no firsthand experience with an America that is not an integrated and diverse America, much less a segregated America. While they are certainly aware of race and racism, these are not the defining issues of their generation.

The second phenomenon is the increasing number of people who, across all generations, desire to move beyond race. These individuals are more concerned with character than color. They are more focused on ethics than ethnicity. They are more interested in right and wrong than race and racism. Once again, they fully acknowledge that racism still exists, but endeavor to prevent it from biasing their thoughts or actions and would like to see our country get past it (despite the obvious and inherent challenges to doing both).

....

Part I: Learning the Game is rooted in the Kwanzaa principles of **Nia** *(Purpose), which means "to make our collective vocation the building and developing of our community in order to restore our people to their traditional greatness";* **Kujichagulia** *(Self-determination), which means "to define ourselves, name ourselves, create for ourselves, and speak for ourselves"; and* **Imani** *(Faith), which means "to believe with all our heart in our people, our parents, our teachers, our leaders, and the righteousness and victory of our struggle."*

....

Learning What the Game Is All About

Looking across these interrelated and intertwined eras, America has clearly become more receptive to the entire spectrum of colors within our society. This has slowly opened the door for people of all backgrounds to be accepted for who they are and to fulfill their destiny. But inasmuch as America is closer, it has yet to achieve the post-racial reality being bandied about nowadays. America's prevailing orientation toward race continues to have direct implications for if, and how, Black faces in white places achieve greatness. This speaks again to the four basic questions implied by the four dimensions:

1. Who am I? (Identity)

2. Can I be judged on my merits? (Meritocracy)

3. Is society color-blind? (Society)

2. Do I have equal opportunity to fulfill my destiny? (Opportunity)

Even today, the answers to these questions can be significantly influenced by race.

Part I: Learning the Game is comprised of three strategies that directly address the first two questions. Learning the game essentially means four things:

▸ Learning about yourself

▸ Learning about the world

▸ Learning about your craft

▸ Learning about your game

In the first two strategies, you'll learn more about us and how our experiences help illustrate the importance of being firm about your identity and purpose—the first, and most important, strategy in redefining the game and reshaping America. Strategy 1: Establish a Strong Identity and Purpose relates to defining who you are and why you are here. Strategy 2: Obtain Broad Exposure conveys the importance of exploring the world around you and how that experience not only informs your identity and purpose but also enhances your effectiveness in a global society. While we delve deeply into exposure in the second strategy of this book, we want readers to also note that it is an important component of what it takes to establish a sense of self and direction. The first two strategies are actually interdependent. If you have questions about additional ways to accomplish Strategy 1, you'll likely find your answers within Strategy 2. Through our stories and those of other emerging African-American game-changers, Strategy 3: Demonstrate

Excellence explains the value of demonstrating excellence, being among the very best at your personal and professional craft and understanding the context of your "game" or professional landscape.

Together, these three strategies speak to the what, why, and how of defining yourself and doing what is within your power to excel and be judged on your merits. Successfully establishing a strong identity and purpose, obtaining broad exposure, and demonstrating excellence are part of a foundation that ultimately gives Blacks the ability to forge ahead independently—that is, without being encumbered by society's expectations of who you are and what you can achieve. This is all part of "learning the game." Knowing who you are in the context of your upbringing and the world around you, having a broad worldview and an openness that allows you to learn, and working to be among the best at whatever it is you choose to pursue, puts you in a position to effectively play the game—a concept that we'll tackle in Part II. In fact, everything we discuss in subsequent parts of this book is wholly dependent upon your ability to implement the strategies from Part I in your life.

Jeffrey, Randal, America, and Race

Our stories begin in the early 1970s. We were born in 1971 on the heels of the Civil Rights Movement. The Movement spawned significant legal advances toward equal opportunity in America, including the Civil Rights Act of 1964, which barred discrimination in public accommodations, transportation, education, and employment; the Voting Rights Act of 1965, which made the ballot more accessible to African Americans, especially in the South; and the Housing Act of 1968, which banned discrimination in the sale or rental of housing.

While the Civil Rights legislation of the 1960s was pivotal for African Americans—ourselves included—as we reflect upon our experiences, it's clear that the circumstances that shape our experiences date back to 1954 and the landmark U.S. Supreme Court decision in Brown v. Board of Education, which made it possible for Black children to be educated in the same classrooms as white children.

In the early 1970s, a growing number of African-American families, fearful of gangs, crime, and poor school systems in the inner city exercised their new rights. In 1973, Randal's parents, Elizabeth and Leslie Pinkett of Philadelphia, and Jeffrey's parents, Doreen and Ronald Robinson of East Orange, New Jersey, moved their preschool aged Black sons out of the mostly Black inner cities and into predominately white New Jersey suburbs.

The Pinketts settled in a subdivision 45 miles across the Pennsylvania state line in East Windsor Township—near Exit 8 on the New Jersey Turnpike. Having earned an MBA from the Wharton School of Business at the University of Pennsylvania, Randal's father was starting a new job at a New York investment bank, and the couple wanted Randal and his older brother, Dan, to live in a quiet, affordable community halfway between their father's new job and their relatives in Philadelphia. East Windsor, with just 12,000 residents, was a stark contrast to Philadelphia, with nearly 2 million citizens at that time.

About a one-hour drive away, the Robinsons moved to an apartment complex in Parsippany—a quiet area which, when combined with neighboring Troy Hills, counted about 55,000 people. While it had just 20,000 fewer residents than East Orange, the seventeen-or-so-mile move meant a world of difference. East Orange neighbors Newark—a city still struggling today to overcome problems with drugs and crime. Ronald Robinson was known to say, "After they stole tires off our cars for the second time, it was about time to go."

The Pinketts and Robinsons didn't know each other back then—but both couples had something in common. They found communities that offered better schools and an escape from the escalating violence that permeated the cities they left behind.

The moves weren't without challenges. Not long after Randal's mother began telling people about their plans, she began hearing stories about crosses being burned near where they had put a down payment on a townhouse. Jeffrey's mother, acutely aware that her son was one of just two Black children in their neighborhood and in his school, always had her antennae up, wondering if a skirmish with a schoolmate or being denied full recognition for his hard work (such as earning 22 badges as a Cub Scout while the white scouts had only earned four or five apiece) were racially motivated.

The challenge for us—being Black Faces in these White Places—was attempting to define ourselves as Black males. It's common for young people to struggle to define themselves, but it's particularly challenging for Blacks living in predominately white surroundings to figure out who they are.

We don't want to suggest in any way that Black people who grow up surrounded by many other Black people don't have their own set of challenges. In fact, growing up in a predominately Black environment may simply delay some of the identity struggles we faced early in life. The overwhelming majority of

African Americans will find themselves at some point in their lives living and working in white places. It's also common for Black Faces who are raised around many other Black Faces to be so comfortable—and perhaps so pro-tected—that they haven't been faced with many opportunities to engage people unlike them.

Nevertheless, it was within the communities of Parsippany and East Wind-sor that we began our personal journeys discussed in this book.

Establish a Strong Identity and Purpose

Thank you [God] for allowing me to see myself the way you see me.
—Kirk Franklin, "Imagine Me"

IDENTITY IS NOT particular to African Americans, but it can present some unique challenges. Everyone asks themselves certain general questions: What are my values? What principles do I stand for? What are the beliefs I hold near and dear? However, for African Americans, having specific answers to these questions is of paramount importance, especially when you inevitably find yourself in environments that challenge or attempt to define you based on racial stereotypes, baseless assumptions, or ignorance. Establishing a strong identity can be the difference between *thinking* that people who look like you can succeed at anything and *knowing* it to be the case.

....

Learn more about us by visiting our websites: **www.randalpinkett.com** *and* **www.jeffreyrobinsonphd.com**. *You can also subscribe to Randal's e-newsletter, "Elevate Your Game."*

....

You may be a Black youth growing up in a predominantly white neighborhood, which was Randal's experience. Or you may be a recent graduate from a historically Black college or university experiencing your first foray

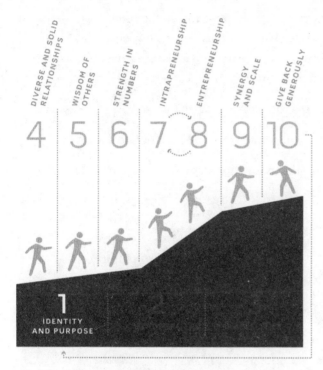

Figure 1–1. The path to greatness (Strategy 1).

into corporate America. Or you may be the sole person of color in a company or a city that lacks diversity. In each scenario, as you become more attuned with your identity, you fortify your ability to stay true to who you are in any situation, and you prepare yourself to effectively deal with any circumstance that challenges your core being.

Identity

As the first dimension of Black faces in white places, identity is a complex subject. But we believe it is an important and appropriate topic to confront early on because establishing a strong identity is a vital component of the foundation on which you can build careers and businesses and undertake other activities that will transform your life and the lives of others. It is also an important consideration for parents raising children in a race-conscious society.

To do this the right way, we'll need to start by defining a few things up-front.

Your identity is comprised of all those things that make you, well, you. Identity represents all of the characteristics for which you can say, "I am . . ." When we talk about identity we are actually talking about three aspects of the same idea, as shown in Figure 1–2:

- *Personal identity* (how you define yourself)

- *Social identity* (how you define yourself in relation to society)

- *Identity negotiation* (the interaction between your personal identity and social identity)

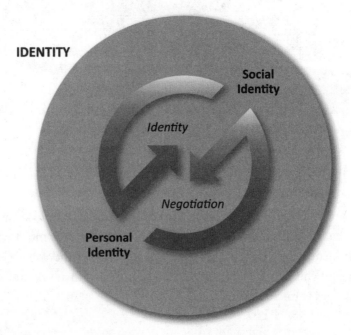

Figure 1–2. The aspects of identity.

Society may seek to define certain people as African American based on their physical characteristics (social identity). However, those same individuals may not define themselves as African American. By contrast, there are people who do not look Black (that is, they could "pass" for white) who still define themselves as African Americans (personal identity). The process of working through all of these considerations is the negotiation of identity.

PERSONAL IDENTITY

Personal identity represents the myriad things that make you unique. It embodies characteristics such as gender, height, weight, physical ability, and race. The formation of personal identity happens early in our lives, and parents play an important role. They tell us if we are a boy or a girl. Parents teach us language and are the first to tell us about our relationship to the world and to each other. These are defining moments that paint a picture of who we are.

For African Americans, you can't underestimate the role of parents in the process of forming a positive racial identity early on. The Pinketts were among a small number of Black parents living in the mostly white and Jewish town of East Windsor, New Jersey, who decided not to leave the development of their children's racial identity to chance. They helped form a group called "Our Kids" that provided opportunities for their children to interact with other Black children through trips to museums and amusement parks and homegrown cultural events like Black History Month programs, where the children starred in short plays. Sometimes the activity was as simple as just getting together at someone's house to have a meal and hang out.

The importance of their identity as Black people was further reinforced in the children through a Kwanzaa celebration. Between Christmas and New Year's, the family lit red, black, and green candles in a Kinara, with each candlestick representing one of seven principles (more on that later). Under the glow of the candlelight the family said out loud what each of those principles meant to them. It is these kinds of experiences—no matter where you live—that can help reinforce a positive self-image.

Of course, there are things that we learn on our own as well. We learn that we are tall or short by comparing ourselves to others. We observe that some students are better at math while we may be better at science. We learn that we are faster or more athletic than other children our age. Both of us learned we had athletic ability, for example—Randal while pursuing several competitive sports from junior high school through college, and J.R. (Jeffrey Robinson) while playing basketball in a competitive league through church.

What we learn about identity on our own is heavily shaped by communities, schools, friends, and extended family members. These influences—for better or for worse—are beyond our parents' control. Parental influence diminishes as we reach adolescence and the influence of peers becomes one of the most significant influences on personal identity, either serving to support a strong sense of who you are or making you question your identity.

SOCIAL IDENTITY

Your *social identity* defines how you view yourself in relation to other people. As you gain greater awareness of self, you are able to further define and position your identity within the context of the broader society. For example, it is intuitively obvious that you speak a language. But it is not until you hear someone speak another language that you begin to define yourself as English-speaking.

Another way to consider social identity is to realize that we each have multiple social identities. Social identity includes, but is not limited to:

▸ *Cultural identity* (membership in a cultural group)

▸ *Gender identity* (the gender with which a person identifies)

▸ *National identity* (membership in a nation)

▸ *Spiritual or religious identity* (belief in a faith)

▸ *Professional identity* (career affiliation)

These broad categorizations, whether deliberate or not, help us decide with whom and where we spend our time and how we think of ourselves. What makes groupings distinct is that "members" of groups typically share certain characteristics, norms, and values.

During our years as engineering students, our identities as academically talented, responsible African-American students were supported and celebrated at Rutgers where we joined the chapter of the National Society of Black Engineers (NSBE). NSBE cultivated a culture that promoted students working together. They'd say hey, we're doing study halls Tuesday night; you all need to meet there and start working on that physics exam because it's coming. We'd work on problems from old exams so that we'd be able to handle the ones we'd encounter on our test the next week.

NSBE believed in recognizing academic performance. Through the first semester we both got "shout outs" for strong performance on our exams. At the beginning of the second semester members were asked to voluntarily share how the previous semester went. Randal stood and said, "I got a 3.9 (GPA). I got an A in almost all my classes." and then sat down. The decision to share came with a great deal of trepidation because he did not know if being academically excellent was going to make him more or less popular. Was he going to get stigmatized or stereotyped as an academic nerd, as a loser, as a geek?

Well, it didn't end up being a problem—in fact, the opposite happened. Randal became a campus celebrity, or at least in Black engineering circles. People whispered on campus, "That's the guy that got the 3.9." or "Did you hear about the Black guy who got straight A's in engineering—him right there."

Black students started to congregate around him. People wanted to study with him. They wanted to come to his dorm. The public nature of his academic performance allowed him to be accepted. It was academics, ironically, that became a conduit for his social connections.

The affirming connections we made through our association with NSBE are just one of many examples of the groups that have helped shape our social identities over the years. We are members of, or are affiliated with, many different kinds of groups, including racial and ethnic, religious, educational, and geographic communities. For example, we are both African-American men, Christian, alumni of Rutgers University, and were raised in New Jersey.

Identifying with a particular culture or nationality, for instance, likely means that you subscribe to the norms, customs, and/or values of that group. At the same time, it also suggests that in identifying with that group you are also helping to shape its ever-evolving norms, customs, and values. In other words, if being African American is part of how you construct your identity, then you not only reflect African-American culture, you also influence African-American culture.

Did our academic performance help encourage a culture of striving for excellence among Black engineering students at Rutgers? We certainly hope so.

IDENTITY NEGOTIATION

There is an interaction between your personal identity and your social identity. They can reinforce one another or they can be in conflict. This negotiation takes place during our formative years, but it also takes place every time we find ourselves having a "Black Faces in White Places" moment.

For example, if you believe you are intelligent and those around you believe you are intelligent, then your identity of being intelligent is reinforced.

But what if you believe you are intelligent, but others tell you that there is no possible way that you are intelligent because people who look like you are not intelligent? This conflict poses a challenge to your identity. Do you really believe you are intelligent, or do you believe what others have said about you or people who look like you?

The *negotiation of identity* is the reconciliation of how you define yourself in relation to society. You must take into consideration how society may seek to define you. Accordingly, there are several "social identifiers" or discernable characteristics by which society can seek to define people. The "Big 9" social identifiers are: race, class, gender, sexual orientation, physical/psychological ability, ethnicity, language, age, and religion.

These characteristics are the markers of human difference through which power and privilege have been differentially distributed and prejudice may accrue. Each dimension meters power and privilege in the dominant culture of America. To the extent that an individual is or is perceived to be white, wealthy, male, heterosexual, able-bodied and rational, European-American, English-speaking, young (or in the "prime" of one's life), and Christian, that individual has unearned advantages of which he or she may well remain unconscious.[1]

So it stands to reason that individuals who deviate from these norms have, in effect, unearned disadvantages of which they may or may not be aware. While a person who embodies the characteristics associated with privilege may enjoy easy success in some areas, a person who does not embody these characteristics likely faces a harder road.

Redefining the game and reshaping America is fundamentally about moving toward a society where advantage and disadvantage are independent of identifiers. But to ignore or deny the gross and subtle effects of these identifiers and the role they play in generating and prolonging inequality, is to ignore or deny the very dynamics that underlie our society.

The reality for Black people is that race and ethnicity continue to be among the most salient of these social identifiers in twenty-first-century America. Consequently, while it is important that we establish a strong identity, it is of paramount importance that we establish a strong *racial and ethnic* identity. Our race and ethnicity must engender a sense of genuine pride.

The navigation and negotiation of identity that takes place in the lives of African Americans can carry a unique set of considerations. Among them is a fundamental decision about how your identity interacts with society. Will you completely *assimilate*—adopt the values of popular American culture—or will you *negotiate*—challenge these norms and leverage your African-American identity in engaging others?

Perhaps one of the best descriptions of the complexity of Black identity in America comes from activist and author W.E.B. DuBois in his classic work, *The Souls of Black Folk*. DuBois describes African Americans as possessing two "warring souls," one African and one American, a sort of "double consciousness" or a "veil." DuBois writes:

> *It is a peculiar sensation, this double-consciousness, this sense of always looking at one's self through the eyes of others, of measuring one's soul by the tape of a world that looks on in amused contempt and pity. One ever feels his two-ness—an American, a Negro; two souls, two thoughts, two unreconciled strivings; two warring ideals in one dark body, whose dogged strength alone keeps it from being torn asunder.*

A strong identity finds harmony between these two perspectives. And while this identity may be informed by your history, it is not defined by your history. We must comfortably embrace our history as both descendants of Africans and residents of America. But we must also acknowledge that while America has come a long way in its perception and treatment of people of color, it still has a long way to go.

Purpose

Purpose is the remaining pillar of the first strategy for redefining the game and reshaping America. *Your purpose is your reason for being.* Purpose answers the question, "Why do I exist?" It explains your existence. It sheds light on what you are living for. It helps define your destiny. And there are a few considerations that can shape how you conceptualize and ultimately come to define your purpose.

▸ *You were made to serve multiple purposes.* Your purpose could be to serve as a loving and responsible parent; to uplift and inspire others through music as a composer; and to mentor young people in your neighborhood. You are not confined to one purpose and, in fact, you may serve different purposes at different points in your life. For example, if you are diagnosed with sickle cell disease, you may dedicate your life thereafter to increasing awareness of how others can live the healthiest life possible with the condition. Life's circumstances, including tragedies, may change or redefine your purpose.

Figure 1–3. Purpose sheds light on why you exist.

▸ *You have an individual purpose and one that is shared with others.* Part of your purpose is particular to you, while in some instances it is intertwined with other individuals. For example, your individual purpose may be to serve as an advocate for quality education in urban schools, while your shared purpose may be to work with others to establish a charter school in an underserved community. We (the authors) have long believed that we have a shared purpose. Throughout this book you will learn about some of the products of our collective purpose, such as the businesses we have cofounded and the ways we have touched people's lives together. In fact, this book is one of those products!

▸ *Your purpose is a higher calling to show you what can be done with your passion and gifts.* Some people argue that your purpose is defined by your passion and your gifts. They believe that those things you are naturally drawn to or that you love to do (your passion) and those things that you naturally do well (your gifts) describe why you were placed on this earth. Passion and gifts are central components of excellence, not purpose (as we'll show in Strategy 3). You may have a passion and a gift for creating music. Your purpose, however, is what you do with that passion and gift.

▸ *Your purpose is determined by nature via nurture.* Some people believe their purpose is determined by a higher power or by "nature," while others believe it is "nurture" or their own will that determines their purpose. We believe it is a combination of the two, where purpose is determined by nature via nurture. Nature uniquely empowers you with the potential to pursue your purpose. However, you must nurture that potential in ways that prepare you for when opportunities present themselves. It is nature that equips you with the potential to compose music or reform the educational system. The extent to which you nurture that potential ultimately determines whether you fulfill those purposes.

▸ *We believe that we were created with a purpose in mind: a divine purpose.* Along these lines, we'd like to share our personal perspective on what purpose means to us: God is the higher power and the "nature" that ultimately determines our purpose. Yet we also accept responsibility to "nurture" ourselves through worship, discipleship, stewardship, and fellowship. This enables us to draw closer to God and reveal His many uses for us. Both of us have an identity that is grounded in the belief that we are children of God. Our overarching purpose is to bring glory to God in everything we do. (In doing so, we choose to serve the purposes identified by Rick Warren in *The Purpose-Driven Life*, an excellent book on the subject of purpose.)

Warren defines a purpose-driven life as a "life guided, controlled, and directed by God's purposes. Consequently, we look to God first, not ourselves, to understand our purpose. We look upward, not inward."

....
Identity keeps you grounded and purpose keeps you going.
....

Identity and Purpose for African Americans
We proudly define our identities as African Americans. We are aware of the rich legacy of excellence established by our people and proudly, if not humbly,

endeavor to continue that legacy. As we look to other African Americans as role models, this legacy is a source of inspiration for us that propels us both as scholars, entrepreneurs, authors, speakers, and community servants. Within the broader context of our lives, our identities also reflect the fact that we define ourselves as husbands, fathers, sons, friends, and much, much more.

Of these identities, it is our African-American identity, our Black identity, that has enormous significance for us and forms the premise of this book. What does it mean to be Black or African American? And, more important, why does it matter?

In many ways, we are asking the same question that other ethnic groups or immigrants to the United States might ask themselves. Our answer is not only about the unique aspects of our community but also about the history, culture, and values of African Americans as a collective. Some critics believe that our emphasis on "Black Faces in White Places" is a throwback to the days of segregation and racial tension. We don't see it that way. We believe that pride in the history, culture, and values of African Americans is a source of strength that helps us better relate to others and empowers our actions at work, school, church, and in society. In fact, without a cultural foundation to our identity and purpose, we have no springboard for achieving greatness.

....
Jonas Salk once said, "Good parents give their children roots and wings. Roots to know where home is, wings to fly away and exercise what's been taught them." Identity represents roots, while purpose represents wings.
....

AFRICAN-AMERICAN CULTURE

What defines African-American culture? As we described above, culture is embodied in the history, norms, and values of the people, organizations, and institutions of an ethnic group. When Dr. Maulana Karenga developed the idea of Kwanzaa in 1967, he drew upon the traditions of West Africa and the historical circumstances of African Americans to create a modern context for African-American culture that could serve as the basis for education, exploration, and excellence in our lives and community. Seven principles, the Nguzo Saba, clarify what makes African Americans unique in the American context and give us a basis for discussing the future of our community.

Umoja (Unity)
To strive for and maintain unity in the family, community, nation, and race

Kujichagulia (Self-Determination)
To define ourselves, name ourselves, create for ourselves, and speak for ourselves

Ujima (Collective Work and Responsibility)
To build and maintain our community together and to make our brothers' and sisters' problems our problems and solve them together

Ujamaa (Cooperative Economics)
To build and maintain our own stores, shops, and other businesses and to profit from them together

Nia (Purpose)
To make our collective vocation the building and developing of our community in order to restore our people to their traditional greatness

Kuumba (Creativity)
To do always as much as we can, in the way we can, in order to leave our community more beautiful and beneficial than we inherited it

Imani (Faith)
To believe with all our heart in our people, our parents, our teachers, our leaders, and the righteousness and victory of our struggle

Source: www.officialkwanzaasite.org

Table 1–1. The Seven Kwanzaa Principles.

These seven principles (listed in Table 1–1) connect us to our roots before slavery and recognize the cultural aspects of the African-American experience. Dr. Karenga's efforts helped to codify much of the cultural capital that was kept in the institutions of the Black community. Strategy 2 encompasses cultural capital in the context of exposure to others, and in that discussion we make reference to the importance of learning, studying, and transmitting the history, themes, and significance of African-American culture. This knowledge is a currency that can and should be leveraged. *If you don't know where you've been, you don't know where you're going.* Therefore, understanding your cultural background is important to developing a strong identity and purpose.

We also believe that the seven principles represent the values that have historically kept our community together when political, economic, social, and institutional forces attempted to tear us apart. We are proud of that heritage, but we had to learn it. It was not taught in our public schools. It was not reinforced in popular culture. It was not always easily accessible. In fact, without our families' efforts, the efforts of teachers like Dr. James Clark who led the Black History Month planning committee at Jeffrey's (J.R.'s) high school, and our personal efforts, we might have chosen not to embrace this identity at all.

Society can misinterpret the fact and assume that being proud of who you are necessarily means that you are critical of others who do not share your characteristics or traits. For example, some people would argue that to be proud of being Black, or to be pro-Black, means that you are anti-white. Or if you are an advocate for women, then you are at odds with men. You can and should celebrate all of the characteristics of your identity and purpose while simultaneously honoring, acknowledging, and celebrating the characteristics of others who may be different from you. Throughout this book, you will see how the pride instilled in us by our parents gave us the strength to overcome certain challenges. This same pattern emerges as we describe the experiences of other accomplished African Americans in subsequent chapters. The great people we profile are proud of their identity and transparent about their purpose. Rather than deny their identity, they embrace it with ease. Rather than shy away from their purpose, they pursue it with passion.

As it relates specifically to identity and purpose, the signature challenges for African Americans, particularly for our youth, are twofold. The first challenge is developing, navigating, and negotiating identity, at times in a relative vacuum. In the absence of societal reinforcement (i.e., role models or mentors), the navigation of identity takes on a different dimension. Who should I emulate? What values should be important to me? This is not to suggest that a Black identity is dependent on having Black role models, but rather that it can simply be more difficult.

The second challenge is embracing one's "nature" or calling and "nurturing" one's potential in positive ways in a world with so many potentially negative or even limiting images, messages, assumptions, and stereotypes. This includes everything from history books that begin African-American history with slavery, to demeaning music videos, to the dearth of African Americans at the upper levels of almost any profession or industry. For example, as African-American men, we know that there are many who would try to stereotype us according to what they read in newspapers and see on TV and in music videos, making us out to be hustlers, "ballers," and pimps. But if we believe that God created us for a divine purpose, we confidently chart a course that is different from these stereotypes.

OUR SPIRITUAL FOUNDATION

Spirituality has always been a cornerstone of African and other cultures, and it has been an important building block for what each of us has become. We'd like to share with you our thoughts on the relationship between our own spirituality, identity, and purpose.

Reading, studying, and pursuing God's word has led us to four important lessons for our lives related to our identity and purpose.

1. A solid spiritual foundation has grounded us in a set of principles for living well

2. A solid spiritual foundation has provided boundaries for our actions and has been instrumental in developing a conscience that limits unhealthy actions and unproductive activities

3. A solid spiritual foundation has helped us prioritize what is important in our lives.

4. A solid spiritual foundation has helped us establish a belief system that puts our lives and living into perspective

These four lessons have been essential elements of our identity and purpose because they provide a context that is beyond the activities of every day. The development of this aspect of our identity and purpose has been of paramount importance to us as Black faces in white places.

Jeffrey's Story

We were one of two Black families in our apartment complex in Parsippany. The other had a son named Raheem, and together, at least for a time, we made up the entire Black population at Intervale Elementary School.

While race wasn't foremost on my mind, the first crush I remember having points to at least some awareness that I was different from most of the kids around me and perhaps that I wanted to be romantically linked with someone who was also Black. I was playing drums in a band made up of students from several schools in the area. I remember having a crush on Esperanza Escobar who played the flute on the opposite side of the band. And it was very simple for me because she was the darkest one around. There were no Black girls in the band. I remember saying to myself, "I don't have a crush on any of these other girls here." Using my eighth grade logic I thought, 'I'm Black and she's sort of Black. Let me talk to her."

By the time I got to high school, I was a good student and was on the honors or higher-level track in school. And as much as it served as an academic benefit, it was a social hindrance. I was the only Black student in my classes and later one of just a few.

I may never know for sure, but I think Dr. Clark, the only Black teacher at my high school, deliberately got me involved with the Black History Month planning committee at my school because he wanted to keep me connected to the Black community. I never had a class with Dr. Clark—he was the chair of the department that taught remedial courses—but he made sure I was involved with the other Black students, even if only for a portion of the year. I wasn't even sure why I was doing it at first, but it became one of the most meaningful events in my high school career and helped me to raise my Black consciousness.

It was during high school that I started to understand the significance of being "the first." Dr. Clark or my parents would often wonder aloud—or pronounce—that I was the first Black person to win a student office at my school or to be the president of the National Honor Society. I never lost that feeling that what I was doing meant something.

Other than during Black History Month events and a special two-period politics class during my senior year, I didn't get to interact with Black students. I simply didn't get to know them and they didn't get to know me because we weren't in the same classes.

Near the end of high school, one of my four Black classmates, named Tanya, having had the chance to get to know me in that politics class, realized I wasn't all that different from the other Black students. One day, she revealed that others thought I was "this smart Black guy." All these years later Tanya's exact words are fuzzy, but I recall that she said something suggesting that the other Black students thought that in some way, I had forgotten them.

While the Black students may have thought I was partying with white kids every weekend, I was actually spending more time taking part in church activities and didn't get a lot of invitations to hang out with my white classmates. A lot of parties would happen on a Friday or Saturday night. I never got a real strong invitation until late, very late in my high school years. Sometimes I went and sometimes I didn't. It didn't mean much to me.

Watching the PBS documentary *Eyes on the Prize*, which chronicled the Civil Rights Movement, influenced my views about race and racism. Seeing Black students integrating Central High School in Little Rock, Arkansas, burned in my consciousness. I remember thinking if I had to go to school there, I would have to fight every day. All they wanted to do was go to school, and there was a bunch of white people trying to stop them. I definitely wasn't militant but perhaps for the first time in my life I became very interested in my history as a young Black man in America, because I had a better sense of how some people might view me in the broader world. All of these experiences helped to shape my identity by giving me perspective on how my life fit into a cultural and historical context.

Randal's Story

Our townhouse in East Windsor kept my mother connected to her city roots. When she and Dad were looking for houses, they gravitated to the townhouse instead of one of the many free-standing homes in the area because Mom didn't want to be isolated. She liked the idea of neighbors being close by. We went from a big, diverse city to a small, largely Jewish suburban township. The neighborhood and our schools were mostly white, and so much of our social circle was made up of white kids.

At times, being the only Black student in so many of my classes—I was the lone African American in every class except gym—made me feel self-conscious. When topics like the Civil Rights Movement came up, I felt like the spotlight was on me. I felt like I had to speak for all Black people and felt pressure to represent Black people in a positive light.

Although I didn't have a lot of Black friends at high school, I was popular. I was voted homecoming and prom king, "best personality," and spoke at my high school graduation. I left high school on a high note—with lots of friends and a scholarship to attend Rutgers. It would probably have been a shock to my high school friends to find out just how challenging my first year of college really was.

During my first semester at Rutgers, I walked in predominantly white circles and predominantly Black circles with dramatically different levels of ease. The former represented a world I was all too accustomed to from my years growing up in a largely white neighborhood. The latter represented a world I desperately wanted to connect with at a deeper level despite limited interactions with Black peers in my hometown.

I wasn't looking to divorce myself from my white friends. They were all great friends, but I still felt like there was something missing in my life. Instead, I was hoping to establish a wider range of friendships with Black people. This tension I felt inside was more than just your typical adolescent struggle to "fit in." It also reflected unresolved issues related to my identity. I found it difficult to fully define myself with very few meaningful relationships with peers who looked like me. I wanted to find more balance with the hope of finding myself, and I figured college was my last chance to do it.

I didn't connect with a group of Black students right away. When Friday night rolled around and Black students were hanging out together studying or socializing, I was hopping on a bus, by myself, and heading to the parties I was told I would find at the predominantly white fraternity houses on College Avenue. What I was yearning for was an opportunity to explore who I was, with people who were more like me. And as I sought out ways to make this transition, my identity began to evolve right before my eyes.

I will never forget the first meeting I attended of the Rutgers chapter of the National Society of Black Engineers. As I looked out into the all-Black room of students, I felt anxious, apprehensive, and to some extent optimistic. I was nervous because I was worried about whether I would be accepted, yet at the same time, I was hopeful that this could be the beginning of an important new chapter in my life.

I sat down, almost in the middle of the room. There was a guy sitting next to me, and he looked like he didn't know too many people either. He turned to me and said, "Hi. I'm Jeff Robinson."

Jeff, whom I later came to know as JR, told me he was from Parsippany, New Jersey. We continued to talk and had a really good rapport for an initial meeting. It became clear that we had a lot in common. We grew up in similar neighborhoods, attended similar high schools, and had similar interests.

That immediate connection with JR and that Rutgers NSBE meeting planted a seed that would grow into close relationships with other African Americans, African Caribbeans, and Africans, which continue to this day. Of all those relationships that began as a result of NSBE, JR and I formed a special bond. Today, he is my closest friend, business partner, and collaborator. Our connection from that day was a validation of where we had come from and a reinforcement of where we were headed. Not only did I get academic and professional support from JR and my fellow NSBE members, but I also learned about Black history and Black culture in a way that instilled pride in my people, shaped my identity as an African American, and ultimately helped me become the man I am today.

The Randal Pinkett who graduated from Rutgers was a much different person than the one who first arrived on campus. I was a better person, with a different walk, talk, style, and sense of self. I resolved my inner tension and found the balance I was searching for. I finally felt complete.

Self-Determination: Your Identity as an Asset and Your Purpose as a Source of Power

Establishing a strong identity and purpose is the foundation of redefining the game and reshaping America.

▶ *A strong identity is a tremendous asset.* Your ethnicity, your uniqueness, your culture, and your diversity—all aspects of your identity—are perhaps your greatest contributions to anything you do. Inevitably, there are times when society may suggest that your ethnic identity should be suppressed or that it is a liability. We argue the opposite: that your ethnic identity should be amplified because it represents a personal, strategic competitive advantage that no one else can replicate. What makes you unique is also what enables you to make truly unique contributions. This is an idea we will revisit with Strategy 4: Build Diverse and Solid Relationships. Rather than assimilate and absorb every aspect of the dominant American culture, you should be critical of the values associated with the dominant culture and evaluate what aspects of your personal identity you are not willing to give up. At times, the prevailing wisdom will be at odds with the values you hold as your own, much like the principles of Kwanzaa can be at odds with popular cultural norms. A strong identity reflects an appreciation of your uniqueness, and the dignity associated with knowing it is something you value and that society should value.

▶ *A well-defined purpose is a tremendous source of power.* Knowing and embracing your purpose engenders confidence in your capacities and command of your capabilities. For us, when we came to believe that God ultimately shaped our purpose, we realized that our power came from Him and Him only. This was an empowering revelation! Coming to understand your particular purpose unleashes a power within you that can transform your life and the lives of others.

▶ *A strong identity gives you a solid sense of self.* A strong identity is an acknowledgment of what makes you, you. It reflects those traits that you choose to hold near and dear to your heart.

▶ *A well-defined purpose gives you a definitive sense of direction.* When society suggests that you should go in one direction, it is your purpose that gives you the self-confidence to know that you can choose to go down another path. It gives you the strength and the stamina to withstand any negative influences or messages from society. According to Lewis Carroll, the author of *Alice in Wonderland,* "If you don't know where you are going, any road will get you there." Purpose is what points you in the right direction.

▶ *A strong identity grounds you. It allows you to define yourself on your terms, as opposed to others defining you on their terms.* A saying that we both learned in college is that "if you stand for nothing, you will fall for anything." Well, similarly, if you do not define yourself, others will define you.

▶ *A well-defined purpose gives your life meaning.* People often make reference to the need to "find themselves" or identify the "meaning of life." These are both attempts to find their purpose. In his book *The Purpose-Driven Life* (Zondervan, 2002), Rick Warren writes, "Without a purpose, life is motion without meaning, activity without direction, and events without reason. Without a purpose, life is trivial, petty, and pointless." A purpose allows you to situate yourself within society and to see the interconnectedness between your purpose and that of others. A purpose gives the essential and much-needed meaning to your life.

Identity answers the questions, Who am I? and What makes me unique?
Purpose answers the questions, Why do I exist? and Where am I going?

The process of establishing a strong identity and purpose ultimately leads to self-determination, which means defining who you are and why you exist (see Figure 1–4). Identity speaks to who you are. Purpose speaks to why you exist and where you are going. Identity is your anchor. Purpose is your compass.

Together, identity and purpose give you the strength and the stamina to withstand the inevitable challenges of being a Black face in a white place and an agent of societal change. Without self-determination, it is much easier for the game to redefine you than for you to redefine the game.

When people say, "You should never forget who you are and where you come from," they are saying you should always maintain a strong identity and sense of purpose.

The Interdependence of Strategies 1 and 2

One of the most effective ways to establish a strong identity and purpose is to *obtain broad exposure* to the world around you, which is our second strategy. Strategies 1 and 2 are closely related and, in many ways, interdependent. The order of the two strategies could easily be interchanged.

Your identity and purpose are major factors in determining the kinds of exposure and experiences you seek. Conversely, the exposure and experiences you seek can significantly shape how you construct your identity and define your purpose. Arguably, the cycle between the two is never-ending, as you will see in the next chapter.

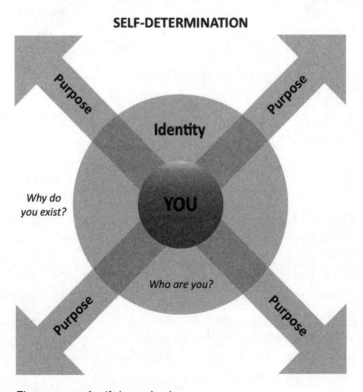

Figure 1–4. The concept of self-determination.

Obtain Broad Exposure

We must not cease from exploration. And the end of all our exploring will be to arrive where we began and to know the place for the first time.

—T. S. Eliot

DRAW A CIRCLE on a piece of paper. Within that circle write "Comfort Zone." This first circle represents your reality today. It represents all of the things you do now; the things to which you are accustomed and the things you are comfortable doing.

Now draw a larger circle around the first circle and in the space between the two circles write "Growth Zone." This space between the two circles represents possibilities. It represents opportunities for growth and positive change. Finally, draw a line with an arrow that begins on the first circle and ends anywhere on the second circle, and just above the line write "Discomfort."

This is a visual depiction of growth and development—both personal and professional (see Figure 2–2). And as the picture implies, any time you move beyond your comfort zone you are likely to experience some kind of discomfort. You cannot do the same things and expect a different outcome. Or, stated differently, if you keep doing what you're doing, you will keep getting what you're getting.

Figure 2–1. The path to greatness (Strategy 2).

Discomfort can have multiple interpretations. There's emotional discomfort, which manifests itself in the form of anxiety, disappointment, or fear. For example, it is not uncommon to feel a sense of anxiety right before giving your first public speech. (In fact, it is not uncommon to feel anxiety anytime you have to give a public speech!) You might experience physical discomfort, such as a pain, shortness of breath, or fatigue. Athletic training is the perfect example here. You could feel discomfort in the form of frustration, unhappiness, or dissatisfaction when you are trying to forgo or discontinue certain behaviors, such as when you are trying to cut down on some of your favorite foods in order to eat healthier. But, regardless of the type of discomfort, what is common across all of these examples is the likelihood of growth as a result of each experience. The anxiety you experience before a speech is necessary for you to develop as a public speaker. The pain you feel during intense sports training is necessary for you to improve as an athlete. And the dissatisfaction you may experience by cutting down on certain foods is necessary for you to live a healthier lifestyle.

Your Comfort Zone and Growth Zone

You have a *comfort zone* that is reflected in your daily experiences and the things to which you are typically exposed: the people with whom you regularly spend time; places you are accustomed to going; even traditional ways of thinking. But you also proba-bly have had moments that you look back upon and say, "I'll never forget when I did X," or, "That was a time in my life I will always remember." What may have been a typical or straightforward experience for others was a transformative experience for you. It could have been something as seemingly mundane as a trip outside of your neighborhood or something as elaborate as a

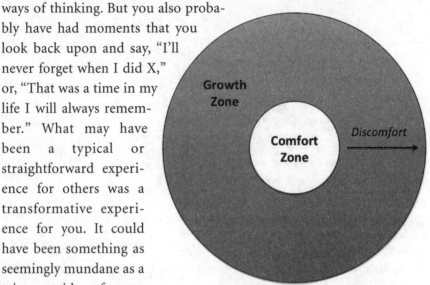

Figure 2–2. Outside your comfort zone lies your growth zone.

tour of multiple foreign countries. These experiences took you beyond your comfort zone and into your *growth zone.*

It is only when we seek experiences that bring about a healthy level of discomfort—those experiences that challenge us to do things we normally would not do—and when we are exposed to differences—perspectives, places, people, and possibilities that are dissimilar from the ones we are accustomed to—that we grow and develop. The fundamental premise of Strategy 2 is that when we actively seek the broadest possible exposure and the widest diversity in experiences it not only makes us a better person, it also makes us better prepared and better equipped to redefine the game and reshape America. But it does not happen naturally because oftentimes we confine ourselves to our comfort zones. Broad exposure and diverse experiences that push you further into your growth zone must happen deliberately, because they are key to your future success.

Top performers are not just comfortable with discomfort—they actively seek discomfort. They are constantly in search of ways to grow and improve upon their abilities. When it is time to perform—when it is "game time"—they draw upon the skills they have developed (we will revisit this idea in Strategy 3: Demonstrate Excellence). Similarly, you should actively seek opportunities to obtain broad exposure. Your ability to redefine the game is significantly bolstered by your ability to draw upon diverse experiences and varied perspectives. Or, as stated by Jean Riboud, a French billionaire credited with building the world's leading oilfield testing company, Schlumberger Ltd.: "If you want to innovate, to change an enterprise of society, it takes people willing to do what is not expected." Redefining the game requires that we all do something that is not expected—something that takes us beyond our collective comfort zone and into our growth zone.

Look at Figure 2–2 again. The beauty of the diagram is that there is always the possibility of drawing additional circles. As your comfort zone becomes larger, your growth zone can also become larger. The possibilities—for you and our society—are endless.

Why Moving Beyond Your Comfort Zone Is Important

Moving beyond our comfort zone was an important aspect of our personal development. Some of this was by default, because it was inherent to our experience growing up as Black Faces in White Places. However, there were also points in our early years that our parents deliberately exposed us to other cultures, activities, circumstances, and people, all of which expanded what we thought the world was or what we thought was possible. All of these experiences helped us develop as individuals.

Having a broad set of experiences will allow you to:

▶ *Cultivate a greater appreciation of yourself and others.* To develop a strong identity and purpose (as discussed in Strategy 1), it is important to understand the links between who you are and where you are going, and their historical and cultural context. African Americans are linked to the experiences of other people of African heritage spread around the world. This is called the African Diaspora, and exposure to other members of the Diaspora is invaluable. People of African descent live across the globe—in the United States but also in Brazil, England, Germany, the Caribbean, and the African continent, of course. Exposure to the experiences and history of people from these places not only situates your own African-ness in a global context, but also places your life experiences in perspective.

▸ *Expand your worldview.* Limited experiences can lead to a limited worldview. If we do not experience a diversity of ideas in our lives, we sell ourselves short in this regard. In an increasingly global economy and interconnected world, it is a disadvantage not to know about global issues and concerns. Generally speaking, Americans have used our relative affluence and geography to isolate ourselves from the rest of the world. For example, in many countries, people speak more than one language, but most U.S. citizens only speak English. Broader experiences can help you develop an understanding and appreciation of other perspectives. This is a valuable tool in your toolbox, one that allows you to better understand the people you encounter in business, academia, and other settings. With this tool, you will be able to recognize and evaluate opportunities in a global context—which is important as our world grows more interconnected.

▸ *Build cultural capital.* "Cultural capital" is a term used to describe the resources that shape how you think and act in a local and global context. This set of resources (i.e., connections, experiences, and insights) is acquired and cultivated. Attending cultural events, learning languages, and engaging in activities related to your culture are examples of building cultural capital. These experiences make the connection between the present and history; they help you understand how culture and society are interconnected. There are many nuances you can learn from being immersed in your own or other cultures. Exposure to ideas and cultures, people and places, is a valuable asset that should be developed throughout your life.

▶ *Broaden your horizons and sense of limitless possibilities.* Broad exposure allows you to see the world beyond your immediate surroundings and instills a sense of limitless possibilities. For example, exposure to the life stories of successful African Americans motivates us to see new possibilities for ourselves. Familiarity with Black Wall Street, one of the wealthiest African-American communities of the early 1900s in Tulsa, Oklahoma (which was eventually devastated by a race riot), empowers us to see new possibilities for our communities. Knowledge of our history in America from the slave house to the White House renews our sense of possibilities for our country and our global society.

....
If experience is the best teacher, exposure creates the best classroom.
....

As we meet people, travel to and from places, and learn about new possibilities on a daily basis, we expand our perspective and add more tools to our tool belts. These tools empower us to think creatively, innovatively, and differently about how to overcome challenges and seize opportunities. It was early exposure that significantly shaped our careers as engineers and business owners.

Randal's relationship with Wayne Abbott began, as we mentioned in Chapter 1, as children growing up in New Jersey. The Abbott family was from St. Thomas and had moved to Twin Rivers—just a few miles from East Windsor—at around the same time as the Pinketts. Growing up, Randal and his brother Dan spent a lot of time with Wayne at each other's homes and were all part of the "Our Kids" group.

Years later, Wayne helped ease the transition into life at Rutgers for both of us. It was Wayne who made sure we knew about that first NSBE meeting where we met and connected with other Black students with similar interests. Wayne was that guy on campus who tried to connect students with opportunities and information—and in that vein he invited Randy to Black Expo in 1993.

R.P. I had never really witnessed, in person, Black business owners. I had known of a few and heard of a few, but I can't say that I had ever really touched one, unlike, say, a doctor. So going to Black Expo, where you had

Black business owners lined up in a huge convention center for as far as the eye could see, was jaw-dropping. I was like, "Wow. Not only are Black folk running companies, we are doing it in numbers." I walked up and down the convention center just to look at people who had all kinds of businesses. Wayne almost had to drag me out of that Expo by my ankles because I could've stayed there for the rest of my life.

Similarly, the genesis of Jeffrey's decision to pursue engineering came from what some might consider an unlikely source. J.R.'s dad never went to college and worked as electrician, but he deliberately exposed JR to the possibility of being an engineer by taking him to electrical trade shows.

J.R. One time, my father saw this guy from PSE&G that he knew, and he said, "That's a Black engineer." That was a big deal to my dad because this was the guy who designed the systems that my dad would eventually install. His name was Mel Hinton, and he was the man who used to talk to me about going to Rutgers. He'd say, "You should think about going to Rutgers to be an engineer." My dad wasn't sure I was going into engineering, but he wanted to show me what other people did. It made an impression on me.

Wayne Abbott provided a vision for Randal and others for becoming an entrepreneur. New York's Black Expo blew Randal away; his first experience attending the National Society of Black Engineers convention had a similar effect in terms of his view of African Americans pursuing careers in technology. Similarly, J.R.'s dad, himself not a college graduate, deliberately exposed J.R. to people and information that ultimately inspired him. This is the power of getting out and exposing yourself to something different—and being open about where that exposure may come from.

Pursuing Broad Exposure and Diverse Experiences

Strategy 1 expressed our belief that self-determination is an important asset for those who endeavor to redefine the game and reshape America. Having a strong identity and purpose provides the ever-so-important base from which you can springboard. There are also a number of game-changing benefits to having broad exposure and diverse experiences.

As African Americans, we are constantly aware of how our experiences are different from those around us. We not only see that difference as an asset, but we also see it as something that must be cultivated through broad exposure so that we become more effective change agents in a global society. Here are some reasons why:

▸ *Enhancing leadership and citizenship.* Insight into others makes you a better leader and citizen. If leadership is about inspiring and influencing other people, then a leader with broad exposure is a leader who will be able to better relate to those he leads. Citizenship is an idea rooted in the concepts of community, democracy, and service. By deliberately pursuing experiences beyond our comfort zone, we are better able to relate to other communities, engage in democratic processes, and serve others.

▸ *Reducing prejudice.* Actually, this is a two-way street. When you are exposed to different experiences, you learn about others and are more likely to move beyond the stereotypes that lead to prejudices. By stretching yourself and going into situations and events where Blacks may not be fully represented, you also give others a chance to learn about your life and experiences as an African American.

▸ *Promoting creativity and innovation in solving problems.* When faced with challenges in life, the person who has had a diversity of experiences will have either: (1) a wellspring of options to choose from, or (2) a set of experiences to draw on to find a creative solution to a problem. Experts refer to the extremely valuable ability to analyze different situations from different perspectives using fancy phrases such as *cognitive complexity* and *multidimensional thinking.* Such thinking enables you to be more creative, more insightful, and more innovative in your approach to both personal and professional matters. It fosters an ability to effectively navigate inevitable situations that force you to move beyond your comfort zone. It gives you a broader set of tools to effect change.

▸ *Fostering compassion for others and, therefore, more effective service to others.* Community service has been a part of our life experience since we were in elementary school. Our parents stressed the fact that some people were not as fortunate as we were and that it was important for us to help others in some way. "There, but by the grace of God, go I," we learned.

We must always ask: For whom are we reshaping America? Why does the game need to be redefined? It is one thing to ask these hypothetical questions, but it is quite another to have answers based on intimate knowledge of the circumstances other people face. Such knowledge ultimately helps you to be more effective in your service to others. When your experiences move you from being self-centered to other-centered, you become aware of the things that need to be changed and are better equipped to actually make the changes. Naturally, we will revisit this theme in Strategy 10: Give Back Generously.

> *For parents and other adults who play a role in the life of a young person, involvement is the close cousin to exposure. Your active involvement can ensure that a young person is exposed to as much of the world as possible.*

Looking Back, Looking Ahead

Strategy 2 is interlinked with both Strategies 1 and 3. The relationship is shown in Figure 2–3.

Looking back to Strategy 1, one of the most effective ways to help establish a strong identity and purpose is to gain broad exposure and diverse experiences. As you endeavor to define who you are and where you are going, it is exposure to people, places, possibilities, and the like that expands your horizons. Equally, a strong identity and a well-defined purpose help frame the kinds of exposure that can best serve you.

Experiences that do not reflect your identity (i.e., an American traveling abroad) or your purpose (i.e., a business person meeting with a community activist) are experiences that often take you into your growth zone. What is

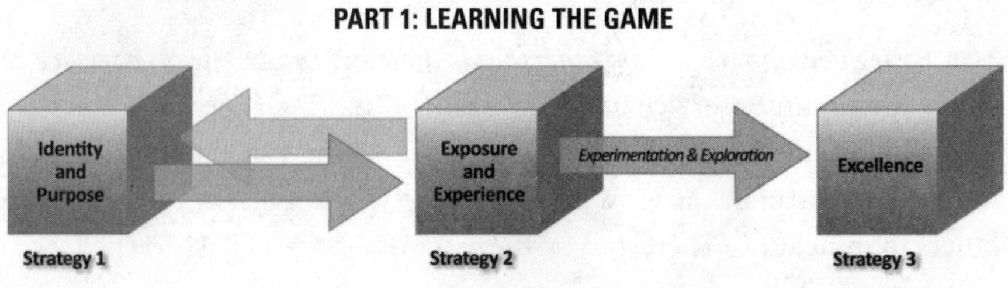

PART 1: LEARNING THE GAME

| Identity and Purpose | Exposure and Experience | Experimentation & Exploration | Excellence |

Strategy 1 — Strategy 2 — Strategy 3

Figure 2–3. Learning the game: relationship between Strategies 1, 2, and 3.

even more powerful is that, as a result of growth experiences, you may re-examine or reshape your identity and purpose in very transformative ways. The American traveling abroad may have a greater appreciation and sense of pride of what it means to live in the United States after returning home. The business person meeting with an activist may change her behavior to become more involved in the community. To the extent that identity and purpose are like a burning fire that evolves over time, experience and exposure provide the fuel to the fire.

You may wonder, "Are my identity and purpose limited by my experiences?" The answer is, "No." In the words of Aldous Huxley, "Experience is not what happens to you. *It is what you do* [emphasis ours] with what happens to you." Your identity and purpose are only limited by *your interpretation* of your experiences. Self-determination is informed but not defined by what you are exposed to—we believe it is up to you to choose your own path. (We believe it is ultimately in God's hands.)

Broad exposure and diverse experiences naturally lead to opportunities for experimentation and exploration. You must be willing to step out of your comfort zone and allow life's journey and your natural curiosity to lead you down new and different pathways. The journey will help you identify your *passion*—those activities you are naturally drawn to—and your *gifts*—those abilities you are naturally blessed with.

Looking ahead to Strategy 3, passion and gifts represent two of the four facets of excellence, as it is defined in the next chapter. Strategy 2 allows you to pinpoint the areas where you can, and must, demonstrate excellence.

STRATEGY 3

Demonstrate Excellence

When you can do the common things in life in an uncommon way, you will command the attention of the world.

—George Washington Carver

AMERICANS OF every race, creed, and color shed tears on January 20, 2009, as Barack Obama, a Black man, was sworn in as the forty-fourth President of the United States. Commentators and ordinary Americans proclaimed that Blacks in the United States had "overcome." Americans living and traveling abroad noted that they were suddenly regarded more favorably. This was a new day. America changed forever.

Well, not so fast.

In the first fifty days of Obama's presidency, what many African Americans feared would happen to the nation's first Black president began to occur. The criticism of the Obama administration's actions to revive the crippled economy came from pundits, economists, and ordinary citizens—some of whom voted him into office.

The new administration was slammed for not articulating a cohesive proposal. When it released its plan for stimulating the economy, it was criticized for not simultaneously having a plan to revive the ailing housing market—as if an economy that unraveled over the previous eight years could be fixed overnight!

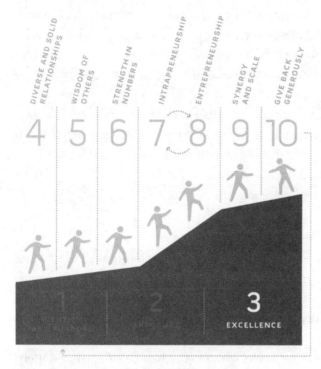

Figure 3–1. The path to greatness (Strategy 3).

And in one striking example, the new president was suddenly presiding over the "Obama Bear Market," according to news stories and media pundits. There's no dispute that stocks fell—a bear market is defined as a drop of 20 percent or more in the stock market—and early in Obama's presidency stocks suffered a steep decline.

What we find interesting—but not necessarily surprising—is how pervasive the term "Obama Bear Market" suddenly became. Media Matters for America, a not-for-profit media watchdog group, did a search through a media database and found ten instances of the phrase "Obama Bear Market" in just the first fifty days of Obama's presidency. By contrast, Media Matters found only ten uses of the phrase "Bush Bear Market" during George W. Bush's entire eight years in office, despite the fact that he presided over *two* bear markets, the first in 2001 and the second in 2008, when stocks fell more than 40 percent.

Later on in Obama's first year, as he addressed Congress and the nation to explain his approach to health care reform, South Carolina Representative Joe Wilson shouted, "You lie!" It was a rare and distasteful outburst not typically hurled at the commander in chief of the United States in a formal setting. It was so unsettling that it left many African Americans—and media outlets—wondering if other presidents had been treated this way. The *New York Times* did some research. In recent history it only found evidence of Republicans snickering and making faces at one another when former president Bill Clinton was talking about a plan to pay for the health care plan he proposed during his presidency.[1]

One Playing Field, Two Sets of Rules

In the book's introduction, we defined four dimensions of the "Black Faces in White Places" experience, asking the question: Can I be judged on my merits, or will race always be a factor?

In the case of President Obama, many African Americans—and perhaps even some non-Blacks—might have wondered, suspected, and, in some cases, been completely sure (even without the benefit of Media Matters' analysis) that Obama was being judged so swiftly and harshly because of his race. Our point is that while there are likely several factors that led to President Obama's treatment, the experience is not particular to him. It is a phenomenon that many African Americans have experienced at some point in their professional lives.

For example, several studies have confirmed that Black job seekers have a harder time than whites, including those with degrees from respected colleges. The same is true for job applicants with Black-sounding names when compared to applicants with white-sounding names. In fact, there is evidence that a college degree was a *greater* liability for African Americans during the months after Obama's election as the economy continued to decline. This suggests that education made the playing field less even, not more even, for Black college graduates. According to the *New York Times* article on this subject, "The discrimination is rarely overt, according to interviews with more than two dozen college-educated black job seekers around the country, many of them out of work for months. Instead, those interviewed told subtler stories, referring to surprised looks and offhand comments, interviews that fell apart almost as soon as they began, and the sudden loss of interest from companies after meetings." The article continued, "Whether or not each case actually involved bias, the possibility has furnished an additional agonizing layer of second-guessing for many as their job searches have dragged on."[2]

Therein lies the dilemma that even the most objective African Americans—regardless of their level of income, education, or socioeconomic status—deal with each and every day, whether they are applying for a promotion or going up in front of a judge to fight an unfair speeding ticket in a suburban area with few non-Black residents.

The concept of meritocracy (a society that is based solely upon merit) is one that is considered by anyone who has ever been (or plans to be) the only Black in a predominantly white classroom, office, boardroom, or other situation. We may ask ourselves: How do the people in these white places view me? Are the decision makers evaluating me based on the content of my character or the color of my skin? If America is supposed to reward those who work hard and follow the rules, why doesn't that always seem true for African Americans? Why does there sometimes appear to be one playing field yet two sets of rules?

Remember our discussion in the Introduction about Randal's experience during *The Apprentice* finale? When it came down to the hiring decision, Donald Trump certainly wanted to hire the best performer, but he also hinted he wanted to hire the second best. By all objective criteria, Randal was the better candidate, and yet there was just enough room in the mind of the decision maker to hand the same victory to the runner-up.

Randal's decision to not share the title was met with lots of criticism. Those defending Randal were overwhelmingly African-American supporters while critics were largely whites. The unusual and unexpected turn of events in Randal's case demonstrates the complexities of Black life. "The only difference between what happened to [Pinkett] and what happens to African Americans all the time at work is that it happened to him before millions of people," says Alfred Edmond, editor-in-chief of *Blackenterprise.com,* who wrote about the show.

Meritocracy is an elusive idea in America. For generations, conventional wisdom among Black Americans has held that to succeed, you must always be the best—often to the point of being two or three times as good as your white counterparts. This message has been passed down as if it was "the Gospel truth"—a deeply rooted belief held by hardworking families raising their children in the projects, along with middle-class families striving to send their children to college and affluent Black families mingling with society's upper crust.

One of the many interesting aspects of the reality television show *The Apprentice* is how it sometimes reveals the social dynamics of real life. Would Donald Trump make the same suggestion if the runner-up was also African American or if the races were reversed? In fact, during the first season of *The Apprentice,* when, arguably, the final two candidates were closer in ability and performance, and one, Kwame Jackson, was Black and the other, Bill Rancic, was white, Trump decided *not* to hire both—he chose Rancic.

The challenge here is that American society tells us that we will be rewarded for being the best, but sometimes when we are the best, another set of rules based on nepotism, cronyism, or some arbitrary criteria seems to apply. The way this plays out in offices and classrooms can be blatant, but is often subtle and nearly imperceptible to people who haven't seen the same things happen to people like themselves. This can be demoralizing and can stymie young Black people.

That being said, you might expect us to be discouraged about the power of excellence in shaping success, but in fact, we are big proponents of excellence. However, the complicated dance between what society tells us and what we know from our experience can challenge anyone's motivation. We resolve this conflict in our psyche by understanding that the idea of meritocracy and excellence are related but not identical. Excellence goes beyond whether society rewards us or not. We desire to be excellent because we believe in the work we do and are passionate about the outcomes we want to achieve. Excellence is proactive. Expecting to be rewarded for top performance is reactive. We want you to be proactive.

Defining Excellence

What does it mean to be *excellent?* To be excellent at something means to be extremely good; to be superior; to be among the very best. Being excellent means being at the top of your game, bringing your "A" game. We believe excellence is achieved when you bring empowering beliefs and old-fashioned discipline to the intersection of your true passion and God-given gifts. This idea is illustrated as the "Diamond of Excellence" in Figure 3–2.

Demonstrating excellence is the third and final foundational strategy—after establishing a strong identity and purpose (Strategy 1) and obtaining broad exposure (Strategy 2)—for learning the game. It is foundational because a commitment to excellence is a prerequisite for the remainder of the strategies. Being exceptional at what you do can significantly enhance your ability to network (Strategy 4) with others. Someone is much more likely to mentor you

Figure 3–2. Excellence defined: four facets of the Diamond of Excellence.

(Strategy 5) if you have proven yourself as someone who can get things done. Your ability to make meaningful contributions to any team, department, group, or organization (Strategy 6) is predicated on excellence. It is difficult, if not impossible, to advance in your career at a school, corporation, or nonprofit organization in the absence of a track record of accomplishment (Strategy 7), and the same is true for any entrepreneurial pursuits (Strategy 8). And, finally, you cannot find synergy with others if you aren't bringing something to the table (Strategy 9). In each instance, it is excellence that sets the stage for great things to happen in your life, in your community, and in our society (Strategy 10).

THE FOUR FACETS OF EXCELLENCE

Many of us are taught that hard work and discipline will lead to success. Discipline is a key component, but for African Americans who want to redefine the game and reshape America, discipline alone is simply not enough. Similarly, being good at what you do is not enough. You must be excellent.

There are four facets on the Diamond of Excellence:

- ▸ *Gifts* (the talents and abilities you naturally possess)

- ▸ *Passion* (the interests and motivations you naturally possess)

▸ *Discipline* (the time, effort, and hard work you are willing to put forth)

▸ *Beliefs* (the translation of your thoughts into empowering actions and outcomes)

Understanding each of these facets and their relationship to one another helps you understand how to be excellent—both generally and specifically for Black Faces in White Places.

Gifts. We firmly believe everyone is blessed with a multitude of abilities or forms of intelligence. These capacities constitute your *human capital* or the knowledge, experience, training, and abilities you possess. In his book, *7 Kinds of Smart*, Thomas Armstrong, PhD, offers a wonderful definition of intelligence. Armstrong defines intelligence as "the ability to respond successfully to new situations and the capacity to learn from one's past experiences." Like us, Armstrong is a proponent of the groundbreaking work of Harvard professor Howard Gardner, PhD, on multiple intelligences. In his book *Frames of Mind* (Basic Books, 1993), Gardner has described up to nine forms of intelligence, as shown in Figure 3–3 (our personal perspective is that we think of them as gifts from God that should be used to benefit others and glorify God). Here are Armstrong's observations about each of these multiple intelligences:[3]

1. *Linguistic Intelligence* ("Word Smart"). According to Armstrong, "The first kind of smart, *linguistic* intelligence, is the intelligence of *words*. This is the intelligence of the journalist, storyteller, poet, and lawyer. It's the kind of thinking that brought us Shakespeare's *King Lear,* Homer's *Odyssey,* and the tales of the Arabian nights. People who are particularly smart in this area can argue, persuade, entertain, or instruct effectively through the spoken word. They often love to play around with the sounds of language through puns, word games, and tongue twisters. Sometimes they're also trivia experts because of their ability to retain facts in their mind. Or alternatively, they're masters of literacy. They read voraciously, can write clearly, and can communicate meaning in other ways through the medium of print." This is undoubtedly one of the intelligences displayed by Alice Walker, author of *The Color Purple,* or mystery

writer Walter Mosley; poets such as Maya Angelou; lawyers such as John-nie Cochran; journalists such as Gwen Ifill; public speakers such as Les Brown; and hip-hop lyricists such as Queen Latifah.

2. *Logical–Mathematical Intelligence* ("Number Smart"). According to Armstrong, "The second kind of smart, *logical–mathematical*, is the intelligence of *numbers* and *logic*. This is the intelligence of the scientist, account-ant, and computer programmer. Newton tapped into it when he invented calculus. So did Einstein when he developed his theory of relativity. Traits of a logical-mathematically-inclined individual include the ability to reason, sequence, think in terms of cause-and-effect, create hypotheses, and look for conceptual regularities or numerical patterns, and enjoy a generally rational outlook on life." This is undoubtedly one of the intelligences dis-played by scientists such as Dr. Shirley Jackson; engineers and technologists such as Dr. Mark Dean; researchers such as Dr. James West; and astronauts such as Dr. Mae Jemison.

3. *Spatial Intelligence* ("Visual Smart"). According to Armstrong, "*Spatial* intelligence is the third kind of smart and involves thinking in *pictures* and *images* and the ability to perceive, transform, and re-create different aspects of the visual-spatial world. As such it's the playground of architects, photog-raphers, artists, pilots, and mechanical engineers. Whoever designed the pyramids in Egypt had a lot of this intelligence. So too did individuals like Thomas Edison, Pablo Picasso, and Ansel Adams. Highly spatial individuals often have an acute sensitivity to visual details and can visualize vividly, draw or sketch their ideas graphically and orient themselves in three-dimensional space with ease." This is undoubtedly one of the intelligences displayed by architects such as Beverly Greene; artists such as Jacob Lawrence and Claude Clark; photographers such as Gordon Parks; and pilots such as Bessie Coleman.

4. *Musical Intelligence* ("Music Smart"). According to Armstrong, "*Musi-cal* intelligence is the fourth kind of smart. Key features of this intelligence are the capacity to perceive, appreciate, and produce *rhythms* and *melodies*. It's the intelligence of a Bach, Beethoven, or Brahms, and also that of a Bali-nese gamelan player or a Yugoslavian epic singer. Yet musical intelligence also resides in the mind of any individual who has a good ear, can sing in tune, keep time to music, and listen to different musical selections with some degree of interpretation." This is undoubtedly one of the intelligences displayed by musical artists such as Alicia Keys, Michael Jackson, Whitney Houston, and Mary J. Blige; composers such as Duke Ellington and Prince; songwriters such as Nina Simone, Quincy Jones, and Ne-Yo; and DJs such as Red Alert and Kid Capri.

5. *Bodily-Kinesthetic Intelligence* ("Body Smart"). According to Armstrong, "The fifth intelligence, *bodily-kinesthetic,* is the intelligence of the *physical* self. It includes talent in controlling one's body movements and also in handling objects skillfully. Athletes, craftspeople, mechanics, and surgeons possess a great measure of this kind of thinking. So too did Charlie Chaplin, who drew upon it in order to perform his many ingenious routines as the 'Little Tramp.' Body-smart individuals can be skilled at sewing, carpentry or model-building. Or they may enjoy physical pursuits like hiking, dancing, jogging, camping, swimming or boating. They are hands-on people who have good tactile sensitivity, need to move their bodies frequently and get 'gut reactions' to things." This is undoubtedly one of the intelligences observed in dancers such as the Alvin Ailey Dance Theater; athletes such as Venus and Serena Williams, Usain Bolt, or LeBron James; surgeons such as Dr. Ben Carson; and actresses/actors such as Halle Berry and Will Smith.

6. *Interpersonal Intelligence* ("People Smart"). According to Armstrong, "The sixth intelligence is *interpersonal.* This is the ability to understand and work with other *people.* In particular, it requires a capacity to perceive and be responsive to the moods, temperaments, intentions, and desires of others. A social director on a cruise ship needs to have this intelligence. So does an administrator of a large corporation. An interpersonally intelligence individual may be very compassionate and socially responsible, or manipulative and cunning like Machiavelli. But they have the ability to get inside the skin of another person and view the world from that individual's perspective. As such they make wonderful networkers, negotiators, and teachers." This is undoubtedly one of the intelligences of educators such as Lisa Delpit; business executives such as Pamela Thomas-Graham; civil rights leaders such as Benjamin Jealous; and community activists such as Angela Glover-Blackwell.

9 KINDS OF SMART

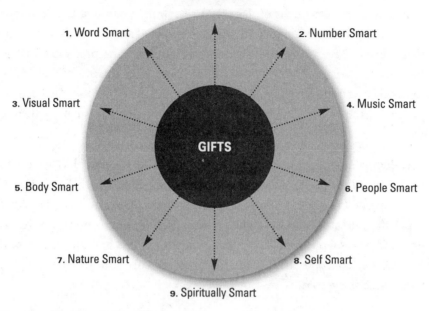

1. Word Smart

2. Number Smart

3. Visual Smart

4. Music Smart

GIFTS

5. Body Smart

6. People Smart

7. Nature Smart

8. Self Smart

9. Spiritually Smart

Figure 3–3. Nine forms of intelligence.

7. *Naturalist Intelligence* ("Nature Smart"). According to Armstrong, people who are highly competent in this intelligence are nature lovers. They would rather be out in the woods hiking or collecting rocks or flowers than indoors. On the other hand, if being indoors involves studying animals, insects, stars, or other living systems or natural formations, then their motivation is likely to soar. They sometimes feel more affiliation with animals than with human beings. This is undoubtedly one of the intelligences of veterinarians such as former Miss America Debbye Turner; farmers such as Gary Grant; biologists such as Fatimah Jackson; and environmentalists such as Margie Eugene-Richard.

8. *Intrapersonal Intelligence* ("Self Smart"). According to Armstrong, "The final intelligence is *intrapersonal* or the intelligence of the *inner self.* A person strong in this kind of smart can easily access her own feelings, discriminate between many different kinds of inner emotional states and use her self-understanding to enrich and guide her life. Examples of individuals intelligent in this way include counselors, theologians, and self-employed businesspeople. They can be very introspective and enjoy meditation, contemplation, or other forms of deep soul-searching. On the other hand they might be fiercely independent, highly goal-directed and intensely self-disciplined. But in any case they're in a class by themselves and prefer to work on their own rather than with others." This is undoubtedly one of the intelligences of psychologists such as Drs. Na'im Akbar and A. Kathleen Hoard Burlew; entrepreneurs such as Earl Graves; theologians such as Bishop Vashti Murphy McKenzie; and counselors such as Dr. Thomas A. Parham.

9. *Existential Intelligence* ("Spiritually Smart"). Gardner has begun to speak of a ninth intelligence—existential intelligence, which is concerned with ultimate *life issues.* According to Armstrong, "Such questions as, 'What is life?' 'What's it all about?' 'Why is there evil?' 'Where is humanity heading?' and 'Does God exist?'" are strong starting points for exploration into these deeper concepts. Dr. Gardner defines the core abilities of existential intelligence as twofold:

▸ To locate oneself with respect to the furthest reaches of the cosmos—the infinite no less than the infinitesimal, and

▸ To locate oneself with respect to the most existential features of the human condition—the significance of life, the meaning of death, the ultimate fate of the physical and psychological worlds, such profound experiences as love of another human being, or total immersion in a work of art."

This is the intelligence of formal or orthodox leaders of religious institutions: ministers, pastors, priests, bishops, and imams, but it can also permeate countless other roles previously mentioned, such as writer, artist, and scientist. This is undoubtedly one of the intelligences of Bishop T.D. Jakes, Iyanla Van Zant, and Reverend Bernice King.

The good news is that you possess *all* of these intelligences! Of course, you are likely to have some areas of strength and some areas of limitation. But as we talk about demonstrating excellence, we want you to be crystal clear about one thing: You are blessed with gifts in each area! In fact, the majority of people are generally very good at two to three intelligences and good at the rest as well. The beauty of multiple intelligences is that unlike our educational system that narrowly focuses on only two intelligences—writing and math—this theory embraces the diversity of abilities that naturally reside in us all.

While gifts reside in all of us, it's not always easy to recognize them early. When he was an elementary school student, Jeffrey discovered that he loved reading and analyzing maps, learning science, and public speaking. He wasn't just passionate about these activities; he was also good at them.

His parents cultivated these gifts by giving him atlases and letting him be the navigator on family trips. They took him to science museums, gave him science books, and worked with him on science projects. They listened to him practice his speeches and applauded his efforts. Looking back, it was clear that Jeffrey was cultivating his visual-spatial intelligence through maps, his logical-mathematical intelligence through science, and his linguistic intelligence through public speaking. His favorite subjects in school were science and social studies. With that in mind, it makes sense that he has degrees in urban studies (maps and science), civil engineering (math and science), and specializes his work in urban entrepreneurship and economic development (social science and lots of reading and writing).

Computers were an early source of inspiration for Randal. Back in the early 1980s, when school districts didn't have computers and there wasn't a mandate from the Board of Education to get them, a math teacher at his school, Mr. Mastoris, won a technology grant and purchased a Radio Shack TRS-80 computer that cost $7,500 for the students. He personally installed the system and learned how to program it using BASIC, one of the earliest computer languages. Randal didn't like to read, so he would make up book reports for class, creating the author and the story and writing a fictional book report rather than having to read the actual assignment. But for Randal, math and computers were fun. He and his brother, Dan, spent a lot of time during and after school writing programs that could print their names across the screen or count from 1 to 100 by 2's. Later, when their dad bought them a Commodore VIC-20 home computer, Dan and Randal created their own video games instead of buying cartridges for their Atari video game system—a clear display of "number smarts."

Stereotypes from television and film would tell you that someone like Randal—a person gifted at math, science, and technology—wouldn't have the best interpersonal skills. Pop culture has branded people who have and use these kinds of gifts as nerds—the guys that don't get the girl and whose only student activities are the math and chess clubs.

But Randal was also involved in student government at an early age—running his first race (for vice president) and losing in the third grade. He didn't let the loss deter him; he ran for secretary in fourth grade and president in fifth grade—winning both offices—a feat that was accomplished through his interpersonal or "people smarts."

Given the early display of his gifts in math and science, it makes sense that Randal's educational and entrepreneurial pursuits are centered on his being "number smart." His early experience running and winning elections shows his "people smarts"—skills that are needed as CEO of BCT Partners and that certainly helped him win *The Apprentice.*

Passion. What are the things that you just love to do? What really fires you up and gets you motivated? You should do some soul searching here to really think about those areas that have interested you throughout your life. If you haven't already, you should ask yourself the following questions to help reveal what you are passionate about:

- What would you do if you knew you could not fail?

- What would you do if money was not a concern in your life?

- What one thing do you dream about doing that you've never told anyone?

- While you're driving your car or taking a shower, what do you fantasize about doing?

- Who do you know that's doing something you'd like to do?

- What are five things that you want and five things that you're good at?

- When you were young, what did you know you would do when you grew up?

- What would you regret not having done if your life was ending?

Source: Taken in part from Cheryl Richardson's *Life Makeovers* (Broadway Books, 2000).

The answers to these questions lie at the heart of your passion. Gifts are those things that you are naturally able to do. Passion represents those things that you are naturally drawn to do. We believe one of the keys to excellence is finding the intersection between your gifts and your passion. In other words, those things you are naturally drawn to do should necessarily tap into those things that you are naturally able to do.

You may know someone who is passionate about something but not gifted to do it well. We see people like this all the time when we've watched the auditions for the performing artist competition *American Idol.* Many people who attend the auditions are passionate about singing, but are not gifted singers.

Passion is an essential element of excellence. It is your passion that produces drive, development, and devotion. You are *driven* to learn more and know more about things for which you are passionate. You are committed to your personal and professional *development.* And you are *devoted* to a lifetime of learning and progress around that passion.

So if you're still in search of your passion, be patient and continue to explore new possibilities and experiment with different opportunities that may lead you to your gifts and your passion. The good news is that everything we discussed in Strategy 2 applies here as well. In other words, experiences and exposure can lead to exploration and experimentation, which can ultimately lead to discovery and determination of your gifts and passion. The same principles in Strategy 2 concerning ways to explore and experiment with your likes, dislikes, strengths, and limitations and move beyond your comfort zone are exactly what you should do to reveal your gifts and passion.

When you find and develop your passion, work doesn't feel like work and the results have the potential to change and improve lives. Take, for instance, Dr. Treena Livingston Arinzeh, an associate professor of biomedical engineering at the New Jersey Institute of Technology. Coming up with a better solution for surgeons using stem cells for cartilage repair was a challenge that she was so passionate about she could barely stay out of the lab.

"We had another material we were working on, but it just wasn't that flexible in terms of use," she explained to us in an interview. The surgeon she collaborates with suggested finding something that would make the procedure less invasive. "And that became a challenge. We started thinking about it and now we've come up with something that's very neat, and we're very excited. I'm just so excited that's all I can think about. What's the next step? Hurry up. Well, then, I'll get in the lab. My students are taking too long. Let me do it. It's that type of thing. I just really enjoy discovery and new challenges."

You may find Dr. Arinzeh's passion daunting—and that's okay; science and medicine isn't for everyone. But fortunately, for some people the fusion of those fields is fascinating. The discovery and innovation resulting from their work likely will someday improve your life or the life of someone you know.

But you won't discover your passion without having experiences and exposure. Taking a music class may lead you to experiment with the drums, flute, or trumpet. Exposure to an entrepreneur may lead you to explore selling lemonade, or seek out a local business owner to shadow for one day, or search the Internet for profiles of successful business people. An event at your church or religious institution may spark a curiosity in matters related to human existence, prompting you to join a study group of classic religious texts or attend a lecture at a nearby school of divinity. From among all of these experiences, your gifts and passion may be revealed. We are confident in saying that as long as you keep looking, if you don't find your gifts and passion, your gifts and passion will find you. With persistence, eventually you will see signs of progress or reinforcement that you are moving in the right direction.

Discipline. To become excellent in those areas found at the intersection of your passion and your gifts, you must develop and apply discipline. According to the Merriam-Webster dictionary, discipline is "training that corrects, molds, or perfects the mental faculties or moral character." Discipline is not only the pursuit of perfection in your skills and abilities, but also the pursuit of perfection morally and ethically. You could say that discipline is developing an expert *competence*, with moral *character*, and an unwavering *commitment*.

No one is perfect, but we can strive for perfection. To do so requires some good-old-fashioned-roll-up-your-sleeves-and-don't-be-afraid-to-get-your-hands-dirty hard work, along with the perseverance to deal with adversity and overcome obstacles. Of the facets of excellence, discipline is tried-and-true. Discipline speaks to the countless hours of rehearsal needed to become an excellent jazz saxophonist; the early mornings, late nights, and long days required to become an excellent journalist; and the years of study and laboratory work needed to become an excellent scientist.

Malcolm Gladwell, in his book *Outliers: The Story of Success* (Little, Brown, 2008), presents the case that it takes 10,000 hours of practice to become an expert at something. Why? Because several studies have shown that world-class musicians and athletes have practiced their craft for more than 10,000 hours to become excellent. In fact, according to Gladwell, their excellence had less to do with their natural ability (although of course that helps) and more to do with the time they put into practicing and developing their abilities.

We both put many hours into our pursuit of entrepreneurship and research. Some of that time was spent in academia earning degrees, but long before that we began our first venture together as students at Rutgers, which we'll discuss in more detail in the chapter on finding strength in numbers (Strategy 6).

Any gift, no matter how abundant, is still raw talent. Discipline transforms your natural gift into expert *competence.* Someone with a natural ability in writing (linguistic intelligence) transforms into an expert poet; a gift in visual perspective (spatial intelligence) leads to your becoming an expert photographer; a raw talent in singing (musical intelligence) enables you to become an expert vocalist.

While it is very easy to observe the *product* of discipline in others, it is significantly much harder to see the *process* of discipline in others. When we see expert lawyers in the courtroom, or expert athletes on the playing field, or expert educators in the classroom, there is often a disconnect between what we see and our understanding of what it took for them to get there. We don't necessarily "see" their struggle. We don't necessarily "see" all of the sweat, blood, tears, and sacrifice behind their story. What we "see" is the end result.

When we see Fantasia Barrino win on *American Idol*, we don't see all the hours of practice or the mountain of rejections she faced before getting her big break. When we see Kevin Garnett or Shaquille O'Neal win a basketball game, we don't see the time they spent on the basketball court, practicing day after day after day. All we see is fifty-point performances and slam dunks, so it's easy to assume they were able to get there with little effort. For example, Venus Williams established a practice regimen of six hours a day, six days a week, at the age of 11, which was four years *after* she was already identified as a tennis prodigy. That alone amounted to 7,488 hours of practice in just four years.

The simple truth is that *nothing in life worth having comes easy.* If you are a performing artist and you want to be excellent, you've got to practice hard. If you are an athlete and you want to be excellent, you've got to train hard. If you aspire to be excellent in anything, you've got to work hard. This is a timeless life principle.

Furthermore, make no mistake: While discipline is a skill, it is also a choice. You *choose* to develop and apply discipline to your areas of life. Discipline means making a personal commitment to becoming excellent. It is an internal standard that you bring to your work. Along with your beliefs, discipline undergirds your ability to persevere in the midst of challenges.

Maya Angelou, Earl Graves, Bill Cosby, and Patrick Ewing are among the collectors of the work of artist Alonzo Adams. Early on there were signs that Adams had artistic ability: When he was a boy, even though there was an orange crayon in his box of Crayolas, he figured out how to create the color orange on his own.

But developing his craft took work. "From an early age I always wanted to be better than everyone else as far as executing a drawing," Adams told us in an interview. When his peers began spending time at clubs, he hung out sometimes, but often he could be found practicing in his studio. And now, with famous actors and athletes as customers, he still spends hours perfecting his craft. "When people see the shows, they see all the work up on the walls, but they don't see the hours I put in getting ready for the shows. They don't see me working twenty hours out of a day on a piece of artwork, forgoing going here or doing this or doing that, painting around the clock; they don't see any of that," he said. "All you see is the Alonzo Mournings and the Patrick Ewings, and the Dikembe Mutombos and the Stephon Marburys, and the Jasmine Guys. You see all these people buying my artwork, but you don't see what it took to get me to the point where these people are interested in buying the artwork. And that's taken a lot of time, that's a lot of sacrifice."

....

Discipline puts you at the top of your game.

....

MORALITY AND DISCIPLINE

And do not forget, going back to the definition, that discipline is not only about perfecting your mental faculties, but also your moral *character*. When you develop disciplined character and keep a moral and ethical perspective based on a strong identity and value system, your work will have responsible outcomes. Consider the negative impact of an excellent scientist who lacks a moral conscience to guide his research, or a gifted reporter whose moral character is fixed in a way that allows her to use her ability and influence to discredit innocent people. We've seen the outcome of skilled police officers who don't apply a solid ethical foundation to their work.

Here again, Strategy 1, establishing a strong identity and purpose, can help you make moral choices and develop your ethical base. And as you will see in Strategy 5, seeking the wisdom of others, mentors can also play an integral role as well.

Beliefs. If, as discussed in Strategy 2, you are thoughtful in obtaining broad exposure, your experiences can expand your horizons, pushing you beyond your comfort zone and challenging you to grow in positive and powerful ways. But it is important to note that it is not our experiences that determine who we are; instead, it is the *meaning and interpretation we assign to those experiences* that ultimately shapes us.

In *Release Your Brilliance* (New York: HarperCollins, 2008), Simon T. Bailey describes how people who have achieved personal and professional success understand the connection between *thoughts, beliefs, actions,* and *outcomes.* Bailey is a speaker, author, and consultant whose work aims to inspire individuals to take charge of, change, and transform their lives. Experiences naturally generate *thoughts* and *ideas.* In any given day, you are likely to generate lots of thoughts and ideas. For example, after reading the earlier discussion on multiple intelligences in this chapter, you may have wondered, "Which of these intelligences represent my strengths?" You may

look back on your life experiences and recall instances when you were com-
plimented on your rapport with animals, or particularly enjoyed an outdoor
excursion, or received top grades in a botany or ecology class. As a result,
you may interpret those events to draw the conclusion that you are truly
blessed with the naturalist intelligence—or that you are "nature smart."

We tend to accept or reject thoughts about ourselves based on the meaning we attach to previous experiences. When we build up enough experiences
in support of (or in contradiction to) a thought, those thoughts become
beliefs. The evidence that composes our beliefs isn't confined to our real
experience: A dream or vision may hold the key to what we ultimately
believe is our path. The mind makes no distinction between real experiences
and those produced through our imagination (there is an entire body of
work around how imagining certain outcomes, such as a peak performance,
helps condition the mind and body to achieve peak performance).

Regardless, your belief that you are truly blessed with any ability has the
ability to shape you in very powerful ways. Why? Because our beliefs help
determine our *actions* and our actions can lead to certain *outcomes* (see Figure 3–4). For this reason, beliefs are a core component of demonstrating
excellence. Two people could experience the same events that lead to the
same thoughts, but it is their beliefs that can lead them to dramatically different actions and outcomes.

A belief that you are truly blessed with gifts and passion will engender a
greater sense of confidence, or a willingness to persevere in the face of
adversity while pursuing these endeavors. Going back to the person who

Figure 3–4. Your belief system.

recognizes he has naturalist intelligence, his gifts and passion for nature may
lead him to earn a degree in environmental science, pursue a career as a
zookeeper, or dedicate time to championing animal rights. But this will only
happen if he *believes* it can happen. This is an example of what author and
peak performance expert Anthony Robbins describes as empowering beliefs

in his national bestseller, *Awaken the Giant Within* (Simon and Schuster, 1991). *Empowering beliefs lead to actions and outcomes that benefit us, benefit others, and benefit society.*

Perhaps the most empowering belief is *faith*. The Bible defines faith as "the substance of things hoped for, the evidence of things not seen" (Hebrews 11:1). Personally, our faith is deeply rooted in our Christian beliefs and, hence, it is derived from living according to God's will. It is also expressed by two acronyms: (1) F.A.I.T.H.: Feeling As If Things Happened and (2) Having F.A.I.T.H.: Having Full Assurance In The Heart. Faith is what enables you to produce an outcome in the absence of experiences that suggest it was possible. Faith is a significant part of what enables people to accomplish breakthrough performances, attain personal records, and blaze new trails. Faith can enable any number of "firsts"—the researcher who achieves a scientific discovery; the entrepreneur who steps out to start her dream business; the athlete who sets a world record; the principal who turns around a previously poor-performing school; and the community leader who reduces crime in a neighborhood that was written off by others.

Strategy 1 emphasized the importance of establishing a strong identity and purpose. Along those same lines, here we pose the following questions: What are your hopes and dreams? What are your aspirations? Or, more important, what would they be right now, right at this very moment, if you replaced any beliefs about what you think you can't do, or think you shouldn't do, or think is not possible, with the empowering beliefs that you can, you should, and you will! Remember the powerful words of an unknown author: "When you come to the edge of all the light you know and are about to step off into the darkness of the unknown, faith is knowing that one of two things will happen: Either there will be something solid to stand on or you will be taught how to fly."

....

"Faith without works is dead." (James 2:17) An empowering belief without discipline is also dead. The unfaithful say, "I will believe it when I see it." The faithful say, "I will see it because I believe it."

....

REDEFINING EXCELLENCE: CONGRUENCE

Gifts and passion are the facets of the Diamond of Excellence that we identify *naturally*, while beliefs and discipline are nurtured and applied *deliberately* (see Figure 3–5). You are naturally drawn to and are able to do certain things, but you deliberately choose to have empowering beliefs and to apply discipline. Everyone has gifts and interests, but not everyone has

Figure 3–5. Natural and deliberate facets of the Diamond of Excellence.

Figure 3–6. Redefining excellence.

the right beliefs and discipline to become excellent. The alignment between your genuine passion and God-given gifts, combined with empowering beliefs and the competence, character, and commitment resulting from discipline, leads to *congruence* (see Figure 3–6).

Congruence is a form of *self-mastery*, or being the very best you can be. Some people call it "flow" or "harmony," while others call it "optimal or peak performance" and being "in the zone." Congruence is made possible by implementing the previous strategies: a strong identity and well-defined purpose (Strategy 1) and broad exposure (Strategy 2). But regardless of what you call it, the basic idea underlying congruence is that all of the facets of excellence come together and are focused in the same direction in a way that reflects who you are and where you are going.

You demonstrate excellence when you bring your "A game."

Why You Must Be Excellent

As you can probably tell, the topic of excellence is very important to us. Certainly, a large part of our story of excellence and success has been finding and cultivating our gifts and passion. We've also spent time developing discipline and empowering beliefs that have propelled and anchored us as we built our careers, businesses, and work, to make an impact on society.

There are three reasons why excellence should be important to you:

▸ *Excellence defines the value you bring to the table.* When working with others, demonstrating excellence helps define what you specifically bring to the table that is valuable. Excellent people need to be around other excellent or excellence-aspiring people. We believe synergy is created when like minds get together and contribute to the conversation, project, or team. Once you achieve excellence in an area, it is important to identify others who are excellent to form high-performing teams. This is a precept we'll discuss in Strategy 6: Find Strength in Numbers,

▸ *Excellence in one area can be translated into excellence in other areas.* If you become excellent in a particular area, you know what it takes to develop excellence. You understand how to put gifts, passion, discipline, and beliefs together to be an expert. You might even say that you have developed a habit for excellence. By "cracking the code" of excellence, the next time you need to become excellent you know exactly what to do. Journalist and political commentator Roland Martin's career, for instance, has spanned multiple communication platforms. Whether as executive editor of the *Chicago Defender* (the largest Black daily newspaper in the United States), the host of a radio show, editor at a magazine, or political commentator on the cable news network CNN, Roland's commitment to excellence in one area has led to excellence in the next.

▸ *Excellence opens doors to opportunities.* People who have achieved excellence in one area are also perceived by others as being fully capable of achieving excellence in another area, which often leads to new opportunities. They know you have worked hard already and now they expect you to be just as excellent in a new endeavor. Jeff Johnson, host of BET's *The Truth with Jeff Johnson* and commentator on Tom Joyner's radio show, had been working with Russell Simmons and the Hip Hop Summit Action Network when he "accidentally" got an opportunity to move into a career in front of the camera. "I didn't want to be on TV; I had no plans on being [on] TV. I wasn't singin' and dancin' for producers, like 'Let me on.' I didn't have a demo tape I was shoppin' you know, none of that," Johnson said to us in an interview.

But when he found out that Stephen Hill, a programming executive at BET, liked his work and voice while with the NAACP and requested a meeting, it led to his having a regular political spot on the network's *Rap City* show. "As a result of that," Johnson said, "we went from doing commentary on *Rap City* to me covering the 2004 Democratic and Republican national conventions for the network on the entertainment side, which led to me getting my own show, the *Jeff Chronicles*, . . . which just blossomed into me doing specials for the network in different parts of the world. So it was an accidental opportunity that was connected to almost a decade of work. I don't want to give the impression that they decided randomly to give Jeff Johnson an opportunity. I was given an opportunity as a reflection of work I had done in another place."

Game-Changing Strategies for Demonstrating Excellence

Mediocrity is unacceptable for Black Faces in White Places. Finding congruence with gifts, passion, discipline, and beliefs results in the excellence needed to propel your personal and professional success. Here we present several game-changing strategies to demonstrate excellence.

GO DEEP AND WIDE

The beauty of the theory of multiple intelligences is that we all possess all of the intelligences, albeit to varying degrees. When Randal was completing his graduate work at MIT, his pastor, Rev. Dr. John Matthew Borders III, gave him some advice that has stuck with him to this day. As Randal recalls:

> Pastor Borders told me, "You've done very well during your time here in Boston. But as you're finishing your degree, you need to begin thinking about what it is that you want to be known for years from now." He explained that although there were several paths I could pursue with my career—as a professor, an entrepreneur, a corporate executive—I should

*focus on one and "get grounded." He told me to get to know everything
and everybody within the space I decided to pursue: the thought leaders,
the best practices, the leading companies or organizations, the magazines
and publications, the conferences, the websites, and more. In choosing to go
the route of becoming a full-time business owner, I have heeded his advice.*

We interpret this advice as "going deep." Going deep means immersing
yourself in a field or industry or area of expertise for a period of time to
become excellent within that space. It means answering Pastor Borders's
question, "What do you want to be known for?" Do you want to be known
as an excellent teacher? An excellent pharmacist? An excellent nurse?

We expand on his advice to include that you should not only go deep, but
you should also "go wide." That is, while you should certainly immerse
yourself in specific areas, mostly likely your areas of greatest strength or
interest, you should still seek to develop yourself in a range of other areas.
This is one of the reasons we encourage young people and students to get
good grades in all of their subjects. Although you may love English and find
math uninteresting, developing your abilities across the board means you
must study hard in every subject.

Going deep and wide also rings true for professionals, although at some
point you must decide whether you want to pursue becoming a *technical/func-
tional expert* (i.e., a scientist or a university researcher) or a *general manager*
(i.e., the manager of a group of scientists or a university dean).

In *Breaking Through: The Making of Minority Executives* (HBS Press,
1999), Harvard professors David Thomas and John Gabarro studied
minority executives who reached the upper levels of corporate America
(becoming CEOs, CFOs, COOs, and other "C-suite" executives) and
minority managers who reached a plateau in their careers. They found
that early in their careers (when they were "breaking in"), the minority
executives had fewer departmental changes than the minority managers.
Based on this finding, Thomas and Gabarro concluded that the minority
executives were able to deepen their technical and functional knowledge.
During their mid-careers ("breaking away"), the minority executives
began to move beyond their technical and functional expertise to develop
more general managerial and judgment skills that would propel them to

the C-suite. Finally, in the later stages of their careers ("breaking through"), the minority executives pursued stretch and strategic broadening assignments (e.g., task forces, special projects, provisional assignments), as well as high consequence/high visibility assignments (e.g., new product introductions, new plant or facility launches, departmental or divisional turnarounds) to achieve success. In summary, it is clear that the minority executives went deep early in their careers and then later went wide.

RECOGNIZE THAT EXCELLENCE IS YOUR BEST ALLY

Even as society makes valiant attempts to live up to the ideals of a meritocracy, studies demonstrate how Blacks can be viewed differently. In *Breaking Through*, Thomas and Gabarro call this state of affairs the "Two Tournaments"—where minorities play a separate "game" than their white counterparts, wherein the rules, benchmarks, and rewards are different.

How do you combat it? Seek objective evaluation criteria that are documented and reviewed jointly by you and your adviser or supervisor. If you demonstrate excellence using objective criteria, then there can be no doubt in anyone's mind that you got the job done and achieved results.

Never allow racism to take you off your game.

LEARN YOUR GAME

In the first part of this book, we made repeated references to learning the game, but what is most important is for you to learn *your* game.

A large part of learning your game is mastering your professional *craft* by demonstrating excellence in your work, as discussed in this chapter. However, based on our experience, this is just the tip of the iceberg. Zack Lemelle, chairperson of the Information Technology Senior Management Forum, the only national organization dedicated exclusively to fostering upper-level executive talent among African-American IT professionals, agrees. Lemelle told us in an interview:

> *It's been ingrained in us from a very young age, "Get out there. Work hard every day. Do the best you can. And you'll grow in your career*

and do well in life." That's been ingrained in us by our parents, by society, from day one. They don't teach us the unwritten rules of the game. They don't teach us how the game is really played. They don't even call it a game. And so we come into this work world thinking that if we bust our butt, and put in twelve-hour days, and work on the weekends, and neglect our families, and we work very, very, very, very, very, very hard, then we will achieve high levels of success in life. Now having said that, there is an element of truth to that, but it is indeed relegated to the small minority. In most cases, when you get to certain levels within an organization, it takes a lot more than just performance to excel to the next level.

The other part of learning your game is mastering your professional context: being a student of your professional landscape or environment. To accomplish this, you must determine the following four things:

1. Your *position in the game,* or the field or sector you will pursue as a career.

2. What you define as success or *winning the game.* By defining what success means to you and constantly reevaluating what it means to you at each stage in your career, you are able to stay true to who you are (identity) and where you want to be going (purpose).

3. Who are the *players in your game,* including:

   ▸ *Decision makers* who control outcomes, such as how budgets are allocated, how resources are distributed, and whether and to whom bonuses or incentives or contracts are awarded.

   ▸ *Gatekeepers* who control pathways to entry, movement, and advancement by determining who is hired, fired, promoted, and reassigned.

   ▸ *Influencers* who are well respected within their field for their knowledge, experience, expertise, or wisdom.

4. The spoken and unspoken *rules of your game* that govern pathways to advancement in your organization:

▸ *Spoken rules* define what's expected of you: What is your job description, and how do rules in the employee handbook apply? And, importantly, what are the criteria for evaluating your performance or the firm's performance?

▸ *Unspoken rules* have to be learned by studying the career trajectories of those who have reached the senior or executive level within your organization, or built successful companies in your industry, to discern whether certain kinds of assignments, experiences, credentials, or expertise are helpful, if not mandatory, to advance. Learning the unspoken rules also involves seeking the wisdom of mentors, which we will discuss in Strategy 5: *Seek the Wisdom of Others.*

DO NOT PRIORITIZE PRESTIGE, PROMOTIONS, OR POSITIONS OVER PASSION

Books such as Ellis Cose's *Rage of a Privileged Class: Why Do Prosperous Blacks Still Sing the Blues?* (HarperCollins, 1993) have brought to light a silent rage that engulfs the last generation of African Americans who bought into the idea that they had to abandon their passion to advance in their organizations. They made enormous sacrifices to get to the top of the ladder and looked back with anger because they were not happy with the sacrifices they made along the way. We believe that if you follow your passion, you will be happier about the steps you have taken.

In *Breaking Through,* Thomas and Gabarro reached a similar finding. The minority executives they studied had fewer promotions than the minority managers who never reached the executive level, suggesting that the executives were unwilling to pursue advancement at the expense of passion. This was exactly the case for Don Thompson, president and chief operating officer of McDonald's USA, who oversees the nearly 14,000 U.S. restaurants for the world's largest fast-food chain. Earlier in his career, he rejected opportunities to move up the corporate ladder because the positions did not tap into his passion. During an interview with us Thompson said:

> *I believe you have to enjoy what you do. You have to really enjoy it, to the extent that you look forward to coming in every day or traveling to that city or being on the road 50 [percent] or 60 percent of the time.*

You can advance to a point very quickly where you find yourself miserable and totally unhappy, and you'll come right back down the rungs on the ladder. What I have been able to do and been blessed to do, I have enjoyed every single phase, as a matter of fact, [and there have] been several . . . positions that I wanted to stay in longer when I was asked to move to the next position. And so you definitely have to enjoy it. You have to have passion around it, and you have to enjoy it in good and bad times.

IDENTIFY THE RIGHT JOB ASSIGNMENT FOR THE RIGHT NEED AT THE RIGHT TIME

As stated by Earl Graves in his book *How to Succeed in Business Without Being White* (HarperBusiness, 1997), "Your career is your own private business." This means you must be in the driver's seat and you cannot rely on a company to look out for your interests.

You must think about your career like entrepreneurs think about their company and ask the following questions: How do I market myself? How do I maintain my own competitiveness? How do I develop my core competencies? How do I ensure that I'm obtaining the best value for my services? How do I achieve my short-term and long-term goals? The answers to these questions partly lie in constantly seeking out job assignments you are passionate about, that challenge you, and that deepen and broaden your skill set. But you must also be entrepreneurial in how you act. You must be creative, innovative, and willing to take risks in managing your career. We refer to this as *strategic career management,* or identifying the right job assignment for the right need at the right time.

MAINTAIN A COMMITMENT TO EXCELLENCE

Don't allow prejudice, the low expectations of others, or inevitable challenges to derail your commitment to excellence. Excellence isn't a silver bullet against racism, but it is perhaps the best counterstrategy. It can clearly expose the actions of others who are being racist or whose efforts are unjustified, making it painfully obvious to observers that their actions are based on some prejudice or preconceived notions. Excellence makes it much more difficult for others to deny you what you are due.

From Independence to Interdependence

Strategy 3 represents the last of the foundational strategies comprising Part I: Learning the Game. At each subsequent step along the way to greatness, we will revisit the core values associated with excellence: passion, courage, resilience, perseverance, commitment, and hard work. These values permeate every strategy, every principle, and every piece of advice found in this book. And, as you will eventually see, these values describe the basic characteristics needed to learn the game, play the game, master the game, and ultimately, redefine the game.

Looking back, it should be clear that the Part I strategies all promote self-development leading to *independence*. A strong identity leads to *self-esteem*. Identity combined with a well-defined purpose leads to *self-determination*. Excellence leads to *self-mastery*. Exposure enhances all of the aforementioned. And the totality of these strategies engenders independence—which means being inner-directed and *self-reliant*.

Strategy 3 is also a jump-off point to move beyond independence. The strategies discussed hereafter build upon one another en route to redefining the game and making a truly lasting impact. Looking ahead, as we transition from Part I: Learning the Game to Part II: Playing the Game, we move from strategies promoting independence to those that build relationships and promote *interdependence*. Building diverse and solid relationships (Strategy 4), seeking the wisdom of others (Strategy 5), and finding strength in numbers (Strategy 6) are all extensions of Part II's core theme: *connectedness*.

P A R T   I I

PLAYING THE GAME

You have to commit, be a team player, learn the rules of the game. And then you have to play better than anyone else.

—Dianne Feinstein

Most people are familiar with the expression "six degrees of separation." Six degrees popularly conveys the theory that we are all only six degrees, or six relationships, away from anybody else. (We've heard it said jokingly within the Black community that our degrees of separation are two!) Regardless of the exact number, we believe it is intuitively obvious to conclude that our degree of separation is going down as time progresses. So, despite the fact there are 6.7 billion people on planet Earth, "it's a small world after all," as the old children's song suggests.

As a result of globalization, the proliferation of technological advances, and increasing societal diversity, our world is becoming more connected every day. These three trends have changed the game significantly and have implications for today's African Americans when compared to the experiences of those who began their careers in the 1960s, 1970s, and 1980s.

Three Trends in a More Interconnected World

The United States is becoming increasingly diverse. More than one-quarter of the population now consists of Latinos, African Americans, Asian Americans, Pacific Islanders, American Indians, and Alaska Natives. According to U.S. Census Bureau projections, these so-called "minorities" will make up a majority of the U.S. population by 2050. Minorities are projected to become the majority of the population in Texas within the next decade, and in New York and Florida within the next twenty years. They already make up a majority of the population of California (60 percent).

The proliferation of mobile phones and PDAs, wired and wireless Internet devices, high-definition television, and other technological developments have transformed the way people live and interact. Not only have we witnessed many technology innovations, we have also adopted technologies at a faster rate over time. Compare the number of years it has taken various technologies to be used by 25 percent of the U.S. population:

Technology	Years to Gain 25 Percent Market Share
Airplane	54
Electricity	44
Telephone	35
VCR	34
Microwave	30
Television	26
Personal computer	15
Mobile phone	13
Internet	7

Source: The Book of Knowledge, Merrill Lynch, 1999.

Technology, whether we like it or not, is enmeshed in the human experience. E-mail, text messaging, instant messaging, and social media—blogs, social and professional networking websites, and wikis—are allowing us to become more interconnected than ever before. Looking ahead, it is safe to assume that we will adopt newer technologies at even faster rates.

Finally, globalization has different meanings to different people. It can refer to interconnected markets for goods and services across national borders and seas. It can mean greater contact with other cultures resulting from fewer travel restrictions, technological links, and media exposure. It also can represent the increased flow of data and information across the globe. But no matter what words you use to describe it, there is no denying that our world continues to move toward a more global society.

In light of these trends, "playing the game" in the twenty-first century is about two things: (1) establishing your own level of *connectedness,* or building meaningful, productive, and mutually supportive relationships that are global and diverse, and (2) leveraging those relationships to effectively navigate your game while also helping other like-minded people to do the same. Naturally, navigating your game—that is, your professional landscape (i.e., the environment comprising your organization, industry, and sector)—can and must be accomplished by leveraging societal diversity, utilizing information technology and social media, and acknowledging the influence of globalization.

Relationship building, which can ultimately lead to connectedness, represents the transition from learning the game (Part I) to playing the game (Part II) and from independence to interdependence.

....

Without self-determination and excellence you are not even in the game—you're on the bench.

....

Relationship Building: The Power of Connectedness

One of the books that had a significant influence on us while at Rutgers was Stephen R. Covey's *The 7 Habits of Highly Effective People* (Simon & Schuster, 1990). In his book, Covey writes (emphasis ours):

> *The techniques and skills that really make a difference in human interaction are the ones that almost naturally flow from a truly **independent** character. So the place to begin building any relationship is inside ourselves, inside . . . our own character. As we become independent— proactive, centered in correct principles, value driven and able to organize and execute around the priorities in our life with integrity— we then can choose to become **interdependent**—capable of building rich, enduring, highly productive relationships with other people. . . . Independence is an achievement. Interdependence is a choice only independent people can make.*

The strategies covered in Part I of our book set the stage for Part II, because *true relationship building begins within yourself first.* More specifically, establishing a strong identity and purpose (Strategy 1), seeking growth opportunities beyond your comfort zone (Strategy 2), and demonstrating a level of excellence or self-mastery (Strategy 3) can lead to independence. An independent person is then better able to form the valuable bonds that lead to interdependence.

As illustrated in Figure II–1, all three strategies in Part II: Playing the Game represent roads that lead to the strategies in Part III: Mastering the Game. Pay close attention to the next three strategies—building diverse and solid *relationships*, seeking the *wisdom of others*, and finding *strength in numbers*—but also keep in mind where we are heading. Relationships signify the basic construct for several concepts introduced in Part III, such as intrapreneurship and entrepreneurship. Relationships between people and between organizations also enable synergy and scale, which are important concepts that come into play in Part IV: Redefining the Game.

As we have done throughout this book, Part II will continue to draw upon our knowledge and experience to bring these strategies to life. However, we will also draw more heavily upon the knowledge and experience of

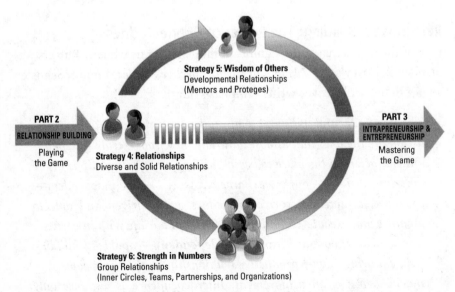

Figure II–1. Relationship-building strategies are central to playing and mastering the game.

others that we regard as pioneers in relationship building, including George Fraser, Stephen Covey, Robert Putnam, and others. This approach enables us to provide the fundamentals of networking and relationship building in a way that combines tried-and-true, "old school" principles with "new school" strategies that can help you to effectively play the game.

....

*Relationships do not make you a player in the game; the **right** relationships make you a player in the game.*

....

Playing the Game: Relationships, Relationships, Relationships

Relationships are the ties that bind us and lead to a fulfilling personal and professional life. They are the cornerstone of playing the game, because there is little that can be accomplished in life without working with other people. Accordingly, the next three strategies discuss relationships from a number of perspectives.

Strategy 4 covers the foundation of *relationships:* building meaningful ties with diverse people and leveraging the power of networking. Strategy 5 discusses the value of seeking the wisdom of others through various *developmental relationships,* including mentors and protégés. Finally, in Strategy 6, we present our conceptualization of "strength in numbers" and how it manifests itself across a continuum of *group relationships,* including teams, partnerships, and organizations. As you will see, Strategy 4 relationships are the facilitators of the mutual exchange of wisdom we describe early in Strategy 5, and they represent the building blocks for the collaborative action we discuss in the latter part of Strategy 6. In other words, the recurring theme throughout Part II: Playing the Game is relationships, relationships, and relationships.

....

*Part II: Playing the Game is rooted in the Kwanzaa principle of **Umoja** (unity), which means "to strive for and maintain unity in the family, community, nation, and race."*

....

Build Diverse and Solid Relationships

We may have all come on different ships, but we're in the same boat now.
—Rev. Dr. Martin Luther King Jr.

RELATIONSHIPS represent the entry point to the second dimension of Black Faces in White Places: *society*. As we first discussed in the Introduction, this dimension leads to the following question: Is society color-blind? While the answer is a resounding "No," if you agree with us that the African-American identity and culture are assets (Strategy 1), then you agree that seeing color in our society helps us see the full beauty of our society.

We do not desire a world that is color-blind. Quite to the contrary, we desire a world that fully acknowledges color and embraces difference, but does not discriminate based on race, ethnicity, religion, sex, disability, or sexual orientation. In this kind of environment people can enjoy learning from, connecting with, and working with people who are different from them on the issues that collectively affect them.

African Americans can help move society forward by building solid relationships with diverse people across the globe, but the work needed to realize this kind of world starts within each of us.

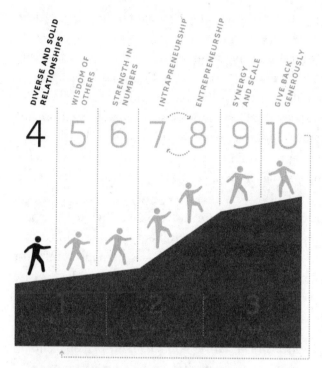

Figure 4–1. The path to greatness (Strategy 4).

Personal Diversity

Diversity is the difference between individuals and among groups. This difference could be along several lines, including the "Big 9" social identifiers discussed in Strategy 1 (race, class, gender, sexual orientation, physical ability, ethnicity, language, age, and religion) and much, much more, including different ways of thinking. The arguments for leveraging diversity have traditionally been applied to organizations, particularly corporations. We refer to this as *organizational diversity.* Computer maker Dell expresses its reasons for encouraging diversity in this way:

> *By continuing to drive diversity initiatives throughout* our organization, *we harness* each individual's *full potential, provide the best* customer *experience [by better understanding their needs], tap the best and brightest* talent, *improve our* **company's** *results, become a better* place *to work, and further our global citizenship efforts in the many cultures* we call *home. (emphasis ours)*[1]

(We note, however, that as of this writing, Dell did not have any African Americans on its executive leadership team.)

The first step for organizations that want to achieve these outcomes is to foster a more inclusive work environment that not only acknowledges and respects differences, but also celebrates differences and taps into them as a source of competitive advantage. Corporations, schools, nonprofit organizations, faith-based groups, and other work, learning, and spiritual organizations must be more receptive and more responsive to people of different backgrounds, including people of color, and view their differences as an asset, not a liability.

In Strategy 1, we made a similar argument from an individual perspective. We discussed the importance of seeing your identity—those things that make you unique (and also make you different)—as perhaps your most valuable asset. Now we take that concept one step further to make the case for *personal diversity.* We can modify Dell's diversity statement and apply it to ourselves to provide an individual blueprint:

> *By continuing to drive diversity initiatives throughout* my personal and professional life, *I harness my full potential, provide the best* human *experience by better understanding* others' *needs, tap the best and brightest talent* in others, *improve my personal results, become a better* person *to know, and further my global citizenship efforts in the many cultures* outside *my home.*

The reality is that we tend to associate with people who are like us or reflect our identity. We often trust others who have similar racial and ethnic backgrounds, grew up in the same or similar neighborhoods, attended the same college or training school, and share affiliations like religion, fraternities and sororities, community organizations, and professions.

If you are an African-American lawyer who went to UCLA and works in a private equity firm, you are more likely to spend time with other African Americans, other UCLA graduates, and other private equity professionals. There's nothing wrong with that. We (the authors) do it all of the time; we sometimes need to do it for affirmation, or reinforcement, or just to enjoy life (e.g., by enjoying an exclusively "Black moment" or a "Black event").

We are not suggesting that you have the most *diverse* personal and professional network. But we are suggesting that you have *diversity* within your personal and professional network. Just like you have to move beyond your comfort zone to pursue meaningful and diverse experiences (as discussed in Strategy 2), you must also move beyond your comfort zone to build meaningful and diverse relationships with people that are not like you. This places you in a unique and powerful position to then leverage personal diversity.

Leveraging personal diversity means operating seamlessly and naturally within many different contexts. You are able to interact with different people more comfortably because you have a greater appreciation of their cultural norms. You're able to work with different teams more productively as a result of previous experiences. You're able to walk in different circles more effectively because you've done it before—even if the circumstances or the context are somewhat different. You're able to play the game, or even different games, because you are not new to the game. In essence, Strategy 4 is yet another way of promoting the ideals of Strategy 2.

By the time J.R. accepted a job at drugmaker Merck & Co. in 1996, the number of African-American employees was growing and some were breaking into the upper echelons of the corporation. J.R. spent three summers interning at Merck and, from that experience, had formed valuable relationships with other interns and full-time employees of many races and backgrounds. Many of those relationships allowed him to perform well at Merck, but those weren't the only important relationships. Forming a bond with Merck's blue-collar workforce, in addition to having a good relationship with the traditional office workers (the so-called "white-collar" staffers), enhanced J.R.'s experience in a number of ways, as he explains:

The only thing that separates you during the day is that some of us are wearing suits and some of us are wearing uniforms, but at the end of the day we are all Black. We would go to each other's houses. We would go and hang out. There were some events, like somebody retiring, [when] we all came together to celebrate. One benefit [was] that a lot of those older Black employees had been there a long time. They knew the real deal. They knew what happened in the past. They knew who had treated who well and who to watch out for. They would tell us things like, "See him smiling in your face right now, but ten years ago, this happened . . . ." So there was some knowledge transfer going on.

African Americans have always been called upon to "code switch," that is, adapt our behaviors to cultures other than our own. In America, that has historically meant learning the game and playing the game of the majority, white culture. But in a global, diverse society, and in a United States where minorities are the majority, we will be increasingly called upon to code-switch according to an even wider array of norms, standards, and customs. You cannot reshape America if you do not have an appreciation of the diversity that is reflected in America. It's not about "us" learning more about "them." And it's not even about "them" learning more about "us." It's about *cultural reciprocity*—creating a culture where everyone sees the value in learning more about one another.

Leveraging personal diversity is essentially a *process*, not a product. It is an ongoing, never-ending process by which awareness, understanding, and connectedness to others enhances us. It should come as no surprise that the basic building block for personal diversity is also the basic building block for the strategies put forth in Part II: relationships.

Every person and organization can benefit from more diversity.

Relationship Building

In *The 7 Habits of Highly Effective People*, Stephen Covey introduces a metaphor for building solid relationships that we have found to be extremely powerful: "the emotional bank account." A financial bank account tallies how much money you have stored in a bank. The emotional bank account describes how much trust you have stored in a relationship. And much like a financial bank account accepts monetary deposits that increase savings (and withdrawals that decrease savings), the emotional bank account experiences deposits that build trust (and withdrawals that degrade trust). Meaningful and productive relationships are predicated upon ongoing and regular deposits in the emotional bank account.

We make deposits to the emotional bank account through acts of kindness, compassion, thoughtfulness, and love. For example, the following are six major deposits suggested by Covey:

> ▸ *Understand the individual.* Learn what is important to the individual (i.e., what constitutes a deposit to them).

> ▸ *Attend to the little things.* Remember that little things (i.e., gestures, courtesies, gifts) mean a lot; little things are really big things.

> ▸ *Keep commitments.* Say what you mean and mean what you say.

> ▸ *Clarify expectations.* Make expectations clear and explicit, and share them up-front.

> ▸ *Show personal integrity.* Conform your actions to your words; be loyal to those who are not present.

> ▸ *Apologize sincerely when you make a withdrawal.* "Fess up" when you mess up.

The emotional bank account is central to our discussion here because it portrays exactly how interactions with others can evolve from networking to connecting to clicking.

In his book, *Click: Ten Truths for Building Extraordinary Relationships* (McGraw-Hill, 2008), relationship-building icon George Fraser writes that relationships often start with *networking,* or "identifying those with whom you wish to build new relationships." The next phase is *connecting,* or "finding, cultivating, nurturing, and building [solid] relationships." Finally, things begin *clicking* when the people in the relationship begin "adding special value to each other and creating synergy." Part II of this book is about networking and connecting. Parts III and IV are about clicking and synergizing.

Black Enterprise founder Earl Graves speaks to the importance of relationship building when he says "networking is a social-first, business-second activity." Having a business card and networking is not relationship building. Although they can both lead to relationship building, at the end of the day, only relationship building is relationship building, and it is based on the following basic principles:

▸ *Invest in your relationships.* You truly reap what you sow. Unless you are willing to commit the time it takes to nurture, develop, and maintain relationships, you cannot expect to enjoy any returns.

▸ *Seek relationships that promote mutual gain.* Relationship building is about giving, not just taking. Seek out opportunities to be helpful to others because what goes around does indeed come back around. You ultimately get out what you put into your network.

▸ *Honor and respect all relationships.* While some relationships may be more useful than others, they are all valuable. So be nice to people on your way up, because you may see those same people again under different circumstances.

The common thread across any deposits into the emotional bank account (including those examples listed previously) is that they adhere to the Golden Rule: "Do unto others as you would have others do unto you." When we treat people the way that we would want to be treated (regardless of how they treat us), several positive things happen. We engender a higher level of trust. We implicitly encourage others to treat people similarly, as a result of our example. We naturally allow people to feel "safe" in their interactions with us and with others. And we move one step closer to manifesting the highest level of solidarity that can exist between two people: *unconditional love.*

....

"It's business, it's not personal" is a common phrase. But since relationships are so important, *"It's business, it's* all *personal"* is perhaps more accurate.

....

Three Compelling Ideas about Relationships

People who regularly interact with one another, or are otherwise connected, are part of the same *network*. There are three compelling ideas about the patterns of relationships and networks in society, how social connections happen, and how they bring advantages to those who know how to use them.

We discussed the first idea, "six degrees of separation," in the introduction to Part II to illustrate how our entire world is interconnected. By the end of this chapter, you'll learn more about two other ideas. The second idea, "the strength of weak ties," turns the notion that the most valuable relationships are with the people closest to you on its head. Finally, the third compelling idea, "bridging network gaps," explains why some people are more likely to be at the right place, at the right time, with the right information, and because of this synergy they are able to wield a great deal of influence.

A basic understanding of these three ideas is central to Strategy 4, as each concept is key to producing extraordinary results.

The Strength of Weak Ties

People often marvel at the length of their longest friendships. We (the authors) have been friends for over twenty years. And we have benefited from our relationship personally, through an enduring friendship that includes mutual love and support, and even financially, through our joint business ventures.

Still, we find that often, the people you know the least can actually help you the most. This idea may seem counterintuitive, and you may be asking yourself, "Why is that?"

The answer is simple and lies in the fact that information tends to circulate within groups as opposed to between groups. Since the people you know very well (your strong ties) tend to know each other, those within your inner circle tend to know the same things. For example, if one of your friends is aware of a job opening, it is very likely that your other friends are also aware of the same opening. It also explains why you may receive the same e-mail several times.

By contrast, if someone with whom you are loosely acquainted (your weak ties) holds information, then it is more likely the information is unique. The old classmate you bump into at the airport may know about a job opening that your friends don't. Information that is of greatest potential value to you is often held by people you do not know very well. Information from these sources tends to be nonredundant and distinct.

STRONG AND WEAK TIES

As shown in Figure 4–2, we can think of relationships along a continuum based on our level of familiarity and the frequency of our interactions. The key to understanding the strength of weak ties is in first understanding the difference between *weak ties*, which lie on the left side of the continuum, and *strong ties*, which lie on the right side of the continuum.

Strong Ties: Close Relationships. Some relationships are stronger than others. By "strong" we mean how close the relationship is between you and the other person and how often you communicate with them. We usually have stronger bonds with family members than nonrelatives because we have a

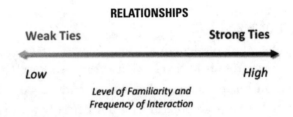

Figure 4–2. The continuum of relationships.

shared background and history. We also tend to have stronger relationships with people we have known for a long time than with people we have just met or who are passing acquaintances. Relatives, close friends, longtime associates, and people you speak with on a regular basis are all examples of strong ties. *Strong ties are characterized by a high level of familiarity and a high frequency of interaction.*

James Coleman (1926–1995) is well regarded as a pioneer in mathematical sociology. His studies influenced U.S. education policy. Coleman saw the significance of a network as being a "net" of support for the members of a network that needed that support. The best example was a strong family unit. If one person was in need of extra assistance, it was the responsibility of the family unit to take care of that person. In this sense, he believed that the network was essential for social support.

Strong relationships bolster the ability for this type of network to be effective in achieving one's goals or positive outcomes in society. This is what Coleman called "social capital." *Social capital* is the value associated with the network of connections that you have. More specifically, it is *bonding social capital* because its value is in how the people in the network stick together to support one another.

We also have strong relationships outside of our family: namely, our friends. Friends are the people we call for advice; we spend lots of time with them when we hang out. Friends can be classmates, neighbors, and colleagues.

....

Strong relationships bolster the ability of a network to be effective in achieving one's goals. Bonding social capital *is the value associated with the support you receive from people in your network.*

....

Weak Ties: Distant Relationships. By comparison, there are other people in your life that are best described as a relatively "weak" tie: a distant relationship. A friend-of-a-friend you only see by chance; a fellow member of an organization you sometimes cross paths with at the annual national conference; a colleague working overseas whom you may reach out to from time to time—all are examples of weak ties. *Weak ties are characterized by a low level of familiarity and a low frequency of interaction.* These people are not as well known to you, and you may not be as comfortable with them as with your strong ties. You are also not likely to be in regular contact with them. Yet these weak ties have information that may be the most useful to you in pursuit of your goals.

Renowned sociologist Mark Granovetter derived the idea of "the strength of weak ties" from several studies in the 1970s about how people found their jobs. In one study, he asked many people who had recently received a job where they heard about this job. The majority of people learned about it from a weak tie.

So what does this tell us? Well, first don't discount casual acquaintances—you never know who might help you. Second, we need to develop and continually use a method to contact and remain connected to the weak ties in our networks. This is an important concept to understand and one that we'll circle back to a bit later, but before we do that, we must explain the final compelling idea: "network gaps."

Bridging Network Gaps

Let's consider the case of Jamal and Imani. They are employees of the same organization. They have equal talent and really only differ in their network ties. As illustrated in Figure 4–3, the shape of their networks is different—and that's not a bad thing, if they have different goals. Each network can assist them in achieving different kinds of outcomes.

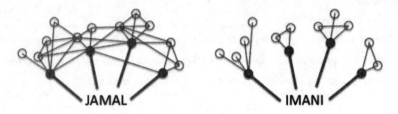

Figure 4–3. The case of Jamal and Imani.

In looking at their networks, consider whose network is better for:

▸ Resource pooling (or bringing people together to achieve a goal)

▸ Autonomy (or not being controlled by others; being independent)

▸ Diverse information (or finding out what you need to know to navigate relationships and get projects done)

▸ Loyalty (knowing who you can trust, who will work hard with you or for you—in other words, who "has your back")

▸ Advancement (knowing who will prepare, recommend, and give you opportunities to grow and prosper)

The shape of each employee's network gives us the answers to these questions. Notice the closeness of the points on Jamal's network. His network is *dense*—many of the people know one another and some relationships overlap. This kind of network is excellent for pooling resources and for loyalty, because there is some trust and cohesion. Trust is built up greatly in dense networks, and accountability is built into the network because all of the people know each other.

Now take another look at Imani's network. There are fewer points on Imani's network and they are spread farther apart. There is not nearly as much interconnection. Imani's network is *sparse*, which makes it great for gaining autonomy and diverse information, since the contacts do not overlap.

Sociologist and business professor Ronald Burt studied the careers of thousands of business people who were making their way through a corporation. He cataloged their career paths, salaries, promotions, performance ratings, and all of their connections to other employees in the company. Several patterns were observed:

- In large networks of people (such as companies and nonprofits), *gaps* between departments, units, and divisions naturally emerged in the organization: teams that did not talk to each other, groups that did not communicate with each other, or people who were unaware of each other, for example. These gaps represent disconnects in the information flow across the organization.

- There were key people in the organizations who bridged these disconnected parts or who were connected to people across their organization.

- Those key people tended to have earlier promotions, higher salaries, and higher performance ratings than others at the same rank.

Experts such as Burt, Coleman, and Granovetter argue that the arrangement of the people and organizations within your network can be a predictor of your professional and personal success. How is it possible to predict the success of an individual based upon her network? Because the structure and other characteristics of a person's network can be compared to the structure and characteristics of other people's networks, we can trace positive outcomes back to the structure of her network.

Burt's theory of how social capital is built is based upon the idea that people who reach across the gaps in the network structure of their organization have a competitive advantage. This is *bridging social capital*, and it is related to how you connect people or groups that do not usually talk to one another through your network. The basis of the competitive advantage for those who effectively bridge network gaps is twofold: (1) the speed by which they receive critical information, and (2) the ability they have to control the type of projects they receive or the type of work they create.

The advantages that people derive from bridging network gaps are centered on *information* and *control*. Along the lines of the former, bridging network gaps translates into expanded access to information and ideas, improved timing and speed of receiving information, and increased opportunities for referrals. The best network will give you advantages because your network will give you right information at the right time. With respect to the latter, bridging network gaps provides an opportunity to have a disproportionate say in whose interests are served in completing a project or program. The best network will give you many opportunities to broker connections between people, groups, and organizations. Here is J.R.'s story about the importance of networking:

> *I remember the first time I really thought about the power of having a good network: I was at my first convention of the National Society of Black Engineers [NSBE] during my sophomore year and looking for an internship at the career fair. I turned down one aisle and I saw a familiar face: Tracy Joyner. I had met Tracy the previous year when she was one of the officers at the Rutgers Chapter of NSBE. Tracy was someone that both Randal and I looked up to because she exemplified where we wanted to go. She was working at Merck & Co. and doing well. I told her I was looking for an internship and she said she would introduce me to the person who was the internship program coordinator for her plant site, Andrea Turner. I remember to this day what she said when she introduced me: "Andrea, here is one of our fantastic engineering students from Rutgers. Can you tell him more about the internship program?" I didn't know Andrea, but because of Tracy's referral, I was in the door.*

> *The rest is history. I gave Andrea my resume, filled out an application, interviewed on site a few weeks later, and got the job. That's the power of networks.*

....

Bridging social capital is related to how you connect people or groups that do not usually talk to one another through your network. If you are adept at bridging network gaps, you gain information and control advantages in your professional and service activities.

....

THE THREE TYPES OF NETWORKS

Every person's network is different. The structure of your network obviously has implications in terms of your access to social capital, but it can also lead to different outcomes. In the case of Jamal and Imani, we learned the difference between *dense* and *sparse* networks. There's a third type of network, too: a *borrowed* network (see Figure 4–4). We'll now explain all three network types in more detail and show how you can network and strategically build relationships, using specific game-changing strategies, in these contexts.

Dense Networks. A dense network is a small network that is tightly connected. It is perhaps more easily described as a small network where everyone knows everybody else. These networks are ideal in fostering support among members of the network.

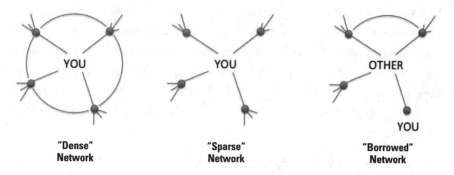

| "Dense" Network | "Sparse" Network | "Borrowed" Network |

Figure 4–4. Three types of networks.

Families are often dense networks. Networks of friends are typically dense as well. Because of the strong communication channels, dense networks are great for communicating complex information. Dense networks are central to our discussion of group relationships in Strategy 6: Find Strength in Numbers, because they enable these groups to function most effectively. The high level of trust that is typical of dense networks works extremely well for getting things done.

But because everyone knows what everyone else knows, dense networks tend to circulate redundant information. Because information is widely disseminated, there is little to no opportunity to control activities or shape the flow of information. Furthermore, because members are so tightly connected or bonded, there is little to no opportunity to bridge network gaps. As a result, *access to social capital in dense networks is limited.*

Sparse Networks. A sparse network is a large network with several independent relationships. Because members of the network are generally isolated from one another, several opportunities emerge: the opportunity to obtain nonredundant, unique, and valuable information from members of the network; the opportunity to control activities, broker information, and broker opportunities among members of the network; the opportunity to shape the flow of information between members of the network; and the opportunity to bridge the gaps between members of the network (i.e., bridging social capital) for mutual gain. As a result, *access to social capital in sparse networks is high.*

If you work in an organization with several departments or satellite offices, the relationships among people are likely to reflect a sparse network. The people *within* each department or office may know each other well. This is a dense network. However, if there are no tight connections *across* all of the departments or offices, the overall organization probably resembles a sparse network. Sparse networks are effective for obtaining diverse information, advancing your career or agenda through intrapreneurship (Strategy 7) and entrepreneurship (Strategy 8), and seizing opportunities for synergy and scale (Strategy 9).

Borrowed Networks. A borrowed network is a network with relationships that are primarily dependent on a second party. Relationships are initiated indirectly through another contact, as opposed to your establishing relationships directly.

For example, let's assume Dwayne is new to his organization and is assigned to work for Stacey, a manager who is well connected to several people at their organization. If Stacey introduces Dwayne to her contacts and they eventually say, "Yeah, I know Dwayne. I met him through Stacey," then Dwayne is borrowing Stacey's network. His relationships with Stacey's contacts are dependent on knowing her.

Borrowed networks can be a very efficient way to expand your own network. It saves time and effort when someone is willing to broker connections to people they have worked to establish relationships with over a long time.

It is much easier to establish a relationship with someone indirectly through a mutual bond (i.e., an introduction or referral) than to try to do so directly without any such context. The network you borrow could be dense or sparse—or even borrowed. In this instance, your network becomes only as good as the network you are borrowing. As a result, *access to social capital in borrowed networks is dependent.*

Of course, the goal in borrowing anyone's network is to ultimately establish your own direct relationships so that you are no longer dependent on the broker. We'll discuss the role of mentors in making these kinds of connections and the possibilities they can lead to in Strategy 5: Seek the Wisdom of Others.

The final thing to know about the three types of networks is that they are not always separate and distinct. For example, you could have a dense network within your department, a sparse network across your organization, and a borrowed network of certain senior-level executives through your supervisor, all at the same time.

Game-Changing Strategies for Networking and Relationship Building

Now that you understand the three compelling ideas about relationships— "six degrees of separation," "the strength of weak ties," and "network gaps"—and the three types of networks, we'll show you how to put these ideas into practice with three valuable game-changing strategies that leverage these concepts and tie them together.

ESTABLISH THE RIGHT NETWORK FOR THE RIGHT NEED AT THE RIGHT TIME

There are benefits to all types of networks. At every stage in your career, and particularly during the early stages, establishing a *dense* network within your team, group, department, or area is important because it can help build credibility with your peers. A dense network contributes to having solid relationships with people with whom you interact regularly.

When you need to establish more influential or powerful relationships that would be difficult to broker directly, a *borrowed* network will be of tremendous benefit. For example, if you are at the mid-stage of your career and you are looking to establish relationships with key decision makers or executive-level sponsors, those connections may be most effectively brokered through a current or past manager, supervisor, mentor, or supporter who has already established those ties. We will elaborate on this strategy in the next chapter.

Finally, at every stage in your career you should seek to establish a *sparse* network as well. This type of network will be particularly helpful when you are looking to connect people or organizations for mutual gain, bridge network gaps to promote more coordinated efforts, or achieve some form of synergy. This idea will be explored more fully in Strategy 9: Synergize and Reach Scale.

We refer to this approach as *strategic networking*, or establishing the right network for the right need at the right time. This approach is in keeping with Strategy 3, which dealt with *strategic career management* and the importance of identifying the right job assignment for the right need at the right time. And it has parallels in Strategies 5 and 6, which, respectively, deal with *strategic mentoring* and *strategic organizational involvement*.

MAINTAIN A DIVERSE NETWORK AT ALL TIMES

Our discussion about personal diversity, "the strength of weak ties," and the benefits of a sparse network clearly suggest there is value in developing diverse and broad relationships: in other words, a network comprised of meaningful ties across various lines of difference (i.e., race, gender, ethnicity, religion, etc.). It is from these relationships that diverse and broad information can flow and rich opportunities present themselves to bridge network gaps.

Further evidence can be found in David Thomas and John Gabarro's study of minority executives and minority managers. Thomas and Gabarro found that the networks of the minority executives who reached the C-suite tended to be more ethnically diverse (with strong ties to both minorities and non-minorities) when compared to the networks of the minority managers who reached a plateau in their careers and never reached the C-suite. The networks of the minority managers tended to be more uniform (exclusively African American or exclusively white).

Maintaining a diverse network means disciplining yourself to build diversity into your relationships. We realize that it may not happen naturally, especially depending on the environment where you work. If so, you will need to be proactive about taking steps to foster your own personal diversity. It could mean attending events comprised of diverse people; joining organizations with members who are dissimilar to you; and even arranging meetings or lunches with colleagues of different backgrounds. Any opportunity that you have to talk to and interact with people who are not like you should be a welcome opportunity to expand your network and your horizons.

BORROW SOMEONE ELSE'S NETWORK TO BUILD YOUR OWN

The same type of network can produce different outcomes for different types of people. Ronald Burt found, in his studies, that men with sparse networks are more likely to get early promotions, whereas women and new hires tend to get early promotions when they have a borrowed network. Think about that for a moment. Why does a sparse network better serve men while a borrowed network better serves women and new hires?

Women and new hires may face particular challenges to establishing credibility in environments that are traditionally male-dominated and that associate age with experience. Hence, Burt groups women and new hires under the term "outsiders." However, when these so-called outsiders established strong ties to a mentor or sponsor with a more powerful or influential network (i.e., when they established a borrowed network), they were able to overcome these challenges. The mentor or sponsor was helpful not only in validating their abilities but also advocating on their behalf for new opportunities.

Given these findings, how do they relate to people of color? A similar conclusion can be drawn for so-called minorities. In many environments, particularly those where people of color are underrepresented and may face particular challenges to establishing credibility, we believe that we, too, can be interpreted as "outsiders" who may similarly benefit at times from a borrowed network. The same could be true for someone who has been with a company for several years but has just transitioned to a completely new department or division. The key is to eventually make the borrowed connections your connections—to translate what may begin as indirect and distant acquaintances into direct and close relationships. When you are an "outsider" you are often best served by borrowing the network of someone who is well connected as a means to ultimately build your own network.

This is a natural segue to Strategy 5, where we will discuss a range of developmental relationships, including mentors and protégés, which can help you along these lines and beyond.

Seek the Wisdom of Others

He who walks with wise men will be wise. But the companion of fools will be destroyed.
—Proverbs 13:20

Never mistake knowledge for wisdom. One helps you make a living; the other helps you make a life.
—Sandra Carey

A single conversation with a wise man [or woman] is better than years of study.
—Chinese Proverb

What Is Wisdom?

THE THREE quotations that open this discussion are powerful descriptions of the value of *wisdom*. Given the tremendous value that is placed on wisdom, this begs the questions: What exactly is wisdom, and what does it mean to possess it?

It is not uncommon to assume that wisdom is a function of age. And while it is indeed the case that many older people in our lives possess a great deal of wisdom, wisdom is not defined by the number of years you have lived.

One part of wisdom is *knowledge*—the things that we know. Everyone has experiences and, as we discussed in Strategy 2, we believe experience is the best teacher. These experiences—both direct experience and the indirect experience of others—naturally translate into knowledge. But acquiring knowledge alone does not make someone wise.

What differentiates wisdom from, say, education is that wisdom implies much more than just learning. Wisdom implies a practical application of knowledge, a level of maturity, and a measure of discernment. Essentially, wisdom combines knowledge with a seasoned ability to distinguish what is

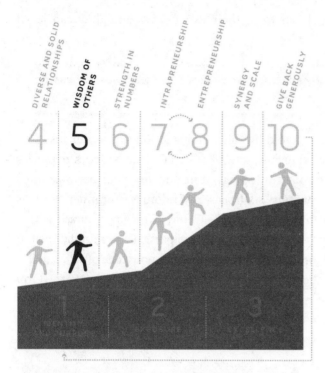

Figure 5–1. The path to greatness (Strategy 5).

appropriate from what is inappropriate, which suggests that the other part of wisdom is *judgment*—the ability to exercise responsible insight. Therefore, *wisdom is knowledge combined with good judgment.* Wisdom can simply be thought of as a blend between "book smarts" and "street smarts," or the combination of learning and good old common sense.

Knowledge + Judgment = **Wisdom**

This is why we are not convinced that just because someone is young that they are not wise. We believe that age significantly contributes to wisdom, but we also believe that wisdom begins to manifest itself at the very moment a lesson is learned. Seeking the wisdom of others is not confined to learning from people who are older than you, or even from those with more experience. Thinking in this way is inconsistent with the fifth strategy for Black Faces in White Places. It is not that other people have *better* experience, but rather, they have *different* experience.

Accordingly, you can learn from their experiences and they can learn from yours.

....
Hindsight is 20/20. By seeking the wisdom of others, foresight can be 20/20, too.
....

Wisdom is ultimately found by cultivating and following your instincts. As Oprah says, "Follow your instincts. That's where true wisdom manifests itself." It is reflected in your gut feelings, your hunches, your personal intuition, your "third eye," or your "sixth sense." Wisdom is your inner voice. As written in the classic Chinese text, *Tao Te Ching*, "Knowing yourself is true wisdom." That is why Strategies 1, 2, and 3 are particularly foundational to Strategy 5. The search for wisdom is the search for knowledge of self, and it is a natural extension of the self-determination that we discussed in Part I. (You will also recall in Strategy 3 that "intrapersonal intelligence," or being "self smart," was identified as one of the God-given gifts or intelligences.) You can *seek* the wisdom of others, but true wisdom can only be *found* within.

The Five Tenets of Seeking Wisdom

We have identified five tenets of seeking the wisdom of others:

1. *There is always something you can learn from others.* Your experience and knowledge base will be bolstered regardless of who is the teacher. We can learn much from younger, older, less experienced, or highly capable people. Observing or listening to the experiences of others can demonstrate what's good or bad, informing decisions about what you would or wouldn't do. As Eleanor Roosevelt once said, "Learn from the mistakes of others. You can't live long enough to make them all yourself."

....
If experience is the best teacher, learning from someone else's experience is a close second.
....

2. *The more you learn, the more you will realize what you do not know.* The possibilities for exposure and experience are limitless and the body of knowledge in our universe is infinite. We could spend a lifetime and still only scratch the surface on what there is to learn. While humbling, this fact

should motivate you to seek the wisdom of others. In doing so, you move beyond what only you are able to learn; you also benefit from what others have learned. This tenet was captured by Albert Einstein's famous quote, "The more I learn, the more I realize I don't know."

3. *Greater wisdom is often found in failure than in success.* A tremendous amount of wisdom can be gleaned from our failures. Take Newark Mayor Cory Booker, for instance. Booker lost one race in 2002 against longtime incumbent Sharpe James before becoming mayor of New Jersey's largest city in 2006. "I learned more lessons in my loss than in my victory," he told us during an interview. "It's one of the professors you can find in life—mistakes and what some people call failures." While it can be difficult to do, time spent analyzing failure for lessons learned is time well spent. Author William Saroyan once said, "Good people are good because they've come to wisdom through failure. We get very little wisdom from success."

4. *When you seek the wisdom of others, you develop your own.* The objective of seeking the wisdom of others is not to blindly adopt their perspectives. Instead, you build up your own, personal encyclopedia of knowledge and judgment. You must filter the experiences of others to draw your own conclusions and cultivate your inner voice. "We don't receive wisdom; we must discover it for ourselves after a journey that no one can take for us or spare us," said writer Marcel Proust.

5. *Do not just seek the wisdom of others; also impart your wisdom on others.* Your experiences—whether they are successes or failures or things you have learned from other people—can add value to another person's life and perhaps help them avoid a pitfall or achieve a goal. Never forget these words of Aesop: "No act of kindness, no matter how small, is ever wasted." We will revisit this tenet at the end of the chapter when we discuss your responsibility to mentor others.

....

Sankofa *is a word in the Akan language of Ghana, West Africa. Its literal meaning is "to go back and retrieve," which is translated to mean "There is nothing wrong with learning from hindsight." One of the symbols for Sankofa is a mythical bird that flies forward with its head turned backward, which reflects a belief in learning wisdom from the*

past to build for the future. The modern interpretation is, "If you don't know where you've been, you don't know where you're going."
....

Developmental Relationships

There is an entire continuum of what we call "developmental relationships" that naturally facilitate the exchange of wisdom.

A developmental relationship could take the form of a peer who comes into your life and inspires you to pursue your dreams. It could be a teacher who helps prepare you for your future. Or it could be a mentor who provides personal and professional support throughout an entire lifetime. The beauty of these and other developmental relationships is that both parties grow wiser as a result of their interaction.

The overarching personal and professional benefit of developmental relationships is not just the opportunity to seek the wisdom of others, but rather, to ultimately cultivate your own wisdom and discover your inner voice. The development of wisdom can help you avoid preventable detours and minimize mistakes. An important by-product of this experience is that it potentially helps you develop into a better person. We believe this is an important aspect of the human experience.

In the professional realm, developmental relationships:

▸ Enable you to seek the knowledge of others who have learned the game and, perhaps more important, played the game effectively, and therefore can teach you to do the same. You need others to teach you to identify the key players in your game, including the decision makers, gatekeepers, and influencers that we discussed in Strategy 3.

▸ Allow you to seek the experience of others who understand the unspoken rules of the game, the subtleties, and the informalities, so that you, too, can "read between the lines."

▸ Facilitate your ability to seek the assistance of major players in the game—people with more power, influence, and connections than you possess. These individuals can help you overcome barriers to reaching the upper echelon of your organization or field, and eventually put you in a position to redefine the game and pave the way for others.

Professional developmental relationships offer support in two areas: (1) *career support* that improves your skills and abilities or advances your professional agenda, and (2) *psychological and social support* (or "psychosocial" support) that helps you process your emotions and build confidence.

Career support can take the forms of:

▶ Teaching new technical or functional skills

▶ Coaching on career decisions

▶ Offering problem-solving advice

▶ Advocacy for promotions

▶ Providing visibility with coworkers and key individuals

Psychosocial support includes:

▶ Affirmation and building self-esteem

▶ Friendship and confidentiality

▶ Encouragement and motivation

▶ Empathic listening and feedback

▶ Counseling and emotional support

The continuum of developmental relationships is shown in Figure 5–2. The level of experience or support associated with a given role increases from left to right across the figure. Along the top of the figure, roles providing

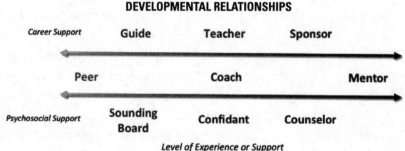

Figure 5–2. The continuum of developmental relationships.

career support are shown. Along the bottom of the figure are roles providing psychosocial support. Roles that provide both can be found in the middle. Note, however, that "role model" does not appear on the continuum in Figure 5–2. That's because anyone, at any level of experience or support, can be a role model. Even a stranger could be your role model. It's not that role models "support" you directly per se. Instead, they indirectly model behaviors or characteristics from which you may learn, or accomplishments to which you may aspire.

These roles are not necessarily separate and distinct. There is tremendous overlap between each of them. For example, a coach can be a teacher, a peer can be a counselor, and a teacher can be a guide. We offer the continuum to paint a complete picture of the range of support that developmental relationships can provide and, conversely, the range of needs that developmental relationships can address.

THE NINE ROLES OF A MENTOR

As you can see in Figure 5–2, "mentor" appears at the far right of the continuum because mentors represent the highest level of experience and support for a "protégé." But the role of a mentor is not a singular one. Mentors often provide several types of support that are encompassed by the nine roles of a mentor, described in Table 5–1.

Going forward, our references to "mentor" are a proxy for one or all of these nine developmental relationships. A mentor could fulfill just one or any combination of the developmental roles. A mentor could simply be a guide. Or a mentor could be a guide, teacher, sponsor, counselor, coach, and role model (although it is rare for a mentor to fulfill all of these roles, as we will discuss later). In this book, *mentor generally refers to anyone who seeks to impart their wisdom to a protégé.*

Similarly, our references to "protégé" are a proxy for any individual who seeks the support of a mentor, like a student working with a teacher or a player who works with a coach. In this book, protégé generally refers to anyone who seeks the wisdom of a mentor.

Next, we will specifically discuss mentoring and the power of mentor/protégé developmental relationships. Again, we focus specifically on these relationships because they can encompass the entire continuum of developmental

Role	Description	Type of Support
Guide	Provides insight to policies, procedures, cultural norms, standards, and obstacles for a protégé	Career
Teacher	Cultivates the skills and abilities of a protégé	Career
Sponsor	Advocates and lobbies for opportunities on behalf of a protégé	Career
Sounding Board	Listens empathetically to issues and offers feedback to a protégé	Psychosocial
Confidant	Offers a trusted perspective on dealing with issues and overcoming challenges faced by a protégé	Psychosocial
Counselor	Offers a trusted, expert perspective on dealing with issues and overcoming challenges faced by a protégé	Psychosocial
Peer	Supports an equal, fellow protégé	Career and Psychosocial
Coach	Helps a protégé develop career strategies and/or motivates a protégé to persevere	Career and Psychosocial
Role Model	Sets a good example that can be modeled by a protégé	Career and Psychosocial (indirectly)

Table 5–1. Nine roles of a mentor.

relationships. We conclude the chapter with game-changing strategies for protégés and mentors, as well as techniques to help you maximize your efforts to both seek wisdom from others and impart wisdom on others.

Mentors and Protégés

For centuries, mentors have been a part of life inside and outside of organizations. The term mentor is derived from the name of Odysseus's wise friend, Mentor, whom the Greek king entrusts with his son's development to become the next king when Odysseus goes off to war. It is a time-honored role in the personal and professional development of others. Some examples from African-American history include the mentorship of Martin Luther King Jr. by Dr. Benjamin Mays, the former president of Morehouse College. Subsequently, Dr. King mentored a young John Lewis, who was the leader of the Student Nonviolent Coordinating Committee during the Civil Rights Movement. In more recent years, as a student at the University of Denver, former U.S. Secretary of State Condoleezza Rice was mentored by the political scientist and international relations expert Josef Korbel (who happens to be the father of former Secretary of State Madeleine Albright). When Rice entered public service another mentor, Brent Scowcroft, brought her into the National Security Council. Scowcroft has been a key adviser to Rice throughout her career.

If you are a science-fiction fan like us, you are familiar with the mentor-protégé relationship between Obi-Wan Kenobi and Luke Skywalker (and later Yoda and Luke) in the *Star Wars* movies, or the relationship between Morpheus and Neo in *The Matrix* trilogy. In the African historical context, the elders of West African villages mentor young people to prepare them for adulthood. Either through rites of passage or other ceremonies, young men and women aren't allowed to become "adults" without someone showing them the way.

FORMS OF MENTORING

In its original incarnation, mentoring was a one-on-one activity. *Traditional mentoring* takes place with one mentor and one protégé over an undefined period of time. Typically there's a more senior person imparting wisdom and knowledge to someone younger and less experienced. The goal of these relationships is to assist the protégé in developing skills for future success. Randal recalls his experience:

> One of my early and very influential mentors was Rey Ramsey. I met Rey at a conference where he was a panelist and I was an attendee. I was finishing my graduate studies at MIT and attempting to launch BCT Partners, [and] Rey had recently left his position as the president of the Enterprise Foundation to establish One Economy Corporation, the social enterprise he cofounded and continues to run. One Economy and BCT were focused on doing very similar work to bridge the "digital divide"— the gap between those who benefit from information technology and those who do not.
>
> During one of our early encounters he said, "I love the work you're doing and I love what you stand for. I'm willing to help you in any way I can because I want to see you succeed. As a community, we need to support one another." I will never forget those words that Rey spoke to me.

Today, there are many variations on this theme and many types of mentoring relationships. Here are a few:

▶ *Transition Mentoring*. This term defines both the duration and the intent of the relationship. In transition mentoring, the relationship occurs during a particular time in a protégé's career, such as when someone is entering into a new organization or even a new department or division. The intent is to help the protégé become acclimated to the culture, politics, and paths of advancement within the organization.

▶ *Group Mentoring*. Group mentoring is when one person mentors several protégés as a unit. Conversations and meetings may take place as a group and be subject to group dynamics. It takes a very skillful mentor to manage this type of relationship, but if mentors are in short supply, this arrangement may serve the need, especially in situations where some mentoring is essential to success (i.e., transition mentoring or mentoring in a youth program). It may also facilitate peer support.

▶ *Team Mentoring*. When a small group of mentors works with a group of protégés it is called team mentoring. In this situation, the team of mentors coordinates its efforts to meet the developmental needs of the team of protégés.

▶ *Peer Mentoring*. Peer mentoring refers to a relationship between peers where one is more experienced than the other. The purpose is for the mentor to help the protégé adjust; in this case, the mentor serves primarily as a resource for answering questions, resolving problems, and providing advice. Some school systems have set up peer mentoring programs between older and younger students and provide training to help both parties function effectively in their roles. Some corporations have peer mentor programs for new hires.

▶ *Reverse Mentoring*. Sometimes a younger person mentors someone older and generally more senior in an organization. This kind of relationship often stems from the idea that senior employees can learn from younger, more technologically savvy ones. We think mentoring is a two-way street and this kind of exchange should happen in traditional one-on-one mentoring relationships.

▸ *Formal vs. Informal Mentoring.* There are formal mentor programs in organizations and, of course, informal arrangements. We define informal mentoring as the kind of pairing that emerges naturally, either inside or outside an organization. Formal mentoring, however, is a structured program developed inside the organization. Table 5–2 summarizes the distinctions.

	Informal	Formal
Duration	Undefined, an indefinite period of time	Defined, a definite period of time
Arrangement	By chance, the two parties gradually assume the roles	By design, the two parties are placed within the roles
Goals	Implicit, not necessarily stated or spoken	Explicit, typically clarified and shared
Organization	Not responsible for monitoring the process	Responsible for monitoring the process
Accessibility	Few people, access is only available to those who are "selected"	Many people, access is available to everyone

Table 5–2. Informal vs. formal mentoring.

Informal mentoring has taken place within organizations forever. But the challenge has been providing equal access for all. Informal mentoring takes place in the so-called "old boys" network, and it tends to exclude women and people of color. Formal mentor programs are a way to get beyond the exclusivity of informal mentoring.

Both informal and formal mentoring relationships can be effective, but formal arrangements tend to be more challenging to develop because you are brought together by a third party. If the organizers of the mentoring program do their homework, they can create pairings that extend beyond the confines of the program. Even after a formal mentoring program is over, the mentor and protégé may want to continue the relationship. That is an excellent outcome of a formal mentoring program.

▸ *Managing vs. Mentoring.* Managers are not mentors. In fact, the roles are quite different. We don't recommend that your manager or immediate supervisor become your mentor while you still work for them. These roles differ along four dimensions: the *period* of the relationship, the *focus* of the relationship, the *commitment* of the parties involved, and the type of *feedback* that is given, as shown in Table 5–3.

Having your manager as your mentor may create conflict—especially if other workers view your relationship with the manager as favoritism or if the manager is asked to recommend people for promotions or identify people who could be let go in a downsizing. So, resist the temptation to just call your immediate supervisor or manager your "mentor."

However, a former manager, someone you worked with previously and already have an established relationship with, might be a great mentor.

	Manager	Mentor
Period	Short-term	Long-term
Focus	Task	Relationship
Commitment	Limited	Broad
Feedback	Specific	General

Table 5–3. Manager vs. mentor

The best way to learn is to teach.

Game-Changing Strategies for Mentors and Protégés

Now, let's review separate game-changing strategies for protégés, mentors, and both.

FOR PROTÉGÉS

Develop a "Personal Board of Directors." A board of directors is a group of people who help a CEO think through strategic issues and make difficult decisions. Protégés should create their own personal "board of directors" or "board of advisers" as another way to seek the wisdom of others and leverage various developmental relationships in their lives.

Identify the Right Mentor for the Right Need at the Right Time. Figure out what type of mentor you will need for different points in your career. This is what we call *strategic mentoring*, or seeking the right mentor for the right need at the right time.

David Thomas and John Gabarro, in their book *Breaking Through,* explain that minority managers who did not make it to the executive ranks often had the wrong mentors for the levels they aspired to in the organization. The mentors were helpful, but only to a certain point. The minority managers kept the mentors as their primary mentors because they felt comfortable with them, but this may not have been the best strategy because they needed mentors at higher levels as they rose through the organization.

Conversely, Thomas and Gabarro also found that successful minority executives had different types of mentors at different points in their career. Early in their careers they had a mentor at the functional/departmental level. During mid-career they had a mentor at the upper levels of management. Later in their careers they had a mentor at the executive level. Understanding that you need different kinds of mentors at different stages is critical, so be open to mentoring relationships with people who have the wisdom you require for your career aspirations.

Be Yourself. We have seen young African Americans come into organizations and try to be someone they are not. It is challenging to enter a place where the culture is strong and be tempted to completely abandon your own identity and assume the dominant culture. This is more challenging if you are still in the stage of your life where you are learning about yourself and establishing your identity. We encourage protégés who are Black Faces in White Places to see your ethnicity as an asset and not to assimilate. When you remain true to who you are, you adapt what you know for use in this new place.

FOR MENTORS

Overcome Network Obstacles. Network obstacles are the circumstances that prevent protégés from having a network that supports their career aspirations. A central role for mentors, particularly mentors to African Americans, is to facilitate a protégé's efforts to overcome these obstacles.

Strategy 4 described how new hires, women, and by extension, members of minority groups may need to "borrow" social capital and relationships from more established people in the organization. Along these lines, mentors can help protégés overcome network obstacles by facilitating access to informal networks and influential contacts that would be difficult to establish otherwise. Because minorities sometimes prefer to interact with other minorities, you should also encourage your protégé to interact with minorities and non-minorities.

Monitor Stereotyping of Your Protégé. In some cases there may be an expectation that an African-American employee may only be able to perform up to a certain level and can't handle more complex or creative work. Monitor your protégé's work assignments and make sure they are appropriate and challenging and that others are not stereotyping her into certain types of jobs or projects.

FOR MENTORS AND PROTÉGÉS

Address the Issue of Race Directly. A potential barrier to mentor/protégé relationships that cross racial and ethnic lines may arise when one party prefers not to discuss race while the other party prefers to discuss race. Studies have found that this situation creates tension and feelings of frustration or disappointment as a result of the perception that the topic is being avoided or even ignored by one party, despite the other party's desire to discuss it openly.

To alleviate this problem, consider having an explicit conversation with your mentor or protégé as to whether race is an open topic for discussion. This will clarify expectations and put everyone on the same page— hopefully avoiding the potential pitfall.

Learn about Each Other's Culture. One of the benefits of mentor/protégé relationships is the opportunity for mutual learning about each other's culture. Diverse mentor/protégé relationships are yet another way to move beyond your comfort zone, as discussed in Strategy 2, and to promote personal diversity, as discussed in Strategy 4. However, this kind of mutual learning does not happen by accident.

Deliberate steps must be taken to explore each other's upbringing, background, experiences, perspectives, and values. This means dedicating time to have these conversations, and displaying a willingness to share your cultures and to learn about the cultures of others without prejudice or judgment.

Become Both a Mentor and a Protégé. We began this chapter by identifying five tenets for seeking the wisdom of others. The first tenet is that there is always something you can learn from others. Conversely, there is always something you can teach to others. That's why the fifth and final tenet is to not just seek the wisdom of others, but also to impart wisdom to others.

Much like networking and relationship building, mentoring is just as much about giving as it is about taking. It is therefore important to seek out opportunities not only to be a protégé of others, but also to be a mentor to others. A college student can mentor a high school student. A young professional can mentor a college student. An executive can mentor a young professional. You can be a mentor at almost any stage of your career.

Mentoring is not just an opportunity; it is a responsibility. No one succeeds in life as a result of their abilities alone. Whatever successes we enjoy are due in large part to people who have helped us. We therefore have a responsibility to do the same for others. Always remember: "Each one, reach one. Each one, teach one."

Seek the Wisdom of Elders. It is an African tradition for young people to seek the wisdom of the elders in their community. As a society, we must never lose our respect or our reverence for our elders. They are the beacons and pillars within our families and communities. We're talking about parents, neighbors, business owners, clergy, educators, aunts, uncles, grandparents, great grandparents, great-great grandparents. Unlike segments of American culture, in African culture elders and senior citizens are held in the highest regard.

Elders should be cherished while we are still blessed to have them among us. They should be regularly sought out for advice and counsel. Their sense of history, wealth of knowledge, and experience is an invaluable resource that we should continually tap into. Moreover, we must create more forums, more mechanisms, and more creative ways to capture their wisdom and promote exchanges across generations. In fact, Randal sits on the board of the National Visionary Leadership Project (NVLP), founded by Dr. Camille O. Cosby and chaired by Dr. Johnnetta B. Cole. This is exactly the work being done by NVLP.

A FINAL WORD ON OUR SPIRITUALITY

Finally, we offer our reflections on how spirituality and seeking the wisdom of others plays out in our lives: We find power in seeking the wisdom of God. We accomplish this by studying His word, reading scripture, practicing meditation, and performing prayer. It is found during our quiet moments when we are able to invoke His presence, hear His voice, and heed His calling. Don Thompson, president and chief operating officer at McDonald's, follows a similar practice to ours. During an interview with us, he commented, "I'm on my knees a lot. I definitely will pray about certain things when I'm wondering, 'Lord, which way should I go? How will this thing work out?' And inevitably I have never been led astray." We've advised others seeking our advice to seek His wisdom by soliciting the advice of their pastor, imam, priest, rabbi, or other spiritual leader. We seek God's counsel on a daily basis to guide us on personal and professional matters. For us, God's wisdom is the ultimate wisdom.

Find Strength in Numbers

When spider webs unite, they can tie up a lion. —African Proverb

The Power of Strength in Numbers: Don Imus Gets Taken Down

April 4, 2007, began the same as most any other day.

For radio personality Don Imus that meant heading off to the studio where his show, *Imus in the Morning,* would discuss the issues of the day, employing a mix of what's been termed "shock" journalism and interviews. This day, U.S. Senator Chris Dodd of Connecticut was on the lineup as the program was simulcast on cable TV network MSNBC and syndicated on radio stations across the United States by Westwood One.[1]

But before his program was over, Imus uttered words that created a firestorm that led MSNBC to drop the program, convinced advertisers to pull the plug on sponsorships, and resulted in his removal from the airwaves.

During a sports segment, Imus, his producer Bernie McGuirk, and sports announcer Sid Rosenberg discussed the Rutgers women's basketball team:[2]

Imus: So I watched the basketball game last night between—a little bit of Rutgers and Tennessee, the women's final.

Figure 6–1. The path to greatness (Strategy 6).

Rosenberg: Yeah, Tennessee won last night—seventh championship for [Tennessee coach] Pat Summitt, I-Man. They beat Rutgers by thirteen points.

Imus: That's some rough girls from Rutgers. Man, they've got tattoos and . . .

McGuirk: Some hard-core hos.

Imus: *(Laughs)* That's some nappy-headed hos there. I'm going to tell you that now.

MSNBC, a division of General Electric's NBC at the time, turned off the camera and CBS Radio, which at the time managed Westwood One, unplugged the microphone—as they should have. But it's unlikely either entity would have walked away from Imus and the millions of dollars in revenue generated from his program if not for the public and financial pressure applied by a variety of individuals and groups.

The "nappy-headed hos" and accompanying comments weren't the first ugly speech uttered by Imus and his gang. Imus, known for his cranky and curmudgeonly demeanor, routinely spouted offensive remarks. So much so that *Chicago Tribune* columnist Clarence Page, a periodic guest on the show, asked him to knock it off. Announcer Rosenberg, according to a *Newsday* article, once recounted on-air telling a friend that tennis greats Venus and Serena Williams had a better shot of getting in *National Geographic* than *Playboy* magazine.[3] Rosenberg also referred to Venus Williams as an "animal."

To be sure, the Imus attacks weren't limited to race. Over the years, his barbs—whether raunchy or rude, sexist or homophobic—were volleyed at politicians, religious leaders, prominent journalists, and other public figures, some of whom appeared on his show regularly.

But when Imus carelessly targeted the Rutgers women's basketball team, he crossed an already-precarious line because he singled out a group of student athletes, not public figures running for office or journalists hawking a book. Going after the Rutgers women, for many, was going too far.

The ire spread swiftly. Bryan Monroe, president of the National Association of Black Journalists (NABJ) and editorial director at Johnson Publishing Co., which publishes *Ebony* and *Jet* magazines, saw an e-mail from one of NABJ's board members about Imus's comments. According to the *Wall Street Journal,* Monroe said, "My first reaction was, 'Oh no, he didn't.'" After conferring with other NABJ board members, Monroe pulled an all-nighter and posted a statement about the comments on the NABJ website, where it caught the attention of Black journalists who forwarded it onto friends and colleagues. NABJ soon demanded that Imus apologize and eventually pushed for his firing.

But NABJ group wasn't alone. Employee affinity groups like the General Electric African-American Forum, the Sprint Nextel Diamond Network, and African-American employees at MSNBC—organizations within corporations that support specific employee groups—simultaneously lobbied for action. NBC News President Steve Capus held a meeting with African-American employees in the news division. The meeting was scheduled for forty-five minutes. It ended up lasting two hours as individuals argued passionately for Imus's dismissal.

Influential individuals also chimed in. Rutgers women's basketball coach, C. Vivian Stringer, held a press conference alongside the entire women's basketball team. "It's not about them [the players] as Black or nappy headed. It's about us as a people," Stringer said. "When there is not equality for all, or when there has been denied equality for one, there has been denied equality for all." American Express CEO Kenneth Chenault, who is African American, pulled the financial services company's advertising from the show. *Washington Week* managing editor and *PBS NewsHour* senior correspondent Gwen Ifill wrote an op-ed for the *New York Times* denouncing Imus's words. NBC's *Today Show* weatherman and host Al Roker wrote several blogs about the Imus comments on his website *www.roker.com*. After his initial post on the subject calling for Imus to be removed from the airwaves, he explained why he spoke out. "Don Imus broadcasts under the NBC News banner via MSNBC," Roker wrote. "This is a reflection of my company. I won't stand for the idea that someone who has the privilege of working under the aegis of NBC News could damage this organization with the taint of racism and sexism." The Imus story was widely reported and well documented in many media sources.

Support came from outside the Black community as well. The National Organization for Women (NOW) sent out alerts urging members to flood CBS and NBC with calls and e-mails to "Dump Don."

Comments made by Capus on the show *Hardball* further showed that the calls to take action came from diverse corners. "I've received hundreds, if not thousands, of e-mails, both internal and external, with people with very strong views about what should happen," Capus said. "I've listened to those people with their comments. And many of them are people who have worked at NBC News for decades, people who put their lives on the line covering wars and things like that. These comments were hurtful to many, many people."

The National Association of Hispanic Journalists (NAHJ) also spoke out. "Imus has freedom of speech," said NAHJ President Rafael Olmeda. "His employers have freedom of association, and if they continue to associate themselves with his patently offensive comments, they show that they are more concerned with ratings and publicity than they are with race relations and the quality of public discourse. Enough is enough. Can him."

In addition to American Express, companies like General Motors, Glaxo-SmithKline, Procter & Gamble, and Staples began pulling ads from MSNBC.

On April 11, MSNBC pulled the plug on its broadcast of the show. On April 12, Imus was fired by CBS. Why were his critics successful? Simply put, they were able to *find strength in numbers.*

Different voices communicated the same message: Imus's brand of hate-riddled speech was no longer acceptable. And while the effort to get Imus removed wasn't broadly coordinated among individuals, companies, and organizations, these groups were successful because:

▸ *The effort focused on an issue, not identities.* The groups that protested focused on a common issue—the insensitive, offensive language that Imus spewed. Groups like the NAHJ, NOW, and NABJ serve different audiences and push agendas connected to their members' shared identity—be it race, gender, or the occupation of their members. The common focus on this issue helped these identity-driven groups turn their independent complaints into a collective roar.

▸ *The approach was multipronged, including individual and collective action.* Efforts came from within the companies that employed Imus; the companies that sponsored his show, like American Express, Sprint, and Procter & Gamble; journalism and business organizations; community and action groups; influential individuals like Stringer, Chenault, Ifill, and Roker; and the general public. Imus and his bosses were hit on all sides from a social and moral perspective—and in their pocketbooks.

▸ *Internal and external pressure forced higher-ups to take notice.* If NBC employees had been alone in their frustration about Imus's comments, many may not have had the guts to risk their own position for a greater purpose. While it's not always ideal, self-preservation is a path that men and women of all races and ethnicities take every day in the workplace. But with the external push for Imus's ousting, employees had the safety net of broad support. Likewise, the external forces had internal voices, and as

Roker expressed in his blog, they didn't want their employer's good name dragged through the mud.

▸ *Established organizations facilitated an efficient, effective, and spontaneous response.* NABJ and NAHJ had processes in place to get the word out to members, to draft media releases, and to make personal calls to key players to express their disgust. The affinity groups within Sprint and GE had an established forum that allowed them to gather quickly and demand an audience with decision makers. With a structure already in place, the groups were able to focus on dealing with the issue rather than spending time on organizational efforts.

The responses to and the results of the Don Imus debacle portray the very essence of this strategy: find strength in numbers.

"Sticks in a bundle are unbreakable." This saying comes from an African proverb that expresses that a single stick can be easily split in half, but combined with a group it can withstand pressure.

We've all heard common sayings like "United we stand, divided we fall," and "All for one and one for all." Management expert Ken Blanchard is known for saying that "none of us is as smart as all of us." The word *team* is sometimes expressed as an acronym T.E.A.M.—Together Everyone Achieves More.

Even "Big Momma" in the popular movie *Soul Food* stated, "One finger pointing don't make no impact. But if you ball all of them fingers up into a mighty fist, then you can strike a mighty blow!"

All of these expressions tell us to do the same thing: *find strength in numbers.* Strategy 6 presents the different kinds of groups with which you can align, explains why connecting with groups is important, and shows how you can do so most effectively.

Group Relationships

Finding strength in numbers can have multiple meanings and interpretations. Here, we discuss the power of strength in numbers through a range of what we call "group relationships"—relationships comprised of two people or more. Whereas Strategy 4 dealt with building *diverse and strong relationships,* and Strategy 5 dealt with *developmental relationships* between two people, Strategy 6 is focused on larger groups.

THE SIX FORMS OF STRENGTH IN NUMBERS

Figure 6–2 presents the six group relationships or the six forms of strength in numbers, ranging from informal family ties and friends to formal organizations. All of these group relationships embody concepts first introduced in Strategy 4. Let's once again review each here (we also provide a summary in Table 6–3 toward the end of this chapter).

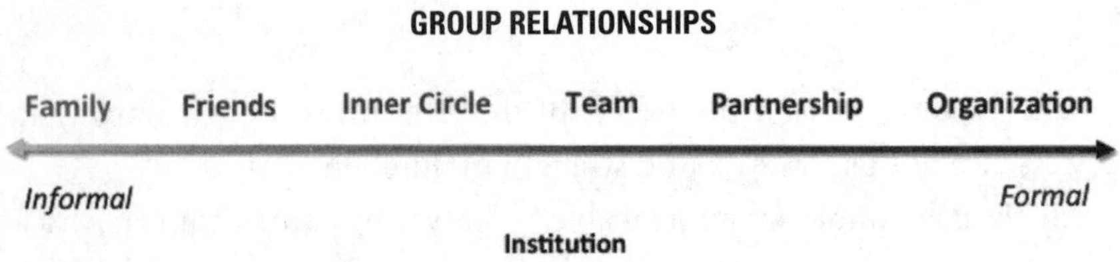

GROUP RELATIONSHIPS

| Family | Friends | Inner Circle | Team | Partnership | Organization |

Informal   *Formal*

Institution

Figure 6–2. The continuum of group relationships.

Bonding social capital—or how people in a group or network stick together—is an important component of an effective group dynamic. Group relationships work best when their structure mirrors *dense networks*—or groups of tightly connected people. The high level of trust that typically characterizes dense networks works extremely well when members of a group need to produce results. Group relationships are further strengthened by the basic principles of networking and relationship building.

The ideas that form the foundation of good group relationships also relate back to the concept of developmental relationships, as discussed in Strategy 5. Group relationships are instrumental to undergirding your personal and professional endeavors because they enhance the wisdom that you gain from more personal, developmental relationships, or at minimum they help you to make the connections that lead to making those personal ties.

For example, Roland Martin credits much of his ascension through the ranks of journalism to his involvement with the National Association of

Black Journalists on the student *and* professional levels. He attended his first convention in 1989. There he met the person who made the connection that helped him get a job at the *Austin American Statesman,* the editor who hired him to become the city hall reporter at the *Fort Worth Star-Telegram,* the person who hired him to be editor of Tom Joyner's *BlackAmericaWeb.com,* and the person who was editor-in-chief when he was hired to work at *Savoy* magazine.

Martin traces his role on CNN back to NABJ's 1989 and 1991 conventions. He recounted this story in an interview with us: "I'm on CNN because I first met Henry Mauldin, who was the head of talent for CNN, and he remembered me from a convention in 1991, and he said [to me], 'We were in a room with all of these bigwigs, [you were] the only student in the room, but everybody in the room knew [you].' Had I not gone to that convention, I would not have been in a position to be in that room."

Essentially, Martin established a borrowed network through connections brokered by Mauldin.

INFORMAL GROUPS

At one end of the continuum are informal groups that do not meet regularly and are not structured to achieve specific goals and objectives. However, despite their unofficial nature, these groups are an extremely important source of strength in numbers. Family and friends are two natural examples of informal groups.

Family members are a group of people with common ancestry, common bonds, or kinship ties. *Friends* are a group of people with a close association. While we do not choose our family, we do choose our friends. There is an expression that we put a lot of stock in—"Show me your friends, show me your future." Some people would say that your circle of friends determines your destiny. Your friends can influence you in many ways—positively and negatively. If you surround yourself with friends, family, and community members who have similar goals, you'll be on your way to positive outcomes.

The point here is that family and friends can have a profound influence on you and can provide the leverage you need to overcome obstacles. We'll get more into this aspect in our next section.

FORMAL GROUPS

At the other end of the continuum are more formal groups organized for a specific purpose. These groups meet regularly to achieve an objective or to conduct a program or initiative. Keep in mind that informal relationships can evolve into formal ones.

In this chapter, we place a particular emphasis on four formal and organized approaches to strength in numbers—*inner circles, teams, partnerships,* and *organizations*. As you will see in Part III: Mastering the Game, these groups are vital components to entrepreneurship, achieving synergy, and reaching scale. We divide these four approaches along two lines—*strength in smaller numbers* (inner circles, teams, and partnerships) and *strength in larger numbers* (organizations).

Strength in Smaller Numbers: Inner Circles, Teams, and Partnerships

In general, finding strength in smaller numbers (groups of two people or more) brings the benefits of:

- Having a cohort of individuals that share your perspective

- Having people who can affirm your goals and dreams

- Developing relationships that provide psychological and social support

- Gaining the knowledge, skills, and education of others

- Networking effectively and efficiently

Now let's specifically define the three points along the continuum: inner circles, teams, and partnerships.

INNER CIRCLES

You may have many friends. But really think about the group with whom you regularly spend most of your time. They are the people you hang out with and communicate with weekly (via phone, text, e-mail, instant messages, or social networking sites), and they are the first to call when you are looking for something to do or need assistance. These are people you would take trips with, given the opportunity. Typically, this is between three and seven people. This is your inner circle, a group of people with strong influence on one another.

Your inner circle is more influential than your general set of friends just by the sheer fact that these people are regularly in contact with you. You also influence them. You have the ability to help and strengthen each other by encouraging and supporting one another through good times and bad, and by holding one another accountable for your goals and objectives. In this context, some people also refer to their inner circle as their "personal cabinet" or their "mastermind group."

At Rutgers, we became close friends with three of our college classmates: Lawrence Hibbert, Dallas Grundy, and Aldwyn Porter. We, along with Aldwyn, were upperclassmen when Lawrence and Dallas were first-year students. Aldwyn, Lawrence, and Dallas comprised our inner circle; they were "our posse," "our crew," and "our brothers." In fact, we shared an apartment with Aldwyn. Lawrence and Dallas were also roommates.

Our relationship was very much like any group of close friends. We hung out together, spent time eating together in the dining hall, and we even partied together. We were also members of the Rutgers Chapter of the National Society of Black Engineers (NSBE). Coincidentally, through a "big brother/little brother" program sponsored by Rutgers NSBE, Randal was Lawrence's "big brother" and Jeffery was Dallas's "big brother." Perhaps most important, we supported each other academically and encouraged one another to stay positive and stay strong.

A variation of the inner circle might be book clubs or discussion groups to which you belong. By design, these small groups are engaged in intellectually stimulating activities. This is a great way to meet like-minded people and to be exposed to new and interesting ideas.

Your inner circle does not have to have a specific purpose, except the general purpose of supporting one another. Your inner circle can be comprised of peers, friends, or more seasoned and experienced people.

Building an inner circle that engenders positive peer pressure and a set of values based on mutual trust, respect, and support (as happened with Larry, Dallas, Aldwyn, J.R., and Randal), and perhaps a shared vision (in our case, the formation of our first business, Mind, Body & Soul Enterprises), can be an important step toward reaching your personal and professional goals. It is no accident that we (the authors) each have five academic degrees, including PhDs. It was a goal we both shared and one that we supported each other in pursuing. We exerted mutual positive peer pressure.

Having an inner circle that exerts positive peer pressure on you to pursue your goals keeps you motivated. When things aren't going well, you have people around you to encourage you to achieve your best. Therefore, choose your inner circle wisely and do things that will keep you linked and allow you to be a positive influence on each other. For actor and author Hill Harper, this means using your intuition. "You usually have a pretty good intuitive knowledge of where other people's hearts are and where they are in terms of you," Harper shared during an interview with us. We should choose people who not only have a good heart, but who are trying to figure out what you are attempting to achieve and want to help you get there. "In other words, they have a vision for your life that is in line with the vision that you have for your own. Those are the types of people you want to surround yourself with," Harper said.

Inner Circle Diversity. There is also the issue of whether to have an inner circle of other Black people or to have a diverse inner circle. We have a few things to say on this subject. Our inner circle was all Black, and we all knew each other and had worked with each other in student organizations. The key to having an inner circle is not necessarily ethnicity but compatibility. It isn't just that you want to be comfortable with your inner circle on a one-on-one basis; it is also how everyone in the group interacts with each other. That will give you the best opportunity to leverage the human and social capital of your inner circle because you will have to spend less time trying to understand where each person is coming from.

Your inner circle is similar to what we referred to in Strategy 5 as your "personal board of directors." Your inner circle is a group of people you would talk to about important decisions, but usually it includes people who are similar to you in terms of experience or interests. By comparison, your personal board of directors or personal cabinet usually has people on it who are more experienced than you are in certain areas and possess wisdom that you may need.

TEAMS

Teams are different from groups. In its simplest form, a group is merely a collection of people. For example, strangers standing in the lobby of a hotel are a group. A *team* is a group of people who work together for a specific purpose—a project, as part of a program, or within an organization. Teams manifest themselves in countless ways: ministries at a church; a hip-hop and R&B group or jazz band; the executive board of a student organization; the committee of a fraternity, sorority, or other association; a dance troupe; the board of directors for a charity; a choir; and, of course, any sports squad. All are examples of teams.

Intellectual capital resides in teams of people. It is the knowledge, experience, and skills resulting from your team's collective effort and is often the source of innovation and intellectual property. In science-oriented ventures, teams of scientists and engineers develop inventions that are then brought to the marketplace. If the team disbands or members leave, the ability for the team to create the next invention may be in jeopardy. Other people may be willing to invest, acquire, or trade for the intellectual capital that resides in a venture or team.

One of our first experiences with innovative teams was when we were on the executive board of Rutgers NSBE. What began as an "inner circle" between ourselves, Aldwyn, Larry, and Dallas later evolved into a "team" when we all served as members of the executive board. Our specific purpose was to fulfill NSBE's mission "to increase the number of culturally responsible Black engineers who excel academically, succeed professionally, and positively impact the community." As a team and fellow members of the "e-board," we fulfilled this mission by working closely together to run the chapter's meetings; coordinate speakers and programs on campus, such as a career fair and a dinner for alums; organize outreach to local high schools; participate in regional and national conferences; and manage the chapter budget. It was through Rutgers NSBE that we honed our team-building skills.

Features of High-Performing Teams. What we have learned over the years is that teams function best and perform at a high level when they have a shared purpose, commitment to that purpose, mutual trust, well-defined roles, and frequent and effective communication.

It is clear to us, looking back, that our team was able to get a lot done because we had many of these high-performing elements in place. We had a common purpose and were committed to it and the NSBE organization. We developed trust and communicated regularly with one another. And we certainly had different roles. Randal was president of the Rutgers chapter. J.R. was the vice president. Aldwyn, Larry, and Dallas were executive board members and officers. We learned each other's strengths and weaknesses by working together.

To get to this level of teamwork, it is important to promote camaraderie among the team. Dedicate time to organizing team-building activities that promote solidarity and collaboration. It may be something as simple as eating dinner together. It could be something as elaborate as spending an entire weekend during the summer participating in icebreakers and games, along with holding strategic planning and organizational development discussions. Two other important considerations are team diversity and team leadership.

Team Diversity. In *Team of Rivals* (Simon and Schuster, 2005), presidential historian Doris Kearns Goodwin explores the relationship between the men who vied for the presidency with Abraham Lincoln. The political genius of Lincoln (which is often referenced, and some say practiced, by President Obama) was to include these rivals in his cabinet and leverage the different points of view to get the best solutions for the nation. His team diversity was based on the various perspectives represented in his cabinet.

Team diversity might be based upon leadership styles, functional expertise, experience, profession, or any other dimension you may think of as relevant for the task at hand. Diversity will lead to different viewpoints. Usually, these disagreements lead to better solutions to complex problems because the proposed solutions are more comprehensive than if everyone had the same perspective.

A harrowing example of what can happen when you don't have diverse and diverging voices on your team is captured in numerous books and movies about the Cuban Missile Crisis during John F. Kennedy's presidential administration. Kennedy had some of the most intelligent men around the table advising him about how to deal with the emerging crisis of Soviet missiles being erected in Cuba. The term *groupthink* is derived from the situation that emerged in those meetings. Dissenting views were drowned out by the race for a speedy and unified solution. The group began to think as one, and it nearly brought the United States to war with the Soviet Union.

The practical takeaway here is that you want your team members to all be committed to a common purpose, but you also want there to be enough difference that you don't all think the same way.

Having people with different personalities and different strengths and weaknesses on your team can be extremely helpful when addressing complex problems. We learned this when we had our first business together and we were trying to figure out how to price our services.

Aldwyn was always the one who pushed the envelope and wanted us to charge more for our services. We tended to be more moderate. In one instance, we developed a proposal to organize a conference for the United Negro College Fund/Citigroup Fellows program. We were shooting in the dark when it came to deciding how much we should charge, because we hadn't yet benchmarked the competition in terms of pricing. Up until that point, we'd been charging just under $5,000 for our conferences.

Aldwyn asked, "What do we have to lose by throwing out a larger number?" At first we thought it was too risky. Eventually, after a good amount of discussion, Aldwyn convinced us to price our proposal at more than double our previous rate—$10,000. As Randal explains:

> I thought that was a huge amount of money! That week, I sat down with Citigroup's vice president, Peter Thorpe, and the program's coordinator, Cathy Grant, to discuss our proposal. The first question Peter asked was: 'Have you ever done a conference for $10,000?' I told him that we had not, but I could guarantee it would be worth it. You know what happened? We got the business! Aldwyn was on point. In retrospect, I should have heeded Aldwyn's words more often.
>
> Aldwyn taught us a valuable lesson that day about avoiding groupthink. If it had been up to the two of us, we would have left some money—okay, a lot of money at that time—on the table that day. J.R. and I appreciate each other because we've often thought alike. We appreciated Aldwyn just the same because he often thought so differently, and that made us a great team.

....

Know your position and play your position on a team—know your role, play to your strengths, and allow the team to compensate for your limitations.

....

Team Leadership. Finally, you must have strong team leadership for any of the benefits to bear fruit. This not only requires some training for those who have not been leaders before, but also requires understanding how to bring out the best in people. J.R. explains our experience:

For Randy, Larry, Dallas, Aldwyn, and me, two things happened over the course of our participation on both the NSBE chapter and regional executive boards together.

First, we quickly learned that the relationships we developed as an inner circle helped to significantly streamline our ability to work together as a team because we knew each other well and got along well. Second, as leaders we charted a course for the organization that the entire team could buy into by respecting and soliciting everyone's varied opinions. While we do not have the hard numbers to prove it, anecdotally, we believe the chapter and the region experienced significant growth in membership, in community outreach, and in academic performance during our tenure.

In fact, because we believed so strongly in our effectiveness as a team, when I decided to become the chairperson for the NSBE National Convention, I convinced both Randy and Aldwyn to join my convention planning committee. By all accounts, the conference was a huge success.

We have participated in and facilitated all kinds of leadership training courses and seminars and have used tools like the Myers-Briggs Type Indicator and the Keirsey Temperament Sorter II offered by AdvisorTeam. (You can learn more about these tools at www.redefinethegame.com.) Yet one of the biggest lessons we have learned and now teach others is that you must understand your own leadership style and the leadership styles of others to be an effective team leader.

PARTNERSHIPS

Partners are the formal members of a venture, initiative, or entity. The partnerships that are formed are formal because they are organized for a specific purpose and are governed by some kind of structure, legal entity, or written agreement. When we think of partners, we think of the people who work together to open a new school, launch a new business venture, or start a new nonprofit organization. Partnerships are serious! These are people you are placing your trust and confidence in to help you achieve your loftiest of goals. You must choose your partners wisely.

Our relationship with Aldwyn, Lawrence, and Dallas evolved beyond that of a "team" during our senior year, when we all became "partners" in our first business venture: Mind, Body & Soul Enterprises (MBS). Randal explains the genesis of MBS:

> *A childhood friend of mine, Wayne Abbott, was almost solely responsible for inspiring us to become entrepreneurs in college. Wayne was a visionary. He was not only the president of Rutgers NSBE during my first year and an early mentor to me, he was also the first student I ever met who owned and operated his own company. At our weekly NSBE meetings, Wayne would always hammer home the message that Corporate America was not the only path for us to follow, and he practiced what he preached. His company, Aware Information Products [AIP], was an on-campus retailer of Afrocentric T-shirts, apparel, and other cultural items, which were increasingly popular among students at the time. Among the Black engineers at Rutgers, Wayne's example was part of an entire wave of social consciousness and entrepreneurship on campus. Recognizing my passion for entrepreneurship, he forced me to ask myself, 'If he can start a business now, why can't I start a business now?' In seeking to follow in Wayne's footsteps, I quickly enlisted the help of the people I knew best—my friends, roommates, and fellow NSBE officers, J.R. and Aldwyn—in launching our first venture. We later reached out to Larry and Dallas to join the partnership, and MBS was formed.*

In this first business venture, we sold compact discs out of our dormitory on campus and used the proceeds to fund high school outreach. We soon learned that we could make money from our outreach efforts and we changed the company name to MBS Educational Services and Training. Eventually, we added a sixth partner, Raqiba Bourne, who had recently completed undergraduate studies at the University of Pennsylvania. Collectively, we ran MBS part-time for seven years while each of us worked fulltime jobs and/or pursued graduate degrees, until Lawrence and Dallas left their full-time jobs in Corporate America to run the company full-time. MBS evolved into BCT Partners, which today is a multi-million-dollar management and information technology consulting firm.

Using Teams to Preview Potential Partners. We are often asked, How did you find your business partners? As you can see, the answer is that we worked on teams (committees, class projects, executive boards) together *before* we even had the business ideas. Working on teams with people allows you to preview potential partnerships. Working on teams with other people is the best way to learn the working styles of potential partners. Through the work of the team you will learn another person's strengths and weaknesses. This will help you to find the right partners and to place them in the most appropriate role.

Another avenue for previewing potential partners is to take a look at your inner circle. There may be people in your inner circle who you already know you want to have as your business partner because you work well together. Our only caution here is that once you enter into a partnership, the stakes are high and the work can become more challenging. If you are going to enter into a partnership with someone who is a good friend or part of your inner circle, you must be able to have frank and honest discussions and not take offense easily. In other words, you must be able to separate what is business from what is personal so that you can have disagreements over "business" but still remain friends. Randal notes that:

> *Although we have sometimes disagreed over issues relating to MBS or BCT, it has never spilled over into our personal relationships. Back in college, we could argue on Thursday about the equity split for the company and then high-five each other in the dark corner of*

a house party on Friday. That is one of the reasons why I loved working with them.

An alternative is to bring people into a partnership with you on a limited or trial basis. This gives you and them an opportunity to test the waters before the stakes are higher. J.R. gives an example:

Technically, Randy, Aldwyn, and I were the original founders of MBS. Larry, Dallas, and Raqiba first came on board only to help with the UNCF/Citigroup Fellows conference because we needed at least five people to pull it off. As part of the team for the conference, it also gave them the opportunity to show us what they could do. They contributed some great ideas for the training materials and did an outstanding job as public speakers. As Randy, Aldwyn, and I were preparing to graduate from Rutgers, we decided to bring them on as full-fledged partners as a result of their performance.

In essence, if you are interested in having someone as a partner, you might want to work with them on a team first. We suggest you put a time frame on this type of involvement so that it is clear what the expectations are.

Strength in Smaller Numbers Leads to Strength in Larger Numbers

If you are already finding strength in smaller numbers, you may be on the brink of creating something new. In Strategy 8: Think and Act Entrepreneurially, we will talk about entrepreneurship and the creation of new ventures both for a profit (i.e., a business) and for a purpose (i.e., a school, nonprofit, or religious institution). Strategy 6 is the beginning of how you get there.

Partners and partnerships create organizations, schools, and businesses. This is how a group of five people becomes 50, and 50 becomes 500, and 500 becomes 5,000. This is how power can be coalesced, how influence can be wielded, and how strength in numbers can be amplified. As you will see in Strategy 9: Synergize and Reach Scale, this power is one of the key ingredients to achieving synergy and reaching scale.

Strength in Larger Numbers: Organizations

Strength in larger numbers represents a second model. Here, a group of people is actively involved in a formal *organization*—an entity that exists to fulfill a specific mission or vision and its values.

COLLABORATIVE ORGANIZATIONS

You find strength in larger numbers through active involvement in a formal organization, but not just any organization. Strength in larger numbers stems from collaborative organizations, or organizations whose efforts lead to ongoing *collaborative action* or *combined action,* such that people take action together (a concept that we'll revisit in Strategy 9: Synergize and Reach Scale). For example, a leadership development program alone does not suffice in this context. But a leadership development program wherein participants tackle societal issues collaboratively does meet this standard.

More specifically, we are referring to collaborative organizations that meet the following five criteria:

1. Organizational mission, vision, and values are defined and clearly communicated and geared toward a societal benefit.

2. Participation is open to anyone, notwithstanding consideration for the demographic focus of the organization (i.e., youth organizations may be open to anyone, but they tend to be comprised of youth).

3. Members work together toward shared goals and objectives.

4. Positions in the organization (i.e., president, committee chairperson, volunteer, etc.) are defined by specific roles and responsibilities independent of who performs those duties; if someone leaves a key position, that person is replaced by someone else.

5. Members communicate and meet on a regular and continual basis (i.e., weekly, monthly, annually) as opposed to only meeting for a finite period (i.e., for a few weeks, a few months, or even a few years).

Collaborative organizations meet all of these five criteria. These organizations generally take the form of clubs, societies, leagues, forums, councils, unions, fraternities, sororities, exchanges, guilds, and other associations. Involvement in collaborative organizations allows you to:

▸ Affirm your identity, purpose, and values.

▸ Develop excellence by exploring your passion, experimenting with your gifts, cultivating greater discipline, and reinforcing empowering beliefs.

▸ Prepare for future roles, including leadership positions.

▸ Create meaningful, lasting relationships.

▸ Coalesce power as you address important societal issues.

▸ Achieve goals you could not achieve on your own.

▸ Become part of something bigger than you.

▸ Serve others and the community.

Some examples include the NAACP, the National Urban League, Black Greek-lettered fraternities and sororities that are part of the National Pan-Hellenic Council, NSBE, NABJ, the National Black MBA Association, Jack and Jill of America, and Mocha Moms.

It is just as important to be clear on what *does not* constitute a collaborative organization. For example, MBS and BCT are not collaborative organizations. Even though they meet most of the five criteria, they are a for-profit company, participation is not open to anyone (criteria number two), and they are not necessarily geared toward addressing societal issues. In Strategy 8: Think and Act Entrepreneurially, we will discuss a special class of for-profit organizations—social ventures—that are specifically geared toward social change.

Organizations that promote the ideals of Strategies 2 and 3 are not collaborative organizations. These organizations primarily, if not exclusively, present either opportunities for exploration and experimentation (broad exposure), or opportunities for personal and professional development to foster excellence. These organizations are, of course, extremely valuable. However, what distinguishes them from the collaborative organizations that constitute the focus of Strategy 6 is that they do not meet criteria number three (shared goals and objectives). They generally promote individual development as opposed to collective action. And while a number of collaborative organizations, as we have defined them, are the sponsors of programs geared toward individual development, *the true lifeblood of a collaborative organization is coordinated, collective action that stems from having strength in numbers and organizing groups of people to make a difference.*

THE FOUR ORGANIZATIONAL DIMENSIONS

As a way to provide you with a way of thinking about which collaborative organizations are right for you, we present four organizational dimensions that can be used to categorize them: *stage, scope, subject,* and *specificity* (see Table 6–1).

Naturally, different organizations speak differently to the organizational dimensions. For example, The Partnership, Inc. is a nonprofit organization dedicated to advancing professionals of color. It offers services to the greater Boston area in a way that very few organizations do: by offering programs that span almost every career stage. This nonprofit's programs are targeted specifically at college students, recent college graduates, entry-level professionals, and mid- to senior-level professionals; it also runs an alumni program that promotes mentoring and community service.

Several examples of African-American *(specificity)* collaborative organizations that operate at the local and national level *(scope)* are listed in Table 6–2, according to their focus area *(subject)* and targeted life-period *(stage)*. Visit www.redefinethegame.com for a more complete list.

If you are not already involved with a collaborative organization such as those listed in Table 6–2, we strongly encourage you to join one or more. J.R. adds:

> *Randy and I are proud members of Alpha Phi Alpha Fraternity Incorporated. Randy was my line brother. We both remain active at various levels of the organizations. The fraternity mission statement is "Alpha*

Category	Description	Examples
Stage	The life-stage or career-stage that comprises the focus of the organization	Youth/college Young adults Adults Seniors Executives
Scope	The geographic scope of the organization and/or the different levels or tiers that comprise the organization	Local Regional National International
Subject	The subject or focus area(s) of the organization	Children and families Grass roots/community Alumni(ae)/fraternity/sorority Professional/industry Affinity groups Religious Political
Specificity	The specific demographic group or social identifier, if any, which predominates or characterizes the membership of the organization	Ethnic-based Gender-based Nationality-based General

Table 6–1. Four organizational dimensions.

Phi Alpha Fraternity Incorporated develops leaders, promotes brotherhood and academic excellence, while providing service and advocacy for our communities." The brotherhood of Alpha Phi Alpha has been invaluable to strengthening our bonds to other Black men, renewing our sense of manhood and fatherhood, reinvigorating our commitment to excellence, and reinforcing our responsibility to give back to the community.

We are vocal advocates and strong proponents of involvement in collaborative organizations. We believe that collaborative organizations have and will continue to play a central and critical role in redefining the game and reshaping America. Much like strength in numbers is a timeless principle, we believe organizational involvement is another time-tested strategy

SUBJECT / STAGE	Youth/College	Young Adults	Adults	Executives
Children and families	Jack and Jill Mocha Moms		Black parents associations	
Grassroots/ community	NAACP Youth and College Division	National Urban League Young Professionals	NAACP NUL	NUL Black Executive Exchange Program
Alumni(ae)/ fraternity/ sorority	School organizations Fraternity/sorority college chapters	School alumni associations Fraternity/sorority graduate chapters	School alumni associations Fraternity/sorority graduate chapters	Alpha Phi Alpha World Policy Council
Professional/ industry	National Society of Black Engineers, NSBE Pre-College Initiative, NSBE Jr. National Black MBA Association Leaders of Tomorrow Urban Financial Services Coalition Mark 1	National Black Graduate Students Association INROADS Alumni Black Data Processing Associates National Bar Association—Young Lawyers Division	NSBE AE NBMBAA UFSC BDPA NBA Information Technology Senior Management Forum National Association of Black Accountants National Association of Black Journalists American Association of Blacks in Energy	Executive Leadership Council ITSMF The Marathon Club
Affinity groups		Black Employee Association (Xerox) African American Leadership Council (Johnson & Johnson) African American Forum (GE)	Black Employee Association (Xerox) African American Leadership Council (Johnson & Johnson) African American Forum (GE)	African American Executive Forum (YMCA)
Religious		The Union of Black Episcopalians	UPE United Black Christians	
Political	National Hip Hop Political Convention	NHHPC Black Americans Lobbying for Leaders of Tomorrow	Black American Political Association of California	Congressional Black Caucus

Table 6–2. Examples of African-American collaborative organizations.

for facilitating change. Granted, organizational involvement is not the only way to facilitate change, but we believe it is among the most viable and effective ways.

However, for involvement in collaborative organizations to indeed serve as an effective mechanism for change, it requires members, at times, to look beyond their individual agendas toward a collective purpose.

....

There are so many organizations doing good work, there is no excuse for not being involved.

....

Have you noticed the diminishing number of R&B groups and bands? In fact, most people are hard-pressed to think of five modern R&B groups or bands that have hit the charts in the new millennium and remained together. At best, you may be able to think about some duets, guest appearances, joint or reunion albums, but not successful, intact R&B groups or bands. Why is that? There are probably several factors that have contributed to this phenomenon, but it is safe to say that this trend reflects a greater emphasis on the individual over the group. Another example is when all-star athletes cannot work together despite the real possibility of winning a championship. These are examples that run counter to the principles of finding strength in numbers. Much like we believe there is something sadly lost in an R&B landscape that is full of solo artists, or a winning sports team that's forced to release one of its star players, we believe collaborative organizations similarly lose when members prioritize their individual agendas over the organization's agenda.

To truly find strength in numbers, we must sometimes sacrifice a bit of our personal objectives to contribute to a greater goal. This is something our business partners have always felt strongly about, especially Larry. We are not contradicting our arguments that you demonstrate excellence (Strategy 3) and not subordinate your passion to other considerations. Instead, we are simply "keeping it real" to emphasize that any collective undertaking—be it a friendship, a marriage, a partnership, or an organization—requires some compromise and some sacrifice. For example, when we formed Mind, Body & Soul Enterprises, J.R. abandoned a company he had already started—Nia Educational Services—to join forces with me, Aldwyn, Larry, and Dallas.

Formality	Form	Function
Informal	Family	A group of people with common ancestry, common bonds, or kinship ties
	Friends	A group of people with a close association
Formal	Inner circle	A group of people with a strong influence on one another
	Team	A group of people who work together for a specific purpose
	Partnership	A group of people who comprise the formal members of a venture, initiative, or entity
	Organization	An entity that exists to fulfill a specific mission, vision, and values, usually comprised of a group of people

Table 6–3. Six forms of strength in numbers.

The need for sacrifice is particularly true as it relates to the ability of collaborative organizations to maximize their strength in numbers. If each individual member did exactly what he wanted to do, the way he wanted to do it, when he wanted to do it, collaborative organizations would crumble. Success not only rests on the ability of organizational leaders to cast a vision that engenders buy-in from their stakeholders, but also the ability of organizational members to do whatever needs to be done to collectively see that vision brought to reality.

Finding "numbers" is easy. All you have to do is create the band, form the sports team, or establish the organization. Finding "strength in numbers" is much harder. To do so, all of the members must remain focused on their united cause and work to stay together.

....
To truly find strength in numbers, we must sometimes sacrifice a bit of our personal objectives to contribute to a greater goal.
....

Game-Changing Strategies for Organizational Involvement

Finally, let's present the game-changing strategies that are specific to African Americans for finding strength in numbers.

IDENTIFY THE RIGHT ORGANIZATION TO ADDRESS THE RIGHT NEEDS AND ISSUES AT THE RIGHT TIME

You must be strategic about what organizations you are a part of and when you are a part of them. The stage, scope, subject, and specificity that constitute the focus of an organization are paramount considerations as you decide which organizations to be involved in. Ask yourself the question: Should a person at this stage in my career or life be involved with this organization? For example, you may have a legitimate reason for working with a college-based organization after you have graduated from college, especially if you are mentoring the upcoming leaders or you are assisting in the transition between terms. However, at some point, you are giving much more than you are receiving. Are you still developing your skills? Are you meeting your own development and professional goals? If not, it may be time for you to move on.

Similarly, ask yourself: What is the real focus of this organization? The answer may help you make a better decision about your involvements. If the scope (local or national), subject (at-risk youth, unemployed adults, etc.), or specificity (African Americans, women, etc.) does not match where you want to make an impact, it may be time to find a different organization.

When Randal transitioned from being a graduate student in engineering to a full-time business owner, he needed an organization that could place him in the company of fellow information technology entrepreneurs and senior-level technology executives. He joined the Black Data Processing Association (BDPA), which provides professional and technical development for African Americans in the field. Around this time Zack Lemelle, then–vice president for information technology for Johnson & Johnson, who also supervised one of BCT's projects at the company, was attending an awards gala where Randal gave a keynote speech. Zack, who later became a mentor to Randal, asked him to speak at the awards ceremony for the Information Technology Senior Management Forum (ITSMF), the only national organization dedicated exclusively to fostering upper-level executive talent among African-American IT professionals and high-growth IT entrepreneurs. Randal describes his experience:

I quickly learned that ITSMF was exactly the organization I had been looking for at that stage of my career. Within a few months of the awards ceremony, I accepted an invitation to become a member and lead their efforts with African-American entrepreneurs in information technology. NSBE was perfect during college. NSBE's alumni extension and BDPA were a great fit during my years as a technical professional. ITSMF was ideal once I became chairman and CEO of a growing technology firm.

Being at the right place at the right time is a theme that runs through Strategy 3 about strategic career management, Strategy 4 about strategic networking, and Strategy 5 about strategic mentoring. Here, too, in Strategy 6, strategic organizational involvement is identifying the right organization to address the right needs and issues at the right time.

COMBINE IDENTITY-DRIVEN AND ISSUE-DRIVEN ORGANIZATIONAL AGENDAS

People are often naturally drawn to organizations that reflect their identity. For example, as African Americans we have naturally been drawn to "ethnic organizations" whose "specificity" is geared toward African Americans. The agendas typically pursued by ethnic organizations rightfully reflect the needs of the ethnicity they represent. We refer to this as an identity-driven agenda, while others may call it "identity politics." A few examples of an identity-driven agenda include the Christian educational society that promotes prayer in schools; the women's organization that lobbies for legislation ensuring equal pay regardless of gender; the predominantly Black association that works to address issues affecting minority communities; or the Cuban-American group that organizes to advance freedom and democracy in Cuba. Quite often their identity group affiliation is even self-evident from their names: the Society for Christian Education (Christians); the League of Women Voters (women); the National Association for the Advancement of Colored People (people of color); the Cuban American National Foundation (Cuban Americans).

We are strong proponents of such organizations and have, in fact, spent a considerable amount of our time working with such organizations. However, we believe reshaping twenty-first-century America necessarily requires combining an *identity-driven* agenda with an *issue-driven agenda*.

As the name implies, an issue-driven agenda is one that is focused on issues, interests, or causes, such as affordable housing, environmental justice, universal health care, poverty elimination, and economic development. Naturally, these issues tend to have an identity spin associated with them. For example, African Americans are disproportionately affected by the lack of affordable housing, environmental racism, access to quality health care, poverty, and the economic gap between the haves and have-nots. However, African Americans alone—and African-American organizations alone—cannot solve these problems. And, in fact, to the extent that the African-American community is not monolithic, African Americans do not necessarily even agree on the issues affecting our community, much less how to address them. It is only when those of us who have some general consensus on issues are able to see and embrace the commonality we share with others across lines of difference that we can truly make a difference together. As evidenced by the efforts of those organizations that called for the firing of Don Imus, as chronicled at the beginning of this chapter, strength in numbers finds its greatest power in large *and* diverse numbers.

There are quite a number of issue-driven organizations in our country, which we also refer to as "general organizations" because they are not necessarily geared toward a particular ethnicity. However, based on our experience, these organizations tend to be predominantly white and are not nearly as prominent within the African-American community as those that are identity-driven. Generally speaking, African Americans are more likely to be familiar with the NAACP or the National Urban League, because of their long-standing tradition of helping our communities, than with Amnesty International or the National Rural Health Association, despite the important work they are also doing. Issue-driven organizations tend to focus on issues that affect society at-large, not necessarily the needs of particular ethnic groups or other identity groups. This suggests that three things must happen.

First, in a diversifying society, issue-driven organizations must consider ways that they can become more attuned and more involved in the issues affecting people of color, which includes diversifying their ranks and promoting closer collaboration with organizations representing people of color. Conversely, identity-driven organizations must both explore ways to collaborate with other identity-driven organizations representing different ethnicities (e.g., predominantly Black organizations working with predominantly Hispanic organizations) and issue-driven organizations that share similar issues (e.g., predominantly Black organizations collaborating with affordable health care organizations).

This is undoubtedly a way to redefine the game and reshape America by building wide-ranging coalitions of diverse people with common interests to achieve shared goals. In Strategy 9: Synergize and Reach Scale, we will take these ideas even further in the context of how these collaborations can reach scale.

BROKER COLLABORATIONS AMONG
ETHNIC AND GENERAL ORGANIZATIONS

We believe it is important to maintain involvement in both ethnic and general organizations. We cannot underscore the importance of this point enough. It is only when you have a "foot in both camps" that you can take informed, proactive steps to create new mechanisms, new spaces, and new structures that help facilitate the discussion, debating, strategizing, and planning that are necessary to build viable coalitions between African-American organizations and other ethnic and/or general organizations.

This involvement could be as simple as becoming a member of another ethnic or general organization. You could lend your perspective to the issues they are wrestling with or build bridges between their organization and your African-American organization. It might mean deliberately putting yourself in a position where you are the sole Black face in a white place, or Latino place, or Asian place, or Native-American place. On a more elaborate scale, brokering collaborations could be manifested in the form of joint, interorganizational meetings, committees, conferences, and task forces comprising representatives from each organization. For example, since the 1990s, Big Brothers Big Sisters of America (a general organization) and Alpha Phi Alpha Fraternity Incorporated (an ethnic organization) have worked together to provide support and mentorship to young African-American males.

Brokering collaboration can also mean building bridges across other lines of difference within the African Diaspora (e.g., religious, geographic, intergenerational, etc.). Reverend Otis Moss III, pastor of Trinity United

Church of Christ in Chicago (and successor to Reverend Jeremiah Wright), is no stranger to crossing lines of religious difference. As a participant and now board member of the Samuel DeWitt Proctor Conference (SDPC), he is involved with convening African-American faith leaders and their congregations from a diverse cross-section of religious backgrounds. SDPC organizes congregations and their leaders to collaborate with others representing the civic, academic, business, and government sectors to address issues related to education, social justice, and economic empowerment. This gives SDPC participants tools they need to mobilize community members. Pastor Moss told us in an interview, "Most Black ministers have been trained in very conservative seminary so they know how to walk you through the Bible, but they really don't know how to make those direct connections to policy and other issues and say that 'This deals with your faith too.' You know, whether a child is able to get decent health care. More and more ministers are admitting that 'I want to take things to another level.' So the Proctor Conference does a marvelous job with that."

Regardless of the form it takes, the point is to take action in bringing together organizations that have shared issues, interests, or causes and to help them find strength in numbers. In Strategy 4, we talked about this very idea in the context of bridging social capital, bridging network gaps, and brokering connections between disconnected or uncoordinated entities. Here, we are simply applying the same thinking to collaborative organizations.

Strength in Numbers Sets the Stage

Finding strength in numbers not only completes Part II: Playing the Game, it also sets the stage for Part III: Mastering the Game and Part IV: Redefining the Game. In these final two parts, starting with the next three chapters, we will synthesize all of the concepts discussed here and in the previous strategies.

Strategy 7: Think and Act Intrapreneurially will talk about intrapreneurship and how to transform existing corporations or government agencies. Strategy 8: Think and Act Entrepreneurally will discuss how small group relationships can spawn new organizations, such as startup businesses or nonprofits. Strategy 9: Synergize and Reach Scale will identify the steps needed for organizations and businesses to evolve into lasting institutions and how collaborative action that is brokered across organizations can have the broadest or deepest possible impact to truly redefine the game and reshape America.

P A R T   I I I

MASTERING THE GAME

Whatever game you want to get into, then you have to learn it. And then after learning it, you've got to try to master it.

—Ice Cube

In the twenty-first century, entrepreneurship is more than just an endeavor, it is an empowering mindset. Being entrepreneurial is an art rooted in the belief that there is always a way to use creativity, passion, and inspired vision to create value in the world. This mindset leads people to create an entirely new school or religious institution that addresses an unmet need; or to transform a corporation to do new things in new ways; or to take something that already exists and make it better.

The Entrepreneurial Mindset

The entrepreneurial mindset takes the underlying spirit of Strategy 2—moving beyond your comfort zone into your growth zone—and elevates it to a higher level. You can easily spot a person with the heart and mind of a true entrepreneur. True entrepreneurs embody the following characteristics:

- *Passion*—a boundless enthusiasm for whatever they endeavor to do; a fundamental love for their work; and a desire to create value

- *Creativity*—an inventive or clever approach to generating ideas and solving problems

▶ *Resourcefulness*—the belief that they can turn nothing into something

▶ *Courage*—a willingness to take calculated risks while maintaining a trailblazer's mentality and the belief that they can achieve anything

▶ *Resilience*—a strong resolve to persevere when faced with challenges, while maintaining a healthy acceptance of failure as way to learn and strengthen oneself

Old-school thinking says the entrepreneurial mindset is confined to people who own a business. Here, we completely explode that notion. One of the key messages from the next two chapters is that entrepreneurship is about using your talents to make a positive impact in your areas of influence, and then leveraging all of the resources at your disposal to create value in the world.

Today, we believe the entrepreneurial mindset is equally applied to any number of pursuits in the government, philanthropic, faith-based, and other sectors, just as it is in business. The person who creates a nonprofit to help cancer patients, the individual who dedicates himself to preserving the environment, and the performing artist who tirelessly brings her craft to underprivileged youth are no less entrepreneurial than the founder of a pet store, the founder and CEO of a multimillion-dollar consulting firm, or even the receptionist who figures out a way to answer customer phone calls in a more timely, efficient manner. In pursuing their respective interests, each one exhibits the entrepreneurial mindset. New-school thinking says that regardless of your field or industry, you can do the same.

Entrepreneurship is not just something you do; it is a way that you think.

Intrapreneurship and Entrepreneurship

While the entrepreneurial mindset is essentially the same regardless of your career path, it plays out differently depending on the context.

▶ *Intrapreneurship* is the application of the entrepreneurial mindset within an established organization. For those that find themselves working in government agencies, large corporations, school districts, community-based organizations, and other environments, we encourage you to "think and act intrapreneurially"—to apply the entrepreneurial mindset in your institutional environment. Your efforts could produce a new product, a new service, a new department, a new agency, a new process, or a new way of doing things. People who are employed by established organizations that apply the entrepreneurial mindset in these ways are *intrapreneurs.*

▸ *Entrepreneurship* is the application of the entrepreneurial mindset to establish a new organization. For those who find themselves looking to create new schools, new nonprofits, new businesses, and new religious institutions, we encourage you to "think and act entrepreneurially"—to apply the principles of the entrepreneurial mindset to creating new entities. Your efforts could produce a new charter school, a new community organization, a new company, or a new church or mosque. People who create new entities and apply the entrepreneurial mindset to their work are *entrepreneurs.*

THE DOUBLE AND TRIPLE BOTTOM LINES
Intrapreneurship and entrepreneurship can also have a social orientation. Just as intrapreneurs and entrepreneurs change the face of their industry, *social intrapreneurs* and *social entrepreneurs* change the face of society. They act as the change agents for society, seizing opportunities others miss to address pressing issues and strengthen underserved communities, and creating new and innovative solutions to change our world for the better. Social intrapreneurs challenge established organizations to play a meaningful role in addressing society's most pressing problems, while social entrepreneurs create new organizations to do the same.

In the next two chapters we will delve even deeper into the concepts of social intrapreneurship and social entrepreneurship. For now, what is important for you to know is that the central and core component of these socially oriented manifestations of the entrepreneurial mindset is an abiding pursuit of the *double bottom line*—that is, achieving both "financial returns on investment" and "social returns on investment."

Social intrapreneurship and social entrepreneurship blur the lines between making a profit and making a difference by combining them into a holistic agenda. The double bottom line is about making a profit *and* making a difference; building organizations *and* building communities; doing good business *and* goodwill; and implementing solid business practices *and* socially responsible behavior. In fact, some social intrapreneurs and social entrepreneurs embrace a *triple bottom line:* financial returns, social returns, and environmental returns on investment. We believe these double bottom line and triple bottom line ways of thinking will characterize successful leaders in the twenty-first century.

> *Thinking and acting like an entrepreneur is certain to elevate your game. Part III: Mastering the Game and the "double bottom line" are rooted in the Kwanzaa principle of Ujamaa (Cooperative Economics), which means "to build and maintain our own stores, shops, and other businesses, and to profit from them together."*

THE ENTREPRENEURIAL MINDSET CYCLE

Fortunately, intrapreneurship and entrepreneurship are not separate and distinct paths. You don't necessarily have to choose one or the other. Nowadays, more than ever, people switch (or cycle) between intrapreneurship and entrepreneurship as they change career paths several times in their lives. You can cycle between both paths (as indicated in Figure III–1) or you may even pursue them simultaneously—pursuing one path from 9:00 A.M. to 5:00 P.M., for example, and the other path on evenings and weekends.

Randal switched between paths and pursued them simultaneously by working in corporate America (at AT&T, then Lucent Technologies) and attending graduate school, all while contributing to MBS Educational Services and Training "on the side," then working for MBS and BCT Partners full-time, then taking a leave of absence to work for the Trump Organization full-time, then returning to BCT Partners. J.R. has pursued both paths simultaneously by starting a career

Part III: Mastering the Game

Figure III–1. Mastering the game: the entrepreneurial mindset cycle.

in corporate America (Merck & Co.), then attending graduate school, and then working in academia full-time, all while maintaining ties to several ventures, including MBS, BCT, and Eden Organix.

Intrapreneurship and entrepreneurship are different sides of the same coin. They apply the same thinking, just in different contexts.

Five Ways to Master the Game

The ability to think and act intrapreneurially and entrepreneurially are the crux of Part III: Mastering the Game. Mastering the game implies that you have essentially achieved five forms of mastery:

▸ *Mastery of self,* which radiates from achieving a level of self-determination, as described in Part I. Identity helps establish your position in the game, while purpose helps reveal what you define as winning your game.

▸ *Mastery of your craft,* which naturally flows from achieving a level of excellence within your field or sector, as discussed in Part I. This helps put you at the top of your game.

▸ *Mastery of relationship building,* which emanates from achieving a level of awareness of the players in your game, and an associated level of connectedness with respect to the interpersonal, developmental, and group relationships relevant to your game, as described in Part II.

▸ *Mastery of your professional landscape,* which stems from achieving a level of wisdom concerning the spoken and unspoken rules of your game (meaning the environment comprising your organization or industry) and establishing yourself as a player in the game, in order to help yourself and others to effectively navigate the game, as discussed in Part II.

▸ *Mastery of the entrepreneurial mindset,* which, once achieved, builds upon your mastery of self, craft, relationship building, and professional environment to produce value in the world. The key to mastering the game is creating value in the world.

Mastery of the game is often evidenced by your accomplishments or your contributions to society, be they small or large. A sign of your mastery of the game might be something tangible: You create a new program, launch a new product, form a new organization, or establish a new business. It could also be reflected in your ability to overcome the challenges associated with reaching the executive level within your organization, growing a profitable company, turning around a failing division, or building a civic association that is making a difference socially, economically, educationally, or environmentally. It could even come in the form of something intangible, such as establishing a new process within your department, implementing a new way of doing business at your company, inspiring colleagues to see new possibilities, or changing people's perceptions in a new and positive way.

Your ability to accomplish these feats requires a certain level of mastery of self, craft, relationship building, professional environment, and the entrepreneurial mindset. To produce anything of value in the world requires a certain level of mastery of the game.

As a basic rule of thumb, you know you are on the path from learning the game (Part I) and playing the game (Part II) to mastering the game (Part III) when you begin displaying intrapreneurial and entrepreneurial thinking, because then your actions fundamentally change from *accepting* our society as the status quo to *transforming* our society into a new reality. It is at this point that you move from being *influenced* by the world around you to *influencing* the world around you. And it is then that you begin to *seek* opportunities, *see* opportunities, and most important, *seize* opportunities that benefit yourself and others. In fact, it is because the entrepreneurial mindset is so distinctive when compared to other ways of thinking and acting that the transition from Part II to Part III represents an inflection point on the path to greatness. Changing your mindset to think and act along these lines is another point of departure to ultimately redefining the game and reshaping America.

In the next two chapters, we discuss how adopting the entrepreneurial mindset can help you achieve greater individual success, both personally and professionally. We will also discuss how it can lead to tremendous benefits for your organization and your community.

A Two-Pronged Approach for Redefining the Game

As we look ahead to Part IV: Redefining the Game, we advocate a two-pronged or two-sided approach, with intrapreneurship and entrepreneurship working in concert.

On one hand, we need people who think and act intrapreneurially (Strategy 7) and have mastered the game to work "inside the system" of existing corporations, government agencies, schools, nonprofits, and faith-based organizations. These intrapreneurs must be willing to challenge existing institutions to be more responsive to the needs of diverse populations.

Intrapreneurs must maintain a strong sense of self-determination (Strategy 1). They cannot lose themselves or their direction while working in established organizations. Intrapreneurs view their culture as an asset that can be a strategic, competitive advantage, not a liability.

These are people who learn the system and master it from within the system, changing it for the better. In doing so, they not only ensure that these institutions are responsive to the needs of African Americans, but all Americans. In J.R.'s role at Rutgers University, he manages a process that invests in entrepreneurs in Newark, New Jersey, helping entrepreneurs run businesses that, in turn, create jobs, pay taxes, and help stabilize neighborhoods. His work as an intrapreneur benefits the entrepreneurs and their employees, the city of Newark, the state of New Jersey, and the country.

And just as we need intrapreneurs working inside the system, we need people who work "outside the system." These entrepreneurs launch new ventures, create new organizations, and establish new institutions. They build wealth, amass power, and compete with existing institutions. Instead of climbing the corporate ladder, entrepreneurs build their own ladders and then reach down to help others climb the ladder with them. Rather than fighting to become partners in someone else's firm, they eventually leave and start their own firms. They are risk takers—jumping off the ship even when they don't know if there is a net to catch them. In some instances, they gain experience and legitimacy from working at existing institutions and later use that knowledge to establish their own institution. Randal has done this by working in corporate America and then breaking out to lead BCT Partners.

Neither approach is better than the other. The best approach is the one that best suits your personal mission, vision, and values.

Intrapreneurship and entrepreneurship are part of a cycle—you don't have to choose one or the other. You can pursue one, then switch to the other, and then back again. Both of us have done so throughout our careers.

Think and Act Intrapreneurially

Yet our best trained, best educated, best equipped, best prepared troops refuse to fight.
As a matter of fact, it's safe to say that they would rather switch, than fight!
—Thomas N. Todd, Esq. ("TNT"), quoted in
the prelude to Public Enemy's "Fight the Power"

WE PROBABLY don't have to tell you that African Americans are under-represented in many professions. Likely you've gone to school or work, industry conventions, and conferences and you are one of the few Blacks in the house.

And as you scan up the ladder into the middle, senior, and executive management ranks, whether it's finance or publishing, entertainment or technology, you'll see the numbers of African Americans thin—and in many cases disappear. The number of state governors—just four in U.S. history—or the number of senators—only five—are just a couple of examples. The number of African-American principals of schools, partners at major investment banks or venture capital funds, or presidents of large philanthropic organizations remains low. In some cases, African Americans have lost ground—in 2008 there were just four Black head football coaches in the NCAA, the lowest number in fifteen years.[1]

In various fields, sectors, and industries, the conclusion remains the same: Despite our country's shifting demographics, in far too many professional environments, African Americans are few and far between at all

Figure 7–1. The path to greatness (Strategy 7).

levels. This is alarmingly true at the upper levels and executive levels. This underscores the need for true African-American intrapreneurs because intrapreneurs are change agents.

African-American Intrapreneurship

Redefining the ever-changing game means working together to level the playing field for everyone. Certainly, people of all backgrounds should be willing to advocate for changes within their organization that will do just that. Unfortunately, it's not a task that many are willing to take on. That's why when we find ourselves as one of the few Blacks in an organization, or perhaps the only Black, it is important that we willingly stand up, speak out, and spawn action. It is no accident that the name of this strategy is both think and act intrapreneurially.

As African-American intrapreneurs we must exercise the judgment to discern between when we can effect change and when certain changes are beyond our current capacity or control—at least for now. Then we can reach a position where we no longer have to abide by the rules, but can change the rules.

THE THREE F'S: FIGHT, FLIGHT, OR FORGO

It could be as simple as how you wear your hair. Management at a conservative financial services firm may view hairstyles like braids or dreadlocks unfavorably, while an Internet company may be more accepting.

Let's assume that you are a graduating senior from college and you've identified your top choice for employment. As an unwritten rule, your hairstyle is not considered acceptable there, but it is something you feel very passionate about as a form of self-expression.

You have a decision to make:

- ▸ *Fight.* Maintain your hairstyle to make a statement, while accepting the consequences of how you may be negatively perceived.

- ▸ *Take "flight."* Simply don't pursue a job there and, instead, seek employment where your hairstyle is accepted. This could send a message to the company that they should reexamine their culture.

- ▸ *Forgo* the issue for now. Change your hairstyle and wait until you are in a more senior position to return to your original hairstyle, and then possibly advocate for changes in the company's culture. This would still make a statement, albeit when the implications to you would be less harmful.

Depending on the circumstances, all three of these choices are reasonable and speak to if, when, and how you want to effect change.

A deeper example is deciding whether to create an organization within your company specifically to support the needs of women or minority employees (commonly referred to as an "affinity group" or "employee resource group"). While these groups have grown in popularity and many companies understand their usefulness, there are many large corporations that do not have any. Some companies have other support structures in place, but in some cases the lack of affinity groups signals a culture that fails to recognize their value.

Say you are a mid-career senior manager on the fast track to senior management and you have grown frustrated by the unwillingness of the company to establish an African-American affinity group, yet you have not done much to make the case. You know from firsthand experience that such an organization would create a more welcoming environment, improve employee retention, and promote networking and mentoring.

Once again, you have a decision to make (from among "the Three F's"):

▶ *Fight.* Work with the company to form an affinity group, understanding that some of your coworkers and superiors may not initially see the value of such a group or may feel threatened by it.

▶ *Take "flight."* Pursue employment at a company that already sees the value of affinity groups.

▶ *Forgo* the issue for now. Revisit it when you hopefully join the ranks of senior management.

Once again, all three of these choices are reasonable. However, at some point, *true African-American intrapreneurs are willing to fight for what they believe.* This does not mean always fighting. The art of intrapreneurship is having the wisdom to discern when it makes sense to fight, when it is better to take flight, or when it is more appropriate in the long run to forgo an issue. African-American intrapreneurship is about choosing your battles wisely, but also about making sure that at the end of the day, you have fought for something. To always take flight or forgo an issue that affects people of color is to do a disservice to the African Americans who will one day occupy your seat.

Tavis Smiley's debate coach perhaps captured the spirit of "fight, flight, or forgo" when sharing with him her four S's. She said, "Always remember, Tavis, how to stand up, speak up, shut up, and sit your behind down."

Game-Changing Strategies for Intrapreneurship

So how do you become a true African-American intrapreneur? The building blocks lie in the previous strategies. Strategies 1 through 6 provided tools, advice, and examples that, when fused together, can transform your experience within an organization.

You started with the foundation of a strong identity and purpose, broad exposure, and a high level of personal and professional excellence so that you can really begin to harness the power of the diverse networks you've built and the variety of mentors and colleagues with whom you've developed strong relationships. Then you found strength in numbers with coworkers inside your organization and on the outside, in professional groups.

Now you can start thinking about your career strategically—like an entrepreneur thinks about her company—and ask yourself the following questions:

- How do I market myself?

- How do I maintain my own competitiveness?

- How do I advance within my organization?

- How do I ensure that I'm obtaining the best value for my services?

- How do I position myself to wield greater influence?

Intrapreneurs must employ the right resources for the right need at the right time. In the same way entrepreneurs respond to the ever-changing dynamics of their customers and put their company in a position to redefine the marketplace, intrapreneurs respond to the ever-changing dynamics of the workplace to put themselves in a position to redefine their industry.

Whereas an employee performs his job responsibilities to contribute to organizations (see Figure 7–2.), an intrapreneur applies game-changing strategies to advance his career and transform organizations (Figure 7–3.).

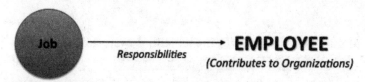

Figure 7–2. Employees contribute to organizations.

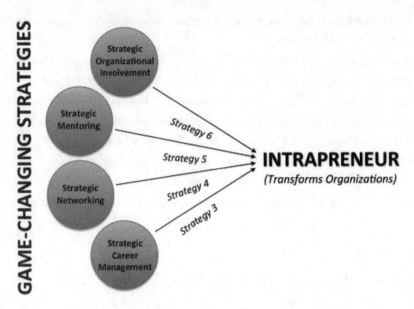

Figure 7–3. Intrapreneurs transform organizations.

These game-changing strategies for intrapreneurship span the areas of career management (Strategy 3), networking (Strategy 4), mentoring (Strategy 5), and organizational involvement (Strategy 6).

To describe the game-changing strategies for intrapreneurship most effectively, we want to present them in the context of a case study.

....
To arrive at Strategy 7 is to say that you have grown smarter (Strategy 3), better (Strategy 4), wiser (Strategy 5), and stronger (Strategy 6).
....

A CAREER CASE STUDY: RHONDA JACKSON

Rhonda Jackson landed her first job in the marketing department at a large consumer products company where she interned through INROADS for two summers.

Early Career. About eight months into the job, things were going well. Her boss, Lauren, was increasingly relying on her and gave Rhonda a large role in important presentations, including a plan aimed at attracting more young customers. She worked well with her mostly white colleagues in her department and occasionally got together with them after work or on the weekends for coffee or drinks.

One day in the cafeteria, she ran into Katie, a colleague in the marketing department. Katie excitedly told her about a recent promotion to another department. Rhonda wondered if there was something wrong with her. Katie was about her age and had the same level of experience. Katie was making big moves while Rhonda was chugging along in marketing—not sure where her efforts would eventually lead. On the other hand, Rhonda liked what she was doing. Lauren was teaching her a lot and advising her on marketing seminars she should attend to deepen her knowledge. She could see that she was not just working in marketing—she was becoming a marketer. She wished Katie luck and decided to stay put for a while longer, building her expertise and taking on more complex assignments.

Early on Rhonda identified two mentors: Stan, the African-American marketing manager who supervised her during her summers there, and her boss Lauren, who is white. But Rhonda didn't get to spend as much time with Stan, because while she was back at school hitting the books during her senior year in college, Stan was making moves of his own, broadening his own skill set by taking a job in operations. So Rhonda made a point to schedule coffee or lunch meetings with Stan every few months to check in and keep him up to date on how things were going for her—and to find out more about his new assignment. Impressed by the positive reports he heard about Rhonda and the tenacity she showed by continuing to reach out to him on a regular basis, Stan made a point to introduce her to several senior vice presidents who he was now working with closely. Rhonda's network was expanding throughout the company.

About three years later, a job managing a small brand opened up and Rhonda was interested. It looked like a great way to move up in the company. She asked Lauren and Stan for their thoughts. Both pointed out that the hiring managers would be looking for a candidate with an MBA. Lauren connected Rhonda with Lin-Yu, a brand manager who used to work in marketing. They talked about how she could continue with the company and position herself for a move, as well as the merits of attending a part-time or full-time MBA program.

Stan suggested that Rhonda take advantage of a company program that would give her a leave of absence to get the degree and pay off her student loans if she worked at the company for at least three years after she finished. So, after four years at the company, Rhonda considered the advice from her mentors and network connections and left to get her MBA, returning two years later as a brand manager.

Mid-Career. When Rhonda began working in brand management, her former boss and mentor Lauren was now heading up marketing and her mentor Stan was second-in-command in operations. She continued her relationships with them and began meeting more senior vice presidents.

By now, she was not only a member of the National Black MBA Association, she regularly attended conferences to hone her skills and was heavily involved with the Leaders of Tomorrow program, aimed at getting more young people to consider careers in business. She also joined the American Marketing Association, the largest marketing association in North America.

While she was gone, Stan and a few other employees founded a minority affinity group at the company and Rhonda jumped in, chairing a committee charged with designing two socially intrapreneurial programs. The first would help employees of color early in their careers learn about, and prepare for, higher-level jobs. The second would help minority-owned and women-owned businesses to pursue contracting opportunities with the company. She sought advice from coworkers like Lin-Yu, who was originally from China and therefore could help Rhonda understand the cultural considerations important to Asians. Hector, a fellow INROADS alum working in human resources whom she had kept in touch with since she started at the company, was able to help her connect with more Latinos.

After making a presentation to a group of senior and executive vice presidents about how her proposed program to help younger employees prepare for higher-level jobs would work, Tim, a Jewish executive vice president in operations, asked Rhonda to join a task force aimed at finding ways to save money without resorting to layoffs. Based on her presentation, he thought she might have ideas that would help the company hold on to workers longer, which would help to reduce the considerable costs, in time and money, the company incurred each year recruiting new employees, training them, and losing ground as those new workers integrated into the culture. She convened a group with representatives from HR, marketing, finance, and operations to design a program. The CEO loved the idea, and with the support of HR and the department heads, the company implemented the plan.

But Rhonda's biggest focus was on moving her brand forward, and she could see that her predecessor's focus on 18-to-34-year-olds offered limited growth. Baby boomers had a lot of money and liked spending it. On a personal level, Rhonda didn't like the way many companies treated more mature women, as if they didn't matter. She set a goal for herself to find some way through her work to make sure women age 40 and older were treated like they were relevant and, at the same time, make money for the company. She fused a passion and a business opportunity to lead the development of a new product, Pronexys, aimed at older women. This launch broadened her skill set into areas such as manufacturing and finance. It went so well that within a year, Rhonda was tapped to manage a larger brand, Exelron, which was in trouble, and she was able to turn that product around in profitability. This assignment forced Rhonda to stretch her abilities as it required her to do business in overseas markets.

Late Career. As a result of Rhonda's success with Pronexys and Exelron, the company tapped her as the executive vice president of marketing and brand management, where she was responsible for overseeing all of the company's consumer brands both domestically and in the emerging markets of Eastern Europe, Africa, and the Middle East. This promotion earned her membership in the Executive Leadership Council (ELC), the nation's premier leadership organization comprised of the most senior African-American corporate executives in Fortune 500 companies. She also joined the board of the American Marketing Association (AMA) and explored ways that ELC and AMA could work together.

Rhonda had also helped the company build a good reputation. Her work exposing minorities and women to opportunities that encouraged them to grow with the company earned many awards. She served as a sponsor to the minority affinity group at the company, providing advice and taking ideas and concerns back to management. She made a point to work with at least two INROADS interns each summer, advising them on career management. At least ten early-career and mid-level career workers at the company consider her a mentor.

Her earlier efforts on the operations task force helped the company find ways to retain workers, encourage loyalty, and improve job satisfaction and earned the company a spot on a prominent business magazine's list of best companies to work for.

By now Rhonda was working side-by-side with both Lauren, who was still head of marketing, and Stan, who by then held the top operations job. The CEO who was nearing retirement marveled at how these three high-level managers worked so well together. It was obvious that the solid relationships Rhonda, Lauren, and Stan had built over the years eliminated many potential bottlenecks. Products went from development to marketing to market almost seamlessly.

The board noticed, too. And Rhonda's name was on the short list of candidates who would succeed the CEO when he retired.

BRINGING IT ALL TOGETHER

By now you may have guessed that "Rhonda" is an idealized version of an intrapreneur who learned, played, and mastered the game by integrating *strategic career management* (from Strategy 3), *strategic networking* (from Strategy 4), *strategic mentoring* (from Strategy 5), and *strategic organizational involvement* (from Strategy 6) as they relate specifically to African Americans and people of color.

You may be asking, is this all really possible? Well, we assure you, this kind of career progression is not only possible, it has happened. Take Lawrence Jackson, for instance, now retired from Wal-Mart. He was, in fact, on the short list of candidates to take the CEO job. When Lee Scott got the position, Jackson moved on and became CEO of another discount retailer, Family Dollar Stores Inc.

Strategic Career Management. Rhonda's case helps illustrate the progression of career knowledge and career management (Strategy 3) that you, too, should demonstrate at the various stages of your career. Early in her career, she deliberately chose to stick with marketing, even while some of her colleagues were trying new things. She scanned her boss's bookshelf to make sure she read the marketing books that her boss felt provided important tenets of the craft and deepened her knowledge at industry conferences. She chose *quality* assignments over a *quantity* of assignments; she sought out positions that *deepened* her technical and functional expertise in marketing as opposed to several short assignments across multiple areas. By the middle of her career she returned to the company with an MBA in tow, thereby *widening* her skill set beyond marketing to include managerial expertise. She landed a job in brand management and, by late career, had managed several brands, and was now heading up the division.

One of the keys to Rhonda's ability to transition from middle management to upper management was her success in undertaking the broadening assignment of the Pronexys product launch and the stretch assignment of the Exelron product turnaround. In Strategy 3, we discussed the importance of having objective evaluation criteria for job assignments. For both products, the evaluation criteria were simple and indeed objective: Either the products would become profitable or they would not. Fortunately, Rhonda's ability to deliver on such high-stakes assignments was just the kind of opportunity she needed to propel her to the C-suite.

She constantly sought out assignments she was passionate about. Old-school thinking believes that to advance your career, you should subordinate your interests and passions to the needs of the company. New-school intrapreneurial thinking suggests that, instead, it behooves both employer and employee to find a natural fit between your passion and your work. It means being willing to make sacrifices in the short term (be it a lower salary, a lesser title, fewer promotions, or otherwise) if a job opportunity is more closely aligned with your personal vision. In summary, strategic career management means *identifying the right job assignment for the right need at the right time.*

Strategic Networking. Rhonda learned to use her networks (Strategy 4) and mentors (Strategy 5) and fused them throughout her career. Old-school thinking is that to advance your career, you should strive for a *sparse* network at all times: establish as many different contacts with as many different people in as many different places as possible—even though they do not necessarily know each other. New-school intrapreneurial thinking suggests that different types of networks have different benefits at different times. This is strategic networking, or *establishing the right network for the right need at the right time.*

Early in her career, her network was dense: She kept relationships with former INROADS interns alive, she developed a new network in her own department, and through the help of her mentor Stan, she began branching out into other areas of the company—meeting people in operations. As she began reaching toward a mid-career level job, Lauren, her other mentor, lent a *borrowed* network connection, Lin-Yu, to aid Rhonda in making her decision to pursue an MBA.

After coming back to the company and joining brand management, Rhonda began more actively using her *dense* and *borrowed* connections and developing more sparse ones. She called on Hector and Lin-Yu for counsel. Her work with the affinity group led her to make a connection with Tim in finance, which led her to convene a committee that cut across multiple departments and allowed her to work with her mentors Lauren and Stan once again and even develop a new mentoring relationship with Tim, who saw her potential and gave her an opportunity to show top executives what she could do by pulling her onto the finance task force.

Strategic Mentoring. As you may have guessed, it's no accident that we've emphasized the diverse ethnic and cultural makeup of Rhonda's mentors (Strategy 5) and the people in her network (Strategy 4). Old-school thinking believes that to advance your career, you should find a mentor who is high-ranking in the company, a non-minority, and one person to address all of your needs. New-school intrapreneurial thinking suggests that, instead, there will inevitably be occasions when you will have different people filling different roles at different times, and that for African Americans, diversity even among your mentors will serve you best. *Seeking the right mentor for the right need at the right time* is the essence of strategic mentoring.

Rhonda's mentors were initially at her *functional level* of marketing (Stan, the marketing manager from her summer internship) and her *departmental level* within the company (Lauren, her boss). It wasn't until the mid-stage of Rhonda's career that she could truly benefit from *upper-level* and *executive-level* mentors. Fortunately, she had maintained her relationships with Stan and Lauren even after both of them had moved into upper management.

Early on Rhonda had mentors of two races, socialized with other African Americans and her mostly white colleagues in marketing, and kept her connection with a Latino from her intern days. Later she made solid connections with an Asian woman and a Jewish man. The successful intrapreneur understands that having relationships with a diverse group is a critical part of managing mentors and networks.

Strategic Organizational Involvement. Lastly, Rhonda found strength in numbers (Strategy 6) in her outside involvements. Old-school thinking believes you should maintain involvement in the same organization throughout your entire career and that the organization should reflect your identity. And while this may still indeed be valid advice depending on your needs, new-school intrapreneurship says *different organizations may address different needs at different times,* which is the fundamental premise of strategic organizational involvement. You should find diversity in your organizational involvement along all four considerations of stage, scope, subject, and specificity.

INROADS was key to Rhonda's early career, creating the opportunity to work at the company. Later, the National Black MBA Association was the appropriate organization as she moved through graduate school and back to her company. These *ethnic organizations* proved extremely valuable to her—allowing her to keep connections with other mid-level Black professionals alive and stay involved in activities that promoted mentorship and could possibly be a pipeline of talent for her company. Her involvement in a *general organization,* the American Marketing Association, was also instrumental in Rhonda's ability to stay on top of industry trends and ensure that she had a diverse network. Becoming a member of the Executive Leadership Council and a board member for AMA during the later stages of her career offered opportunities to make connections between the two organizations, network with people at her level, and expand her relationships internationally as she was deepening her brands' reach into developing markets.

Table 7–1 summarizes all of the game-changing strategies for intrapreneurship, organized by career stage.

	CAREER STAGE		
	Early-Career	**Mid-Career**	**Late-Career**
	STRATEGY 3: Demonstrate Excellence *Strategic Career Management*		
Career knowledge	Technical/functional mastery (deep)	Specialized (deep) or General/Managerial (wide)	Executive or expert (deep and/or wide)
Career management	Quality assignments over quantity	Broadening assignments	Stretch assignments
	STRATEGY 4: Build Diverse and Solid Relationships *Strategic Networking*		
Network type	Dense/borrowed	Dense/borrowed toward sparse	Sparse
Network diversity	Diverse		
	STRATEGY 5: Seek the Wisdom of Others *Strategic Mentoring*		
Mentor level	Functional/departmental level	Upper-level	Executive-level
Mentor diversity	Diverse		
	STRATEGY 6: Find Strength in Numbers *Strategic Organizational Involvement*		
Organization stage	For emerging professionals	For seasoned professionals	For upper-level and executive professionals
Organization scope	Local, regional, national, and international		
Organization subject	Employee groups and affinity groups		
Organization specificity	Ethnic and general		

Table 7–1. Game-changing strategies for intrapreneurship, by career stage.

Social Intrapreneurship and Community Investment as a Competitive Advantage

There has always been and continues to be a positive tension in our lives of striving to balance our desire to pursue professional endeavors, like those illustrated in Rhonda Jackson's case study, with our yearning to advance a social agenda. We are certainly not alone in our desire to pursue a professional path while serving society: Many people—maybe even you—wonder how they can manage both desires. In our own lives, we've had the best of both worlds.

When we founded MBS Enterprises as undergrads at Rutgers with our friends Aldwyn Porter, Lawrence Hibbert, and Dallas Grundy, we had a retail sales division that sold compact discs and cassette tapes out of our dormitory and an educational services division that offered workshops, lectures, and seminars—with an emphasis on reaching minority youths. This was our first experience balancing the *double bottom line* we discussed in the Part III introduction: combining good business with goodwill.

J.R. has built much of his academic career around the study of entrepreneurial endeavors that fulfill a social need. At BCT Partners, Randal has worked successfully with federal and municipal government agencies, foundations, nonprofits, and faith-based organizations to improve the self-sufficiency and quality of life for residents in low-income and underserved communities across the country and across the globe. For several years, BCT Partners was proud to work with Hewlett-Packard and the Association for Enterprise Opportunity to implement a national program that equipped low-income communities with technology labs to train local entrepreneurs.

The key is finding harmony between your personal and professional endeavors by seeking out the synergy between the two. This way you can simultaneously help yourself and others. You can ascend to the ranks of a principal, or an executive director, or a chief executive officer, while at the same time challenging your school, your nonprofit, or your corporation to be more responsive to the needs of the community along the way.

Social intrapreneurs challenge established organizations to play a meaningful role in addressing society's most pressing problems. In this context, the opportunities to combine good business and goodwill are vast for large corporations, so-called "mega-churches," statewide systems of higher education, international foundations, and other organizations. And as all these organizations grow in size, scale, and reach, the resources at their disposal also multiply. Social intrapreneurs who are employed or affiliated with institutions—small, medium, or large—can ensure that some of their resources are properly reinvested in communities in ways that benefit others.

We believe that community investment is not only the "right" thing for your organization in terms of goodwill, but it is also the right thing for your organization in terms of good business. In other words, we believe community investment not only fulfills both organizational or corporate social responsibility, but it is also a competitive advantage that can lead to better performance, such as increased financial returns and improved organizational outcomes.

Gwen Kelly, senior marketing manager at the world's largest retailer, Wal-Mart Stores Inc., shared a similar perspective during an interview with us. "I have responsibility for approving imagery, words, and language that is targeted to the African-American community, but I also realize the larger community sees it as well," she said. "If I do something that is not honoring that community, or is not respectful of that community, then I am not doing my job. Literally, the images I put out there may impact someone for better or worse." Anthony Jerome Smalls, vice president and director of community relations for retailer the TJX Companies, which operates T.J. Maxx and Marshalls, uses his connections inside and outside of the company to advance work in the company and the community along the same lines. "I can use my position as a corporate cupid," he said during his interview.

For a school or a nonprofit, community investment can improve the surrounding neighborhood, strengthen families, and improve the local economy, just to name a few benefits—all of which can help the school or the nonprofit reach and exceed its organizational and operational goals. For a corporation, community investment can help attract better workers, improve employee satisfaction, and build stronger suppliers—all of which can lead to better corporate and financial results. And keep in mind that financial results are not confined to revenue or profits for corporations. For a university, it could be the overall finances that support research and student education. For a hospital, it could be the total budget to deliver services to patients. Financial metrics may be evaluated in terms of public relations or advertising impressions, marketing exposure, products or services sold, brand recognition, or image and reputation building.

However, organizations and corporations do not become more socially responsible by accident. In some instances, individuals or groups of individuals request or even demand certain changes. It takes the dedicated and committed efforts of employees, staff, associates, administrators, executives, and other stakeholders to think and act intrapreneurially by identifying new and creative ways for their organization to make a broader or deeper social impact. And, once again, true African-American social intrapreneurship is about choosing these battles wisely, but at some point being willing to stand up and "fight" for matters of importance.

Whether it is a college administrator who spearheads a university-sponsored community cleanup, or a police chief who leads a department-wide volunteer effort, or a teacher who organizes a school-wide canned food drive, or a corporate executive who establishes an international corporate foundation, or a hotel manager who champions an organizational initiative to donate surplus goods to needy families, each person has taken his or her organization one step further toward helping one more person, and each of them embodies the mindset of a social intrapreneur.

For example, at Prudential Financial Inc. in Newark, New Jersey, Gabriella Morris heads up the Prudential Foundation, which oversees the financial services company's purely philanthropic endeavors and socially targeted investments. When Prudential makes a social investment, the first return must be *social*. Prudential measures these outcomes by how lives or living conditions were improved. Depending on the scope of the project, those metrics could be how many affordable housing units were created, how many jobs were obtained, how much incomes increased, or how much students' grades improved as a result of the investments.

But being a financial services company with expertise in investing, Prudential also seeks a second return on investment that is *financial*. Prudential underwrites loans for socially targeted investments as a regular transaction—albeit with the expectation of a below market rate of return. "We think it is an important function because many of the things we try to finance, the organizations, the people do not have access to capital," Morris shared during an interview with us.

Prudential's focus on education, affordable housing, and economic development has led it to provide loans to finance real estate and working capital funds to forty-eight charter schools, including about twenty-five in New Jersey. The program provided an $800,000 mortgage to North Star Academy Charter School in downtown Newark, which in 2004 achieved a

100 percent college attendance rate. By 2005, the program surpassed the $1 billion mark, with more than $228 million worth of financing going to affordable housing and nearly $30 million supporting minority entrepreneurship.

The Cycle Continues

Rhonda Jackson's case study, which is idealized, and Gabriella Morris's quite-real work at Prudential Financial clearly demonstrate the power of thinking and acting intrapreneurially. Intrapreneurship ties together several key concepts from Strategies 3 through 6. But even this is only half the story. Intrapreneurship and entrepreneurship reflect the same entrepreneurial mindset. They are different parts of a continuous cycle. They are different sides of the same coin. They are different pathways to mastering the game.

Next, Strategy 8 will describe what it means to apply the entrepreneurial mindset to the creation of entirely new ventures—both for a profit and for a social purpose. Then, Strategy 9 will connect these two approaches and paint a picture of how those working inside organizations (intrapreneurs) can connect with those working outside to create new organizations (entrepreneurs), thereby combining their efforts and having the broadest or deepest possible impact.

Think and Act Entrepreneurially

I am a woman who came from the cotton fields of the South. From there I was promoted to the washtub. From there I was promoted to the cook kitchen. And from there I promoted myself into the business of manufacturing hair goods and preparations. . . . I have built my own factory on my own ground. . . . Don't sit down and wait for the opportunities to come; you have to get up and make them. . . . I got my start by giving myself a start.

—Madam C. J. Walker

IN HER MEMOIR, *Success Never Smelled So Sweet* (Random House, 2004), Lisa Price recalls loving scents from an early age. Most of the fragrant rose petals that she was charged with scattering as a flower girl at her aunt's wedding never hit the floor—for Price they were much too precious for that. Instead, a young Lisa dropped a neat line of them all the way to the altar leaving her with a bounty of petals to savor later.

For Price, the saying "the nose knows" takes on special meaning. The scents that she adored in her childhood and turned into a hobby as a young adult later are now generating millions. Today, she is the founder of Carol's Daughter Holdings LLC, which makes and sells a line of body and hair care products online, through company-owned stores, and through major retailers like JCPenney and Macy's.

Price didn't graduate from high school or college and immediately start a successful business. As we have observed and experienced, that's rarely

Figure 8-1. The path to greatness (Strategy 8).

how it happens. Price's life took twists and sometimes difficult turns. From a personal perspective, she dealt with a bad marriage and even personal bankruptcy after years of overspending. Career-wise, she worked at the United Nations, pursued a singing career, and even worked on *The Cosby Show*.

All the while, Price was experimenting with oils—sometimes making fragrances for friends and coworkers. Eventually, she sold some of her creations, which expanded to include all kinds of creams, lotions, and potions—all made in her own kitchen set up at flea markets and then out of her apartment. In 1999, she opened her first store, and by 2001 she began the (not-so-smooth) process of moving the Carol's Daughter operations from her home to a warehouse.

Today, Carol's Daughter counts celebrities, including actress Halle Berry, actor Brad Pitt, and recording artist Erykah Badu, as customers. Songstress Mary J. Blige, rapper Jay-Z, and Hollywood super couple Will Smith and Jada Pinkett Smith invested in the business, helping to fuel its expansion.

More recently, a private equity firm, Pegasus Capital Advisors, has invested in the company and is leading it through an expansion.

African-American Wealth Creation

Lisa Price took a hobby and turned it into a multimillion-dollar business enterprise that attracted investment from celebrities and others. Her experience shows how almost anyone can travel the path from running a small operation to creating wealth for herself and others. Today, family and friends work for her and she has drawn the interest (and money) of numerous investors.

There's a good chance that you are familiar with the *Rich Dad, Poor Dad* book series started by real estate investor Robert Kiyosaki. Kiyosaki uses something he calls the "CASHFLOW Quadrant" to describe how money is made and wealth is created in America.

Figure 8–2. Kiyosaki's CASHFLOW Quadrants.
From *Rich Dad's CASHFLOW Quadrant* by Robert Kiyosaki. Copyright © 1998, 1999 by Robert T. Kiyosaki and Sharon L. Lechter. By permission of Grand Central Publishing.

According to Kiyosaki, you can work for someone else as an *E*mployee. As an employee you generate income from the work you do in someone else's company. You generally do not share in the profits. The second option is to be Self-employed. To be self-employed means that you work for yourself, but you don't have any other employees (or very few). In other words, if you don't work, work doesn't get done, and you don't get paid.

You can be a *B*usiness owner, which is different from being self-employed because you have employees that are working on your behalf. If you are on vacation, work is still getting done and money is still getting made (hopefully). Business ownership, of course, requires systems and processes and that all employees are in sync in order for the business to function smoothly. Lisa

Price made the transition from being self-employed to being a business owner by reinvesting earnings into her business.

Lastly, you can be an *I*nvestor, putting money into other businesses, real estate, or other situations in hope of making a profit. There is a lot that can be said about investing, much of which is beyond the scope of this book. However, we believe wise investments can go a long way toward creating wealth. We recommend that you consider investing in new ventures and businesses seeking growth capital.

There is a big difference between the first quadrant (Employee) and the second and third quadrants (Self-employment and Business ownership), both of which speak directly to being an entrepreneur. When we discuss entrepreneurship in this chapter, we mean formally registering your business with your state and creating a company that is legitimate in the eyes of the law. We don't mean the informal economy, or what some people call "bootleg" businesses. There are important financial benefits to going through these formal processes. If you study the U.S. tax code you'll see that it was written for business owners. You cannot take advantage of any of the rules for business owners without formally setting up a business. Our stance is that you are not in business unless your business is registered. All of your other efforts are just a precursor to having a real business, which includes network or multilevel marketing businesses, such as selling Mary Kay cosmetics, Amway products, Pre-Paid Legal, or Primerica financial services. In these situations you operate like you are in your own business, but essentially you are the marketing or selling unit of a big company. While this model works for many, it isn't self-employment or business ownership in the traditional sense.

There is an even bigger difference between the first two quadrants (Employee and Self-employment) and the second two quadrants (Business ownership and Investor). The first two require that all of the work is done by you before money is made. The second two allow you to make money while you sleep, vacation, or do other things. We've written about various forms of capital throughout this book and now, finally, we get to the one that most people think of first: financial capital. Owning a business or investing is important for anyone who wants to create *financial capital*.

Financial capital refers to cash, savings, investments, real estate, or anything else that has some financial value associated with it—especially if it is easily converted into cash or can be leveraged for cash value. People usually think of financial capital as debt (money you borrow) or equity (money that others invest). Financial capital is important because it allows you to purchase things that you may want or need and to enjoy certain aspects of life.

However, financial capital is not *wealth*. Wealth is not just about how much money you make. It is about how much money you keep, what it is invested in, and how it is used across generations. There are many people with high incomes who aren't wealthy because they spend everything they bring in or do not invest their money wisely in assets that will appreciate (increase value) over time and can be passed from generation to generation. Wealth and ownership are inextricably linked.

We encourage people to strategize about creating wealth, not income. Investing in homeownership is an important step in the process for African Americans. But, as you may have guessed from our backgrounds, our favorite wealth creation strategy is entrepreneurship. We have witnessed the effect that entrepreneurship can have on people, places, and communities. This chapter focuses on entrepreneurship and the way we have used it as a vehicle for wealth creation. More important, we'll show how African American entrepreneurship is a pivotal strategy to position yourself to redefine the game and reshape America.

THE STATE OF AFRICAN-AMERICAN WEALTH CREATION

Here in the United States, we have seen an increasing gap between the wealthy and poor, the "haves" and the "have-nots," the rich and the rest. For example, the 13,000 richest families in the United States now have almost as much income as the 20 million poorest. And those 13,000 families have incomes 300 times that of average families. Moreover, the top one percent of Americans own approximately 40 percent of the nation's wealth; the top 5 percent owns almost 60 percent; and the top 20 percent owns more than 80 percent. If you eliminated homeownership and only counted businesses, factories, and offices, then the top one percent owns 90 percent of all wealth, and the top 10 percent owns 99 percent.[1] As severe as the inequalities are among Americans, they are significantly worse for minorities, and especially for African Americans. For instance:

‣ *African Americans still earn less than their white counterparts.* Even when households with similar educational, occupational, and demographic characteristics are compared, a Black household earns almost $6,000 less than a white household with similar educational, occupational, and demographic characteristics.[2] Clearly, the "cost of being Black" is high.

‣ *While there is considerable income in minority communities, there is also a considerable lack of wealth.* The collective buying power of African Americans, Asian Americans, Latinos, and American Indians is projected to reach $4.5 trillion by 2015.[3] That is income. But, as we discussed earlier, income is not wealth. In terms of wealth, in 2001 the average white household had a net worth of $121,000—including home equity. The figure for an average Black household: only $19,000![4] The median net worth for whites is $88,000, while the median net worth for Hispanics and Blacks is just $7,900 and $6,000, respectively.[5] Furthermore, while minority groups represent approximately 27 percent of the U.S. population and are projected to be the majority by 2050, minority-owned businesses only receive 2.7 percent of all U.S. gross revenues.[6] When juxtaposed against the perception that minority communities are doing well economically, we refer to these statistics highlighting the persistent gaps in wealth as "the illusion of economic inclusion."

WHY WE NEED AFRICAN-AMERICAN ENTREPRENEURSHIP

At this point, you are hopefully asking the same question we ponder every time we read these and similar statistics: How can we build more wealth in the African-American community? There are a number of answers to this challenge. Part of the solution involves increased financial awareness and financial literacy that encourages members of our community to save, eliminate debt, and invest in education and other appreciating assets. However, the most effective way to build significant wealth is by becoming a business owner.

Entrepreneurship is the most viable pathway to creating significant wealth. Thomas Stanley's book *The Millionaire Next Door* (Pocket Books, 1998) explains that seven out of every ten millionaires made their millions through entrepreneurship. Sadly, according to some sources, there are 8 million white millionaires in America and only 35,000 Black millionaires.[7]

It stands to reason that to create more African-American millionaires, we must create more successful African-American entrepreneurs.

We are among the most aggressive advocates for entrepreneurship in America. We have created companies together and consulted with small and medium-size businesses. We've taught entrepreneurship courses at universities, advised political campaigns and policy think tanks on the issue of entrepreneurship, written books on the subject, and we are actively engaged in several business ventures. We believe in entrepreneurship and its power to create wealth, transform communities, and boost the wealth of African Americans. But, we also know that African Americans are behind. With all of the wealth that was created in the last two decades, no Black athletes or entertainers have become billionaires (yet). Both of America's only Black billionaires, Oprah Winfrey and Black Entertainment Television founder Bob Johnson, made their money through business ownership.

White Americans enjoy a 14-to-1 wealth advantage over African Americans, and to close this wealth gap we must close the entrepreneurship gap, which means creating more African-American entrepreneurs. However, to create more African-American entrepreneurs we have considerable work to do. The rate of entrepreneurship among African Americans hovers around 5 percent as compared to 10 percent for whites and Asians, according to U.S. Census Bureau 2000 data. So not only is there an income gap and a wealth gap, there is also a related entrepreneurship gap for African Americans. It certainly seems like a steep hill to climb.

But there is good news:

▸ *African-American businesses are on the rise.* The number of businesses owned by Blacks increased 45 percent between 1997 and 2002 to 1.2 million businesses, and revenue was up 30 percent in the same period to $92.7 billion.[8]

▸ *African Americans have a strong desire to become entrepreneurs.* African Americans (men especially) have the highest entrepreneurial intention of any group studied, according to the Kauffman Foundation.[9]

▸ *African Americans have a rich legacy of success in business.* From Madam C. J. Walker, the first female millionaire (of any race), whose Walker Manufacturing Company employed more than 3,000 people in the early 1900s; to

John H. Johnson, founder of *Ebony* and *Jet* magazines; to Earl Graves, founder and publisher of *Black Enterprise* magazine; to Reginald Lewis, the first African American to own and operate a billion-dollar corporation, TLC Beatrice; to Oprah Winfrey, the first African-American female billionaire and owner of Harpo Productions—the list of African-American entrepreneurs is notable and their accomplishments are significant. We draw inspiration from their stories and the tales of countless others.

For those of you already pursuing your entrepreneurial dreams, we applaud you for your efforts. For those of you who have a young person in your life with an entrepreneurial spirit, we encourage you to nurture it. And for those of you on the fence who are considering taking the entrepreneurial leap, we can only say to you what athletic shoe maker Nike has been saying for years: Just Do It! While we are quick to point out that entrepreneurship is not an easy path and is not for everybody, we want everyone to know that they have the choice to be a business owner should they choose to exercise it, and that not only can it be done, but our people have been doing it for centuries.

If you are working for someone else right now, maybe this is a wake-up call for you to consider taking the entrepreneurial leap. If you already have your own venture, you are taking advantage of one of the best vehicles for building significant wealth.

But we are not big believers in making money just for the sake of creating wealth for your personal benefit. Amassing wealth can create opportunity for others. It helps stabilize our families, build our communities, and put jobs in our neighborhoods. In fact, in one of the studies that Jeffrey Robinson and Greg Fairchild of the University of Virginia conducted, Black business owners were two to three times more likely to hire Black employees than white business owners.

If we have more Black entrepreneurs we will go a long way toward addressing the high unemployment rate in the Black community. Business owners address many issues in communities and contribute to the civic and philanthropic life of an area.

And with respect to the ever-changing game, wealth helps level the playing field by reducing income and wealth inequities. Increasing the number of African-American entrepreneurs has the potential to significantly improve the Black community.

We could write an entire book just on entrepreneurship or social entrepreneurship (in fact, we have written books on each subject already). So we won't try to jam into this chapter everything we've ever learned about entrepreneurship. What we want to demonstrate is how thinking and acting entrepreneurially is a critical part of the journey to redefining the game and reshaping America.

Applying the Entrepreneurial Mindset

Nowadays, perhaps more than ever, regardless of whether you work for a company (an "employee"), run your own business (an "entrepreneur"), or are someone new to the job market (a new "entrant") who is endeavoring to become an employee or entrepreneur, to be competitive in the marketplace you must think and act like an entrepreneur. The once tacit assumption and "contract" between employers and employees—namely, that if you work hard for a company they will keep you in your job—has been broken. It no longer exists. As a result, you cannot risk putting your fate in the hands of an employer. You must take control of your career; you must dare to be in the driver's seat of your destiny; and you must be in a position to pursue your economic prosperity. Regardless of whether the economy is weak or strong, the entrepreneurial mindset of passion, creativity, resourcefulness, courage, and resilience is not just the recommended mindset in the twenty-first century, rather, it is the mandatory one.

So how do you apply the entrepreneur's mindset? It is simple. You should not look for a single "job" that generates a "salary." That's an old-school mindset, where you are thinking and acting like an employee to create income and break the glass ceiling (see Figure 8–3). Instead, you should seek out multiple "sources of revenue" that generate "income streams." That's

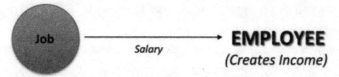

Figure 8–3. Old-school mindset: thinking and acting like an employee.

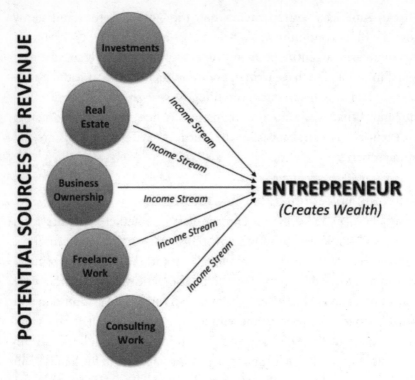

Figure 8–4. New-school mindset: thinking and acting like an entrepreneur.

new-school thinking and acting like an entrepreneur to create wealth and master the ever-changing game (see Figure 8–4).

A job is only one of many potential sources of revenue, and a salary is only one of many potential income streams. For example, investments, real estate (e.g., rental properties), consulting work, fee-for-service work, part-time work, freelance work, auctioning items, network or multilevel marketing, and, above all, business ownership, all represent alternative sources of revenue that can generate income streams. And the beauty of thinking and acting along these lines is that it opens up an entirely new realm of possibility to tap into all of your gifts and abilities, especially if your "day job" is only tapping into a few.

Depending on which of the three E's most closely resembles your current reality—*employee, entrepreneur,* or *new entrant*—you may apply the entrepreneur's mindset in a different way. But regardless of which "E" best describes you, the common theme is to diversify your sources of revenue so that you are not wholly dependent on any single source. Even companies may have several diversified sources of revenue in the form of different products, services, divisions, or lines of business under the firm's umbrella.

If you are a new entrant to the job market—a young person, recent graduate, first-time job seeker, or someone recently laid off—then applying the entrepreneur's mindset means taking a serious look at starting your own business in parallel with interviewing for employment positions. Be sure to consider the entire range of entrepreneurial ventures presented in this chapter. In fact, if you are a displaced worker, don't think of it as being "let go," think of it as being "set free" to pursue these options.

If you are an employee who works for a company, then applying the entrepreneur's mindset means exploring additional ways to monetize your skills and abilities. We'll talk about this in greater detail later in this chapter under the heading of "Profiting from Your Knowledge, Experience, or Expertise."

If you are an entrepreneur who is self-employed or a business owner, then applying the entrepreneur's mindset means constantly pursuing growth opportunities for your company by utilizing all of the concepts and strategies for "entrepreneurship for a profit," encompassed here in Strategy 8. (You'll also benefit from Strategy 9: Synergize and Reach Scale.)

Lastly, if you are more socially oriented, there is something in this chapter for you, too, as we delve deeper into the practice of social entrepreneurship, or what we call "entrepreneurship for a purpose."

In summary, while every section of this chapter may not apply directly to you, we are confident the concepts and strategies discussed will be of tremendous benefit to you in applying the entrepreneur's mindset to your life.

It should come as no surprise that the same quote from Earl Graves that we referenced in Strategy 3 also applies here in Strategy 8: "Your career is your own private business." In other words, while your status may be best described as an employee or a new entrant, you must always think and act like an entrepreneur. Regardless of whether you work as a human relations manager, detective, or nurse—or aspire to pursue one of these careers or any other—the key is to think and act like an entrepreneur at all times.

Game-Changing Strategies for Entrepreneurship for a Profit

There are different types of business ventures for a profit and only you can decide what kind of venture best suits your interests. To best explain these options, let's further separate entrepreneurship for a profit into *lifestyle ventures,* generally small companies that allow you to maintain a comfortable lifestyle, and *growth ventures* that expand and create wealth for you and your investors. Between the two, you have to decide where you want to play in the game.

CREATING LIFESTYLE VENTURES

People who don't want to work for somebody else (i.e., entrepreneurs), want to generate additional steams of income (i.e., employees), or who go into business because they don't have another option (i.e., new entrants) are good candidates for what we call lifestyle ventures. Lifestyle ventures replace or supplement your income.

These smaller-scale businesses provide products and services to the general public. Examples are small retail stores such as the coffee shop, the dry cleaner, the hair salon, and the caterer. These and many other businesses are great for creating a few jobs and for sustaining a comfortable lifestyle for yourself and your family.

In some cases, these are part-time endeavors. For example, home-based retail operations, one-person consulting companies, and custom jewelry makers are typically lifestyle ventures. These types of companies generally do not require a lot of financial capital to start. The key is that lifestyle ventures generate enough income for the entrepreneur and allow her to maintain and, in some cases, improve her lifestyle.

Think about it—there are a lot of small businesses that don't make millions of dollars in a year. According to the U.S. Department of Commerce, less than 20 percent of the 6 million U.S. companies with employees make more than $1 million in a given year. In the African-American business community, about 800,000 firms, only 3 percent have revenues above $1 million, according to the Minority Business Development Agency of the U.S. Department of Commerce. (Of course, we think this number should be much higher, and later in this chapter we have some ideas to share about how to increase the number of growth ventures.) An astounding 99 percent of businesses in the United States are small businesses, which are generally defined as companies with fewer than 500 employees. These companies employ more than half of the country's private-sector employees and create 60 percent to 80 percent of new jobs in a given year, according to the U.S. Small Business Administration's Office of Advocacy. Clearly, it is small and medium-size businesses that make the American economy flow.

Profiting from Your Knowledge, Experience, or Expertise. There are many ways people get into a lifestyle business both part-time and full-time. Some people take their passion for cooking and become caterers for hire. Lisa Price, who we introduced at the beginning of the chapter, transformed her love of scents into Carol's Daughter. Some people take their gift of song or other artistic talent and turn it into a production company. Profiting from your knowledge, experience, or expertise in these ways is a great entry point for a lifestyle venture. Many entrepreneurs have gone this route and made substantial profits along the way. If you have valuable expertise, you may be able to pursue contracts as an independent consultant.

There are, however, two challenges with this approach. First, this type of entrepreneurship is limited by how much time and effort is required by you to create the final product or provide the service. If you work alone or with a small group, you may have capacity limitations that prevent you from growing your business. Second, there may not be a market for your passion or expertise, or it may take a long time to develop the market. In either case, the returns on all of your work may not be enough to sustain your lifestyle. This is why every person who wants to capitalize on their expertise isn't necessarily financially successful. (When you can engage a team of employees, contractors, or business partners, however, the potential to grow the business increases exponentially. That leads to creating growth entrepreneurial ventures, which we talk about in the next section.)

There is certainly a level of autonomy when you have built a small business. Your clients may become your new bosses, but at least you have some choice about where and how you'll complete the client's work. But going it alone has its own set of burdens as well, and potential business owners shouldn't jump into the entrepreneurial world without considering the pros, the cons, and the risks.

If you are a professional and you are going to become an entrepreneur, then make sure you pursue a venture that's worth your time. Some small ventures don't have the potential to generate wealth because the business can't realistically be expanded to a larger scale or the profit-generating potential is very small. Other businesses have the potential to reach a bigger scale and generate wealth (Carol's Daughter is an example), but the entrepreneur has to realize this and pursue the business in a way that will unlock its growth potential.

We know of several caterers who are excellent in the kitchen. They can prepare wonderful meals for any occasion. Yet most of the ones we know are small operations, where one lead entrepreneur does almost everything. These entrepreneurs usually have a few people they can count on to help them when necessary, but for the most part, they are on their own, working out of their home kitchen with the dream of opening a restaurant someday. In our experience, few of these entrepreneurs make the leap from being a one-person show to creating a business that hires people and creates wealth.

But there are a few exceptions. Tod Wilson of Mr. Tod's Pie Factory (whybake.com) bakes delicious pies, cobblers, and cheesecakes. He started off working part-time in his godfather's business and learned about pie making. He figured out that if he was going to generate wealth, he was going to have to take control of the entire operation and build the production capacity. That type of thinking—and subsequent action—is different from just making pies or cakes on the side for friends, family, and anyone else who happens to find out about you. You may have an expertise, but is your vision a small-scale business or a larger-scale enterprise? Mr. Tod was thinking big from the start. In fact, he negotiated a lucrative investment deal as an entrepreneur winner on the reality television show *Shark Tank*.

Marissa Blackwell's love of cooking was a career she pursued in the hospitality industry. She developed her skill managing large operations at a major hospital in New York and working for a large food-services company. She started catering on the side and her customers raved about her food. Her goal was to one day work for herself, but it took a while to assemble the team to convert her small operation into one that could service multiple events simultaneously. Cravings, a catering company, came out of her desire to take her gifts in food preparation and presentation to a larger scale.

Blackwell now has a large catering facility in Newark, New Jersey, and serves customers throughout the state and beyond.

Wilson and Blackwell demonstrate that expertise can generate profit. In both cases, however, these entrepreneurs had to put some serious business thinking into how they would take their passion from something that was a small operation and transform it into a growth venture.

When determining how you want to proceed, remember to consider the vision you have for your business. If you want to have a lifestyle venture that makes enough money to provide a decent income, then more power to you! Capitalize on your knowledge or expertise the best way you know how. Just keep in mind that these types of small ventures are developed differently than the growth venture firms we discuss in the next section.

CREATING GROWTH VENTURES

All-star entrepreneurs like World Wide Technology's David Steward, Microsoft's Bill Gates, Radio One's Cathy Hughes, Google founders Larry Page and Sergey Brin, ACT·1 Group's Janice Bryant Howroyd, and TLC Beatrice's Reginald Lewis epitomize the idea of wealth generation. While Gates and many other successful company founders give back, most people focus on the money they made when they took their companies public or the profits they generate in a given year.

The alternative to lifestyle ventures is these kinds of growth ventures that expand in size or scale and create wealth for the entrepreneur and others who invest in the business. They include franchise businesses and partnerships and other arrangements where business ownership is shared or distributed. Growth ventures are capable of crossing that million-dollar threshold to become businesses that we see heralded in the media because they have made an economic impact on a city, region, the entire country— or even the world! These ventures have several characteristics in common:

 ▸ *They have the potential to scale up and expand to multiple locations and distribution channels.* We can see this in action through following the expansion of Carol's Daughter, which has grown from one store in Brooklyn to have several locations, mail-order operations, and distribution through major retailers and television-shopping networks.

▶ *They generate income for the entrepreneurs/founders/owners and create wealth through shared ownership and equity investment.* If you have lived in or visited the Southeast United States, there's a good chance you've seen and maybe even spent time in some of the structures that helped Herman J. Russell build a legacy for his family. H. J. Russell & Co. grew to become the largest African-American construction firm in the United States, having built notable landmarks, including Coca-Cola's headquarters, the Georgia Dome, and Centennial Olympic Stadium/Turner Field. Today, Russell has stepped aside from the day-to-day running of the company and serves as chairman, with his son Michael B. Russell at the helm as CEO. A daughter, Danata, and another son, Jerome, also hold key positions in the enterprise.

▶ *They leverage the skills, talents, and abilities of many people, not just the lead entrepreneurs.* This is evident in every entrepreneur that we mention and profile for this book—as well as in our own venture, BCT Partners. At BCT, Randal is the face of the company going out and generating deals. We rely on our own team and subcontractors to fulfill those contracts.

▶ *They are prepared for investment, merger, acquisition, and other exit strategies.* In 2007, Rodney Hunt, who owned a 75 percent stake in RS Information Systems (RSIS), told *Black Enterprise* magazine that he was mulling the future of the technology and defense contractor. As CEO, Hunt led RSIS to generate about $328 million in annual revenue. At the time of the *BE* interview, the company had unfilled orders of about $1.3 billion—a level that made it an attractive acquisition target. About a year later, RSIS announced that it would be bought by Wyle, a privately held competitor, for an undisclosed sum.

▶ *They are typically full-time endeavors for managers and employees of the company.* The entrepreneurs we have featured here made a full-time commitment to their businesses. They show that to go the distance, you must eventually be able to put in the time and energy and have a team in place to get the job done.

There is a heightened level of complexity associated with creating (and sustaining) growth ventures. Increased scale means greater complexity. When you have multiple locations you have to have systems and processes in place to monitor operations in these different places. To leverage the skills, talents, and abilities of many people, you have to have a great team and be able to manage them across space and time.

Creating a Winning Team. While people tend to focus on the individual entrepreneur, very few entrepreneurial success stories are accomplished by individuals alone. Our team of Randal, Jeffrey, Lawrence, and Dallas would not have been able to launch BCT Partners were it not for our collective efforts. To create this kind of growth venture, you, likewise, will need to have a strong team working with you. We talk extensively about teams and partnerships in Strategy 6, but we cannot emphasize this point enough.

BEYOND SMALL BUSINESS DEVELOPMENT
TO BUSINESS ENTERPRISE DEVELOPMENT

The question we pose to African-American entrepreneurs is not how we can continue to develop more Black-owned small businesses. We've been doing that for years. In fact, our country is not at a loss for small businesses. Small businesses represent the backbone of our economy.

However, small businesses come and small businesses go. According to the U.S. Small Business Administration, more than 33 percent of small businesses fail in the first two years, and 66 percent fail within the first four years. So, small businesses are created and then they fail. Then more small businesses are created and more fail. Only a select few ultimately succeed. This is simply the reality of entrepreneurship. It is also why the question we pose to aspiring and established African-American entrepreneurs is not how we can develop more Black-owned or operated small businesses, but rather, how can we develop more *business enterprises,* that is, growth ventures, that reach scale?

We need more Black-owned small businesses to evolve into Black-owned business enterprises because business enterprises are critical to generating and retaining significant wealth in minority communities and eliminating "the illusion of economic inclusion," as described earlier. Business enterprises can serve as the cornerstones for job creation and opportunity and, perhaps most important, generate significant wealth for individuals, families, and communities.

Whether we like it or not, in the twenty-first century business land-scape, *size matters*. While small businesses are indeed the backbone of the U.S. economy, it is becoming increasingly difficult for small businesses to remain competitive. For example, over the past few decades we have wit-nessed several mergers and acquisitions among long-standing, multina-tional corporations that we never dreamed would have joined forces: AT&T and Cingular; Bank of America and Merrill Lynch; Wells Fargo and Wachovia; Citicorp and Travelers; Sprint and Nextel; Delta Airlines and Northwest Airlines; Hewlett-Packard and Compaq and EDS; AOL and Time Warner; FedEx and Kinko's; XM Radio and Sirius Radio; and even the UPN and the WB television networks. As already-big companies get bigger, it reduces the number of players in their industry. The remaining players are likely to be larger than ever before, making it harder for smaller companies to remain competitive.

This trend of consolidation raises the bar for African-American entre-preneurs (and those who support their development). True business enter-prises stand the best chance of competing in the marketplace, achieving longevity, and generating wealth for generations and generations to come. We often refer to a minority-owned business as a "minority business enter-prise," or MBE. For us, the operative word is "enterprise."

Social Entrepreneurship

When people use entrepreneurship as a vehicle to transform communities, address social issues, or improve the environment, they are employing entrepreneurship for a purpose. If this describes what you do, or what you desire to do, then you are the kind of person who believes you can achieve the *double bottom line*—"do well" (for yourself financially) and "do good" (for others and the community) at the same time.

The traditional model of capitalism in the United States is to create a company and grow it to be very big and make lots of money. Then, after you've made your millions or billions of dollars (in many cases), you turn your attention to charitable deeds and create a foundation. Some of the major companies and wealthiest families in the nation followed this pattern of wealth creation and then foundation creation. Think of the Ford, Rocke-feller, and Gates foundations. These and other foundations have been used as a significant means of taking wealth generated in business and applying it toward creating social value or change.

Entrepreneurship for a purpose flips the traditional model on its head by creating economic value *and* social value simultaneously. Just like the double bottom line for social intrapreneurs working inside established organizations, you can work on the outside to strike the double line. The core of this idea is called *social entrepreneurship.* In fact, many people are striving for triple bottom lines where they also create environmental value by defending the natural environment or reducing our impact on it.

We take the broadest possible definition of social entrepreneurship so that we can help you understand how creating social and economic value at the same time redefines the game and reshapes America. Here is a definition from a book that Jeffrey co-edited with his colleagues Joanna Mair and Kai Hockerts:

> *Social entrepreneurship is recognized as encompassing a wide range of activities: enterprising individuals devoted to making a difference; social purpose business ventures dedicated to adding for-profit motivations to the nonprofit sector; new types of philanthropists supporting venture capital-like "investment" portfolios; and nonprofit organizations that are reinventing themselves by drawing on lessons learned from the business world.[10]*

Instead of using the terms "for-profit social business" and "nonprofit organization," we use the terms *social venture* and *civic* and *community venture.*

THE FOUR ELEMENTS OF SOCIAL ENTREPRENEURSHIP

From our perspective, four elements must be present for a venture to be considered social entrepreneurship: *social impact, social innovation, sustainability, and success measures.*

▸ *Social Impact: What issue or problem is the venture being set up to address?* Social impact is a key element of a social venture. How a social venture makes a difference and where it wants to create change are important strategic decisions. A social venture can solve challenges at community, local, regional, or national levels. Social ventures are often challenged by the trade-off between breadth and depth of their social impact. How the venture's management and board reconcile this tension is an important strategic consideration.

▸ *Social Innovation: Is the venture using a new approach to addressing the social/environmental issue?* Social ventures break new ground, pioneer new approaches, or develop new models. These ventures need to creatively navigate the economic, social, and institutional barriers to addressing the social need. Social entrepreneurs develop new approaches to addressing social problems or utilize technology to facilitate problem solving. It is important that social ventures use effective innovations for the problem they are addressing.

▸ *Sustainability: Is the venture financially viable? Is the venture positioned to fulfill its mission over the long term?* A sustainable social venture is financially viable and positioned to fulfill its mission. Many social ventures are not sustainable because they rely upon unstable grant-making or government institutions for funding. Alternatively, earned-income or fee-for-service business models are generally more effective strategies for social ventures. Some social ventures are not sustainable because they have not organized their internal resources effectively to fulfill their mission. How a social venture marshals its resources is an important strategic decision that often separates traditional nonprofit organizations from social entrepreneurship. Later in the chapter, we will expand upon this concept of sustainability.

▸ *Success Measures: How does the venture measure its social impact and evaluate success?* Are the measurement tools appropriate for this type of venture? Measurement and evaluation are essential to social entrepreneurship. In addition to the financial metrics used by traditional ventures, social ventures must measure their impact and evaluate their effectiveness. There are many ways to measure and evaluate the social impact of a venture. Depending on the venture, examples of measures include improved student grades, reductions in the incidence of a disease, or decreases in environmental emissions. The key is that the social venture is using an appropriate type of measurement tool that is in line with its *theory of change*. A theory of change is the way that social entrepreneurs define how their innovation makes a social impact or how they think change will be made. It is also a concept we will revisit in Strategy 9.

These four elements guide the way for using the social entrepreneurship approach to address the social and environmental issues in the African-American community and beyond. We acknowledge that social entrepreneurship is not the only approach that can lead to change in the African-American community, but we strongly believe that it is an approach that makes a difference. Emerging social entrepreneurs that consider these four elements when creating and operating their social ventures and business will be more effective and make a substantial impact in our communities.

Game-Changing Strategies for Entrepreneurship for a Purpose

Here we present social entrepreneurship for a purpose in two categories, namely, *civic and community ventures* and *social ventures.*

CREATING CIVIC AND COMMUNITY VENTURES

In this category, we place all nonprofit and community-based organizations, including grassroots, educational, and faith-based organizations, created to address social and/or environmental issues. This category includes groups offering exposure, expertise, and mentoring to schools, churches, and mosques, as well as entities promoting youth development, professional development, and economic development.

We also believe that when you create your own organization of this type that you are being just as entrepreneurial as someone who creates a multi-billion-dollar business enterprise. The only difference is that central to your mission is a desire to make a socially important difference.

Nationally, there has been an explosion of these types of nonprofit organizations. When we say nonprofit organizations, we are referring to the registered nonprofit corporations that have tax-exempt status under IRS code 501(c)(3). Not only do they not pay corporate taxes, but they also are able to accept donations. Individuals who give these nonprofits donations can claim those donations as charitable contributions and reduce their taxable income.

Following Your Passion. We meet many people who tell us that they are not challenged by or passionate about their full-time jobs. Often they say they are passionate about youth development, education, or public health. In fact, it is the disconnect between their "day job" and their passion that causes many people to be frustrated. For some people, starting a new community organization is something that can be more rewarding than being in corporate finance, engineering, or sales.

For example, Angela Glover Blackwell's path to becoming a social entrepreneur began when she graduated in 1967 from an admittedly uninvolved four years at Hampton University and moved into the thick of the Black Power Movement in New York City.

"I went from zero to sixty miles an hour in no time at all because I had literally done nothing. When I was in college I didn't join anything; I didn't lead anything, I just was observing," Blackwell related to us in an interview. "But when I entered the Black Power Movement, life became purposeful and the skills that I had developed—in church, in the community, in debates around my dining room table—suddenly had a place where they could be focused."

And so began a career organizing first in New York City and then in Los Angeles. She earned a law degree at the University of California at Berkeley and became a public-interest lawyer working for organizations like the American Civil Liberties Union and the NAACP. The Rockefeller Foundation recruited her from the Urban Strategies Council in Oakland, which focused on policies that dealt with infant mortality, teenage pregnancy, early childhood development, and school improvement.

But like many of the people we run into who have that social entrepreneurial spirit, something was missing.

"I accepted that offer because I thought it was a way to spread the kind of work that we were doing in Oakland," Blackwell explains. "But I found philanthropy to be frustrating. It wasn't action-oriented enough for me. After three years being there, though, I recognized that what was missing was a policy organization that actually did its policy work from the wisdom, voice, and experience of people who were working locally."

From there, Blackwell fused her experience working with people as a community organizer and her experience in philanthropy to create PolicyLink, which works with people in communities to create sustainable opportunities for people to improve their lives. One successful PolicyLink initiative has been to fight the spread of obesity and other diet-related diseases by attracting grocery stores to underserved areas. When people don't have access to fresh, healthy food options, as is the case in many low-income communities, they aren't able to make better food choices. PolicyLink serves as a consultant to organizations and communities that are trying to make a difference by implementing these kinds of projects.

Bringing your experience and expertise from your profession into the social sector is a great way to make an impact in communities. But, we also want to caution you about creating a new organization for the sake of creating something new. In some cases, it is better to develop your efforts through an existing organization.

The Challenge for Nonprofit Organizations. We believe that creating a new nonprofit organization or civil society organization (CSO) is an entrepreneurial act. The challenge we see with many of these organizations is that after they are created, they stop being entrepreneurial. Sometimes the mindset of the founders shifts from getting off the ground to providing the services or meeting the need and they forget about the resourcefulness and entrepreneurial drive necessary to grow a nonprofit organization. Sometimes, the tax-exempt status and restrictions placed on nonprofit organizations make it difficult for these organizations to be creative. Boards of directors can make things more complicated if they have a perspective that is different from the staff of the organization.

We've seen the amazing work done by civic- or community-based organizations disappear because the sources of their funding—government agencies and philanthropic individuals or foundations—shifted their priorities. Others did not run their organizations like they were businesses. They didn't write a business or an operational plan. They let inefficiency and ineffectiveness creep in. All of this leads to the diminishing of the vital services that you are providing.

Creating and sustaining a small nonprofit organization can be difficult. The hours are long, the pay can be low, and you become emotionally invested in the success or failure of each project or program. You may be following your passions, but we advise that you find team members who are excited about the work that you do but also have the ability to address the operational challenges that every organization has when it is starting out or growing. It is just as important to have people with an accounting or financial background as it is to have people with a passion for the work that your organization does. People with these necessary business skills will help your organization be financially sustainable and effective and efficient at meeting your mission, vision, and organizational goals.

CREATING SOCIAL VENTURES

Social ventures use entrepreneurial and business skills to create innovative approaches to solving social and environmental problems. These are mission-driven organizations focused on the double (or triple) bottom line of social impact and financial growth. Whether they are called social ventures, social purpose businesses, or social enterprises, we consider all of them social entrepreneurship.

They share these characteristics:

- A central purpose of the organization is the desire to make a socially important impact.

- They leverage new approaches (social innovation) to address social and/or environmental issues.

- They create a sustainable business and operational model that allows them to make a social impact over the long term. Among the possible models are earned income strategies, partnerships, fee-for-service, and state or federal contracting.

- They measure and promote their success in addressing specific social or environmental issues.

We meet many people with an entrepreneurial spirit who also want to make an impact on the world. They come to us and usually say something like, "I want to start a nonprofit organization." This statement often reveals old-school thinking. We will often respond with the questions: "Why does it have to be a nonprofit organization? What is it *exactly* that you want to do?"

Old-school thinking says that nonprofit organizations and CSOs are the only type of entities that can meet social needs or address environmental problems. New-school thinking says that the terms *nonprofit* and *for-profit* are only organizational forms. (Remember, we already gave you the technical definition of a "nonprofit, tax-exempt organization" in the previous section.) A social entrepreneur can use either form of organization to achieve social and environmental goals.

If you want to help solve a social problem, you should figure out the best type of organization to achieve your goals. The best approach will allow you to accomplish those goals efficiently and effectively.

Social entrepreneurs can use any of the following methods to address social and environmental issues. Each approach is an entrepreneurial act:

▸ *Creating nonprofit organizations that generate earned income.* An example is Green Worker Cooperatives, a nonprofit incubator for entities that work to solve environmental issues in the South Bronx. Its first cooperative, Rebuilders Source, salvages used building materials from new construction and demolition projects and sells them to the general public below retail prices to generate earned income—while also keeping tons of waste out of landfills.

▸ *Developing for-profit subsidiaries for a nonprofit organization.* Greyston Bakery, a for-profit in Yonkers, New York, was founded to create an income stream for a Zen Buddhist meditation group, but later expanded to create jobs for community residents including former felons and the homeless. The organization grew to become the exclusive maker of brownie mix-ins for the Ben & Jerry's ice cream brand and creates gourmet pastries and wedding cakes.

▸ *Operating a nonprofit organization like a business.* Co-founded by one of Randal's mentors, Rey Ramsey, Washington, D.C.–based One Economy works to help people improve their lives through access to technology and media. The organization works to bring broadband Internet access to low-income communities and creates programming for its Public Internet Channel (PIC.tv), including a series on single motherhood produced and directed by Robert Townsend and thebehive.org, which provides content on finances, healthy habits, housing, and education. One Economy accepts funding to support some of its activities, but also derives a large percentage of earned income from fee-for-service activities such as installing broadband service in low-income housing developments.

▸ *Creating a for-profit business that addresses a social or environmental problem as part of the central mission of its business.* Eden Organix, a Raritan, New Jersey, spa founded by Jeffrey and his wife Valerie Mason-Robinson, promotes taking a natural approach to solving skin care problems through the use of holistic products, instead of using harsh chemicals that could have harmful side effects. Sweet Beginnings is a Chicago-based maker of honey-based spa-quality products that absorb more easily into the skin than many synthetic products. Sweet Beginnings trains and employs residents in the city's North Lawndale community who are often locked out of the traditional labor market due to criminal records or other barriers to employment. Eden Organix creates jobs for women who have fallen on hard times and donates 10 percent of its profits to environmental and other charities.

▸ *Creating for-profit companies whose products and services provide a societal benefit.* Our company, BCT Partners, offers an array of strategic management, technology, and organizational development services to support efforts aimed at producing positive change. Under one contract, BCT works with the U.S. Department of Housing and Urban Development to help public housing authorities that have won grants to better utilize their resources in implementing a community revitalization plan while meeting other grant requirements.

BEYOND NONPROFIT SUSTAINABILITY TO SOCIAL ENTERPRISE GROWTH

Capacity building refers to the multitude of activities geared toward enhancing an organization's ability to function more effectively in achieving its desired outcomes. These activities include training, technical assistance, strategic planning, fund-raising, technology assistance, partnership development, and much more. Old-school capacity-building efforts aimed at nonprofit organizations (e.g., community-based organizations, faith-based organizations, charter schools, CSOs) have focused on achieving *sustainability* or simply maintaining an organization's current level of capacity. In fact, the paradigm of sustainability is somewhat reflected in the language traditionally used by some within the nonprofit sector to describe those who support their work.

For example, some within the social sector refer to their capacity-building supporters as "funders" who provide "funding," while others refer to their capacity-building supporters as "investors" who make "investments." The Merriam-Webster dictionary definitions of some of these terms are as follows:

Invest—1: to commit (money) in order to earn a financial return; 2: to make use of for future benefits or advantages.

Investment—the outlay of money usually for income or profit [profit is defined as "a valuable return"].

Funding—to make provision of resources for discharging the interest or principal; to provide funds for.

These definitions are suggestive of two potential paradigms. The first paradigm—a *sustainability paradigm*—treats resources as funding and discharges these resources in a way that maintains the status quo. It is an organizational paradigm that is willing to accept occasional growth, occasional capacity building, survival, and breaking even. The second paradigm—a *growth paradigm*—treats resources as investment and makes use of these resources to achieve a valuable return on the investment. It is an organizational paradigm that emphasizes continuous growth, continuous improvement, future benefits, and future advantages. The question we pose to those working in the nonprofit, faith-based, educational, community, or civic sectors is: Which of these paradigms best applies to you and your organization?

Perhaps not surprisingly, we are vocal advocates of the growth paradigm. It is the more empowering paradigm. It places a premium on advancement and progress. It is wholly consistent with the entrepreneurial mindset. When a civic, community, or social venture enacts the necessary rigor that promotes organizational growth financially, procedurally, technologically, and operationally along the lines of revenue, budgets, staff development, new systems and processes, and strengthened partnerships, we call this becoming a *social enterprise*. Experienced social entrepreneurs seek to move beyond a paradigm of achieving sustainability to a paradigm of growth that reaches scale and expands the scope of their impact.

Figure 8–5 summarizes the four types of entrepreneurial ventures we have discussed in this chapter—*lifestyle ventures, growth ventures, social ventures,* and *civic and community ventures.*

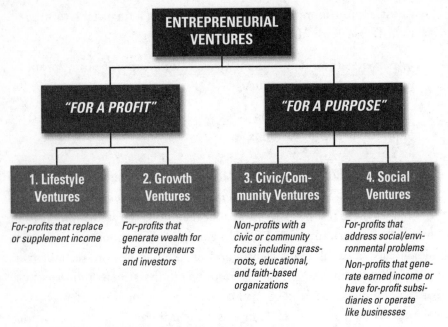

Figure 8–5. Four types of entrepreneurial ventures.

Institution Building

The challenge for the last generation of African-American entrepreneurs was breaking down doors and lobbying government and corporations to even consider doing business with minority-owned firms. The challenges of today apply to both entrepreneurs for a profit and entrepreneurs for a purpose, but in subtly different ways.

Today's generation of African-American social entrepreneurs represents a vanguard of socially conscious, business-savvy individuals who must similarly break down doors to create social enterprises that can grow and reach scale to address the pressing social and environmental problems facing society. African-American entrepreneurs must continue the momentum of their predecessors and work together to build companies that can also grow and reach scale. However, these business enterprises must be oriented toward creating lasting, generational wealth and promoting much-needed economic development in communities across our globe.

Looking ahead to Strategy 9: Synergize and Reach Scale, it's important to note that business enterprises and social enterprises are just a particular class of organizations we refer to as *institutions*. In Strategy 6: Find Strength in Numbers, we introduced the continuum of group relationships that ended with organizations. *Institutions are organizations that stand the test of time.* Institutions are establishments: organizations that will exist long after we have left this world and, in doing so, will continue to uphold their governing ideas of mission, vision, and values.

Government is an institution. It was here before we were born and will likely be here after we have moved on. The existence of government helps perpetuate certain ideals, norms, and standards for generations past, present, and future. The Baptist Church and the Catholic Church are institutions. Many well-recognized corporations such as World Wide Technology, General Electric, CAMAC, and McDonald's are institutions. Viable non-profit organizations like the College Fund and the Red Cross are institutions. To further illustrate what it takes to be classified as an institution, consider the following:

- The difference between an independent consultant and a long-standing consulting firm is that the latter is positioned to become an institution. The independent consultant's impact may be felt for years, but the point of view, processes, and methods that he used to do his work won't fuel another business after he stops working.

- The difference between Oprah as a talk-show host and Harpo Productions, which is owned by Oprah, is that Oprah one day will no longer host a talk show. Harpo is positioned to exist as an institution for years after Oprah has moved on.

- The difference between a nonprofit, church, or school that survives for two, three, or maybe four years and one that remains in the community for a hundred years is that the latter has become an institution.

An institution does not necessarily imply a large organization. A small-, medium-, or large-size organization can be an institution. Size and scale are not the distinguishing characteristics of an institution; rather, it's about staying power and permanence. No organization is meant to truly last forever, but some organizations do last much longer than others. So we're not talking about "Mom and Pop operations" that cease to exist once Mom or

Pop move on. They're great, but that's what past generations of African-American entrepreneurs were poised to accomplish: They opened store-fronts, independent consulting firms, and community groups with a single staff person.

Therefore, the ultimate question put to entrepreneurs and social entre-preneurs alike is the following: *If the founding members or key leaders of your organization were to step down tomorrow, would your organization continue to grow?* If the answer is "no," then there is more work to be done for your organization to be considered an institution. If the answer is "yes," then your organization is likely to be there. One of the primary reasons certain governments, corporations, and nonprofits are institutions is because they have *institutionalized* their ability to replace their leaders. To the extent that you want your organization to have staying power, you must do the same.

As you can see, our definition of institution applies equally to public, private, community, educational, philanthropic, and faith-based organiza-tions. Strategy 9: Synergize and Reach Scale will make clear how to work across all of these sectors—intrapreneurs and entrepreneurs alike—to empower people and build institutions that have longevity and create lasting change.

P A R T   I V

REDEFINING THE GAME

If we don't leverage our collective economic, political, spiritual, and cultural power, we can never expect to control our own destiny in this country.
—Earl Graves, *How to Succeed in Business Without Being White*

We've waited until now to define exactly what we mean by "redefining the game" and "reshaping America" because these concepts are best explained in the context of Strategies 1 through 8. Here we'll explore what it means to redefine the game and, in Strategy 10, we'll do the same for reshaping America. But before we do that, let's quickly review what it takes to be in a position to redefine the game.

Prerequisites to Redefining the Game

Perhaps not surprisingly, the prerequisites to redefining the game are captured in the previous eight strategies. To redefine the game, the following preconditions must be met:

Learning the Game (Part I)

▸ You must know who you are and where you are going so that you remain grounded with a sense of direction (Strategy 1).

▸ You must seek constant, ongoing exposure to new ideas, new ways of thinking, new cultures, and new experiences to promote multidimensional thinking (Strategy 2).

▸ You must maintain a commitment to lifelong learning, growth, development, and being among the very best at whatever you do, in order to possess deep knowledge in certain areas and broad knowledge in other areas (Strategy 3).

In summary, as Mahatma Gandhi said, "You must be the change you seek in your world."

Playing the Game (Part II)

▸ You must foster personal diversity through relationships with people of many backgrounds (Strategy 4) because:

– These relationships help you to understand the broad issues that influence all people, especially disadvantaged people.

– These relationships enable you to mobilize across lines of difference, search for common ground, and facilitate change beyond a single group but for many groups.

▸ These relationships are the fundamental building block of any change effort.

▸ You must learn from the experiences of others and learn from failure to avoid repeating past mistakes (Strategy 5).

▸ You must compensate for your own limitations by leveraging the strengths of others to build strong organizations and leverage team diversity (Strategy 6).

In summary, *change is most effectively accomplished by working with others and learning from others.*

Mastering the Game (Part III)

▸ You must marshal the resources of existing institutions and challenge them to be more responsive to diverse people (Strategy 7), and/or:

▸ You must establish new institutions that are responsive to diverse people and marshal their resources to create wealth (Strategy 8).

In summary, to facilitate change, *you must think and act like a change agent.*

What We Mean by "Redefining the Game"

It is only after you have learned the game, played the game, and mastered the game that you'll be in a position to redefine the game. Here's our definition:

> To redefine the game you must **synergize** by creating mutually beneficial connections between people and between organizations to fulfill their collective purpose, and then **reach scale** by amplifying their collaborative actions to have the broadest or deepest possible impact in a way that levels the playing field for everyone.

That's saying a lot, so we're going to break it down piece by piece in Strategy 9: Synergize and Reach Scale. But for now, there are three things that are important for you to know:

1. *Synergy and scale are the "inputs" or the mechanisms for redefining the game.* Our brand of synergy is achieved by creating mutually beneficial connections between people and between organizations. It is bridging the *network gaps* that exist between people and between organizations (discussed in Strategy 4) to foster *collaborative action* (Strategy 6), and doing so in a way that benefits all parties involved. That means connecting people to other people and connecting organizations to other organizations that can benefit from working together and might not otherwise be connected. Reaching *scale* means going from "each one, reach one" to "each one, reach *one hundred*," or "each one, reach *one thousand*," or "each one, reach *one million*." Scale is like a multiplier: It is an effect that translates collaborative action into *amplified action*.

2. *Making an impact that levels the playing field is the "output" or the outcome from redefining the game.* Impact speaks back to how you define success. It also speaks to your bottom line: financial or social or both (the double bottom line). If you are a statewide elected official, an outcome could mean reductions in crime. If you are the executive director of a national youth program, it could mean increased graduation rates. If you are the founder and CEO of an international public relations and event planning firm, it could mean increased revenues and profits.

3. *Synergy and scale can lead to a "broad" or "deep" impact that redefines the game.* In fact, the appropriate combination of synergy and scale can lead to "the broadest possible impact"—one that is wide-ranging and far-reaching—or "the deepest possible impact"—one that is targeted and penetrating. A broad impact could be felt regionally, nationally, or globally, while a deep impact could be focused on a specific neighborhood, community, or issue (e.g., poverty elimination or environmental justice). Both impacts are representative of what it means to redefine the game.

The transition from mastering the game to redefining the game is the final inflection point on your journey because, like a lever, you are able to multiply your efforts by working with others who share a common agenda. The entrepreneurial mindset cycle and the two-sided approach, with both intrapreneurs and entrepreneurs mastering the game and working together, help fuel the mutually beneficial connections that lead to synergy, scale, and, ultimately, redefining the game, as shown in Figure IV–1.

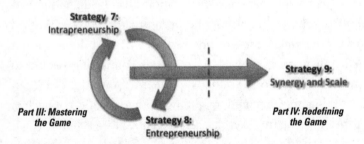

Figure IV–1. From mastering the game to redefining it: intrapreneurship and entrepreneurship to synergy and scale.

Changing the Game vs. Redefining the Game

To be a game-changer is to be a change agent. However, those who redefine the game do not just facilitate change, they change the game itself. Your reach is broader or deeper when you are redefining the game. Redefining the game is about facilitating positive, lasting, widespread change.

"Playing the game" means accepting the rules of the game as they are stated. "Changing the game" means modifying the rules for the better. "Redefining the game" means restructuring the systems that once defined the rules to ultimately bring an end to the game itself. Playing the game and changing the game assume you are still working within constraints defined by other people. Redefining the game means that you are working outside of those constraints. You are redefining the problem, the solution, or how the solution meets the problem. In doing so, you are redirecting how resources flow inside and between companies, communities, government agencies, and organizations locally and around the globe. Because you are now competing on a grand stage, world-class excellence is required.

The fourth dimension of Black Faces in White Places is *opportunity*. This dimension leads us to ask questions such as, "Do I have equal opportunity to fulfill my destiny?" or "As an African American, will I ultimately encounter barriers that others may not necessarily face?" or "Will my life's destiny be denied or encumbered because of my color, or will it be driven and empowered by my color?" The final piece of the puzzle for redefining the game is to facilitate lasting change that positively affects the lives of others and levels the playing field, giving future generations of African Americans and all Americans an equal opportunity to fulfill their destiny.

By synergizing and reaching scale—we can implement solutions to the problems facing African Americans and our country.

....

Part IV: Redefining the Game is rooted in two Kwanzaa principles: **Ujima** *(Collective Work and Responsibility), which means "to build and maintain our community together and make our brothers' and sisters' problems our problems and to solve them together" (Strategy 9), and* **Kuumba** *(Creativity), or "to do always as much as we can, in the way we can to leave our community more beautiful and beneficial than we inherited it" (Strategy 10).*

....

Synergize and Reach Scale

Synergy is the highest activity of life; it creates new untapped alternatives; it values and exploits the mental, emotional, and psychological differences between people.
—Stephen Covey, *The 7 Habits of Highly Effective People*

Creating Synergy

WHEN PEOPLE and organizations work together harmoniously, they can achieve incredible outcomes. This is synergy. Synergy can galvanize change.

We first learned about the concept of synergy when we both read Stephen R. Covey's *The 7 Habits of Highly Effective People*. "To Synergize" is Covey's final habit leading from dependence to independence to interdependence. He writes:

> *Synergy is everywhere in nature. If you plant two plants close together, the roots will comingle and improve the quality of the soil so that both plants will grow better together than if they were separated. If you put two pieces of wood together, they will hold much more than the total of the weight held by each separately. The whole is greater than the sum of its parts. One plus one equals three or more.... The very way a man and woman bring a child into the world is synergistic.*

Figure 9–1. The path to greatness (Strategy 9) .

Clearly, synergy can happen naturally. As we discussed in Strategy 4, when two people just seem to "click" and work together so well it is almost effortless, or when two organizations have such complimentary values, needs, and objectives that they just seem to "fit" together perfectly, synergy has taken place. Synergy manifests the natural harmony that can exist between people and between organizations.

Synergy is also a product of creativity. It is more art than science. Unleashing the power of synergy suspends logic about the possibilities of what can be accomplished. Synergy moves us beyond our comfort zone into the growth zone of Strategy 2. It means fully embracing the characteristics of the entrepreneurial mindset from Strategies 7 and 8. It removes any limitations of our individual and collective imagination.

According to Covey, "The essence of synergy is to value differences—to respect them, to build on strengths, to compensate for our weakness." Strategy 1 explores how our identity helps to define who we are in relationship to society. Understanding and embracing our identity enables us to appreciate what makes us distinct. Strategies 2, 4, and 5 teach us the value of diverse exposure, meaningful relationships with different people, and the wisdom we can seek from others. Strategy 3 encourages us to develop our strengths and turn our weaknesses into assets. Strategy 6 stresses the importance of team cohesion and team diversity.

Synergy brings together all of these strategies and directs us to truly value differences and leverage diversity. Valuing diversity means forming partnerships that cross multiple lines of difference, including ethnicity, gender, geography, and nationality, and fostering an environment that honors and celebrates differences. Leveraging diversity means tapping into each person's and each organization's strengths, perspectives, and assets, to bring out the very best in every stakeholder represented at the table. It requires open and honest communication and meaningful dialogue to understand the varying perspectives of those we endeavor to work with.

Cooperation and collaboration are among the final underpinnings of synergy. Strategy 6 impresses the need to look beyond our individual agendas toward a more collective agenda, and the need to combine an identity-driven agenda with an issue-driven agenda. Both of these points speak to the need for genuine cooperation and true collaborations—relationships and partnerships that are mutually respectful and mutually beneficial, but are also guided by a shared vision for what greater good can be served by working together versus working apart.

"The challenge is to apply the principles of creative cooperation, which we learn from nature, in our social interactions," according to Covey. In the context of redefining the game, we interpret Covey's statement as having two meanings. First, we must apply the principles of synergy and collaborative action—creativity, communication, cooperation, collaboration, diversity, and differences—to the way we work together as people and as organizations to solve the problems being faced by our communities. Second, while synergy *can* occur naturally, that doesn't mean it necessarily *does* occur naturally. We must sometimes be painstakingly deliberate in our efforts to foster synergy.

These deliberate efforts can take the form of:

- Brainstorming sessions to encourage creativity

- ▸ Training classes to foster effective communication

- ▸ Leadership retreats to promote cooperation

- ▸ Strategic partnerships, joint ventures, mergers and acquisitions to govern collaboration

- ▸ Facilitated dialogues to help people value differences and leverage diversity

Ultimately, using these kinds of deliberate efforts, or processes, can lead to effective, collaborative action.

When synergy occurs, it can translate into very powerful results. Sweeping legislation can get passed. Businesses can voluntarily merge or be acquired to create enterprises that can more effectively compete. Educational systems and social service systems can undergo much-needed reform. Community-based programs can be implemented on a widespread basis to families.

There is tremendous fragmentation and unnecessary competition among people and organizations seeking to facilitate change. There are people working individually. There are educational and faith-based organizations working independently. There are businesses pursuing the same goals working in silos. Such isolated actions are either unproductive or counterproductive. Synergy is the antidote.

Reaching Scale and Expanding Scope

At this point in the book, you should know that we are advocates of making significant and meaningful impact in whatever we are doing. In Strategy 6, we are explicit about how important creating and establishing organizations is to making an impact. From here on out, we take a distinctly organizational view toward increasing social and economic impact.

To make a difference in business, education, or in communities, we know that figuring out ways to increase wealth, social change, or both are critical to achieve the broadest or deepest impact. We call this process "reaching scale and expanding scope," and they are key concepts (defined below) for building wealth and addressing the social issues in the African-American community.

When we talk about making a broad or deep impact, we mean making an impact that is about *scale, scope,* and *time.*

SCALE

People often say, "If I can touch the life of at least one person, my efforts will not have been in vain." And we completely agree. But what if those same efforts could reach hundreds, or thousands, or millions of people? That is the underlying thinking for *reaching scale.* It is not necessarily about working harder; it is about working smarter, especially with things that you know work.

For businesses, this means starting small, learning all you can from opening the first office or first store, and then adding multiple stores or offices in different places. It also means creating products or conducting your service on a larger scale so that you can reduce your unit cost and utilize the new efficiencies to the benefit of the business. This is known as *economies of scale,* and many large corporations use this strategy in their operations.

For social-change makers, reaching scale has an additional meaning. Reaching scale also means taking a proven model for change (e.g., strategies, tactics, programs, policies, and approaches) to other locations that could benefit from the effective solution you have come up with. Reaching scale is about moving from "each one, reach one" to "each one, reach one hundred" (or one thousand or one million).

If something works, it should be scaled up. For social-change makers, this is not a cookie-cutter process. Often, these models for change have to be adapted to the local circumstances. There are many stories of organizations with proven business models in a community trying to move that model to another place and failing. To reach scale, you have to really think about what it is about your model that is exportable to other places. It is more about extracting "best practices" or "promising practices" than replication.

SCOPE

A parallel way of thinking about a broad or deep impact is the idea of expanding scope. When a business provides more services to the same customers that is an expansion of scope. When social entrepreneurs expand the service to a local community instead of moving to a different community, this is an example of expanding the scope of impact. To expand scope is to move from offering A, to offering A + B, to offering A + B + C.

Expanding scope means that you desire to change people's lives in a broader, wider-reaching way or a deeper, targeted way. This approach has its advantages. Each time you interact with a customer, client, or community you learn about their needs. That knowledge can be translated into providing better products or services. Rather than trying to find, or relying upon, other customers or communities to achieve additional goals, the expanding scope approach seeks to work with the same people in ways that deliver a wider range of value. This should involve using some of the same resources to provide service A that you are using to provide service B. In doing so, there are *economies of scope* to be gained that will benefit your business or organization. It may also lead to further diversification of your revenue.

To gain the broadest impact, reaching scale and expanding scope must be completed over a long *period of time.* For this strategy to be successful, institutions must be built that can endeavor to carry out the work of scale and scope in perpetuity.

....

Reaching scale represents more than strength in smaller numbers or larger numbers; it represents strength in the largest numbers.

....

Profiles of Synergy, Scale, and Scope

▸ *The Sustainable South Bronx.* After college, Majora Carter didn't want to return to her South Bronx neighborhood of New York City, but she didn't believe she had much of a choice. Around this time she learned that pollution from trucks, debris, and other environmental contaminants was making the community sick. In response to these alarming trends, she founded the Sustainable South Bronx (SSBX), a community organization dedicated to environmental justice solutions through innovative, economically sustainable projects that are informed by community needs.

Under Carter's leadership, SSBX significantly expanded the scope of its work and deepened its impact in the neighborhood by influencing and changing attitudes of the community about environmental issues, getting changes incorporated into the city's plans, and instituting green-collar job initiatives (before that was fashionable). SSBX has been instrumental in connecting community voices with private philanthropy, corporations, government, and industry. Carter, who has since moved on to form the Majora Carter Group, LLC, told us in an interview, "So what I really wanted to do was not only start an organization to advocate against these kinds of really egregious and discriminatory policies that were being impacted against poor communities and poor communities of color, but I also wanted to respond to communities when they talked about what their dreams were for a healthy, sustainable community."

▸ *World Wide Technology.* David Steward found tremendous synergy with a friend, James Kavanaugh, when he brought him in as a partner in World Wide Technology. In fact, Steward gave Kavanaugh a 15 percent stake in the company on just a handshake. WWT is primarily a reseller of information technology products from large equipment manufacturers. Over the years they have reached scale and expanded scope by establishing more than twenty-five strategic partnerships, with companies like Cisco Systems, Dell Computer, HP, Sun Microsystems, Novell, Lexmark, Symantec, VMware, and Sony Electronics, to resell, install, and service their computers, servers, routers, switches, storage devices, and software. The company's relationship with networking gear maker Cisco represents about one-third of its $2.6 billion in annual revenue. "My first job and my biggest job that I have here today, is to serve the people of this organization and serve them well. If I serve them well, guess what? There's going to be a culture of us serving one another, and that spreads out to the relationships of the partners we work with," Steward said. "They know that we're going to put their best interests—and serve them—first, and so they'll want us involved in their deals." Today, WWT sits atop the *Black Enterprise* B.E. 100s list as the largest Black-owned business in the world and continues to have a broad economic impact.

▸ *Amnesty International.* When Benjamin Jealous joined Amnesty International in 2003 as director of the Human Rights Program to take on the issue of racial profiling, he faced a stack of challenges. Because the terrorists who attacked the World Trade Center and the Pentagon on September 11, 2001, were from the Middle East, racial profiling was spreading beyond the larger minority communities in the United States to affect

Arabs, Muslims, Persians, and others. The breadth of the problem required that he use different tactics. Fortunately Jealous, who had studied political science at Columbia University and attended internationally diverse Oxford University as a Rhodes Scholar, was comfortable working in such a context.

"We had to figure out how to talk in a way that was capable of convincing the powers that be that what we were suggesting also just made good sense toward making the country safer," said Jealous, who in 2008 was named president and CEO of the NAACP. "When you're a Black American, both in the American context and in the British context, everybody's expecting you to come in talking solely about your group and only be capable of being an expert on the impact on Black people. So the fact that I was willing to listen, engage, and pay attention to the problem as it related to Muslims, as it related to Arabs, as it related to Persians, as it related to Native Americans, as it related to Southeast Asians . . . that empowered me to be successful in what could have been a very hostile context."

Jealous built a synergistic coalition of organizations representing different minority groups, ethnicities, and religions, including Blacks, Hispanics, Arabs, Muslims, Native Americans, and Asians, that reached scale to include more than 100 groups nationwide. After holding six national public hearings and doing more than a year of research, Amnesty released its report, "Threat and Humiliation: Racial Profiling, National Security, and Human Rights in the United States." Following the report, also in 2004, the U.S. House of Representatives proposed the End Racial Profiling Act (ERPA). This bill was introduced in Congress, but hasn't passed. Regardless, Amnesty's work has already had a broad impact by significantly raising awareness of the issue.

▸ *Harpo Productions.* In 1984, before Oprah Winfrey was a household name, she tapped Jeff Jacobs, an entertainment lawyer, to renegotiate her contract with AM Chicago, a local morning program that she was hired to host about a year earlier. Jacobs convinced her to start her own company, and in 1986 they created Harpo Productions Inc. He then brokered a deal that gave Oprah the right to syndicate *The Oprah Winfrey Show,* bringing it to a national audience and creating a multimillion-dollar enterprise that has reached scale and spawned movies, a magazine, other popular daytime shows, radio programs, and the Oprah Winfrey Network, which collectively represent a significant and broad economic impact. In commenting on her synergy with Jacobs, Oprah told *Fortune* magazine in 2002 that he is "a piranha—and that's a good thing for me to have." Like the relationship between David Steward and James Kavanaugh at World Wide Technology, Oprah showed that she valued Jacobs' contribution to her success—first giving him a 5 percent stake in Harpo Productions and then later boosting his stake to 10 percent.

▸ *Harlem Children's Zone.* For decades many of the same problems that Majora Carter witnessed growing up in the South Bronx plagued neighboring Harlem, where Geoffrey Canada came to work at the Rheedlen Centers for Children and Families. Canada, who is also from the South Bronx, studied education at Harvard. He worked at Rheedlen in the late 1990s, but grew frustrated that its afterschool programs for promoting antiviolence and truancy prevention weren't doing enough to decrease the low graduation rates, criminal activity, and youth unemployment that afflicted the community. So Canada decided to design a program to fill the gaps and transformed Rheedlen into what is known today as the Harlem Children's Zone (HCZ).

The HCZ team put together a program that connects education, health, and youth development issues and that appreciates the complexity of the urban environment. Its comprehensive "cradle to college" philosophy includes programming for parents and babies, preschoolers, and older students. "We had to create a pipeline that started at birth, that ensured our children came into the world healthy and happy, and [that] stayed with these children through every developmental stage of their life until they graduated, and then into college, and then we would stay with this group of children through college," Canada said.

HCZ's strategy for scaling up its efforts was written in the organization's ten-year business plan. In 1997, the agency began a network of programs for a twenty-four-block area—the Harlem Children's Zone Project. In that same year it spread to an almost 100-block area serving 7,400 children and more than 4,100 adults. In 2009, President Obama announced that HCZ would be used as the model for a national program to create programs in twenty "Promise Neighborhoods" and allocated $10 million toward the planning of the initiative through the U.S. Department of Education, along with an appropriation of up to $65 million for "Choice Neighborhoods," a related effort through the U.S. Department of Housing and Urban Development. This could lead to an expansion of HCZ's approach to communities throughout the United States. In this regard, Geoffrey Canada's efforts could result in both a deep impact (across Harlem) and a broad impact (across the country) at the same time.

It is clear from these profiles, and others found throughout this book, that redefining the game can happen at multiple levels. Majora Carter, Geoffrey Canada, and Angela Glover Blackwell (mentioned in the previous chapter) redefined the game at the *community* level, helping organize residents in New York. In earlier chapters we discussed Gabriella Morris at Prudential and Don Thompson at McDonald's, who are working at the *organizational* level to redefine how corporate resources can have an impact beyond the company. David Steward, who sits at the helm of a multibillion-dollar business enterprise, and multibillionaire Oprah Winfrey have redefined the fields of information technology and media, respectively, at the *industry* level. In fact, Oprah's influence extends throughout the globe. Benjamin Jealous, in his role at Amnesty International and now as president of the NAACP, and President Barack Obama, in his position as U.S. Senator and now President of the United States of America, are working at the *societal* level to redefine how our country addresses issues related to health care, education, and economic development. Without all of their efforts to redefine the game in some manner, social change would not have been possible.

The Critical Importance of Synergy and Scale to African Americans

Why are synergy and scale of such critical importance to the African-American community? It is simple. We have many great programs and initiatives, but some are not coordinated with one another and others are not large enough to make a *lasting* impact. How do we deal with this as a community? We have to systematically increase the scale and the scope of our efforts. This is perhaps best understood from the historical perspective that informs our thinking.

ADDRESSING SOCIETAL ISSUES: A HISTORICAL PERSPECTIVE

When some people try to compare the African-American experience to the experience of immigrant groups, we worry that they are not comparing apples to apples.

There are two major ways that the experiences differ. First, African Americans were brought here as slaves. And even when slavery was over, our skin color meant we were easily identifiable for various discriminatory practices, namely, Jim Crow laws. This kind of discrimination was prevalent and well documented by historians.

But the second and perhaps more significant way in which the immigrant experience is different from the African-American experience is numerical. At the end of the Civil War, the population of people of African descent in America was more than 4.5 million. Approximately 10 percent of this population (450,000) had their freedom before the Emancipation Proclamation. Many among that 10 percent were educated and had businesses, families, and influence.

In comparison, during the 1890s and early part of the twentieth century, several immigrant groups—Germans, Italians, Russian, and Polish immigrants—came to America in large numbers. But their numbers were relatively small in comparison to the African-American population. In 1880, less than 2 million German immigrants and 1.85 million Irish immigrants entered America. The African-American population in 1880 was already more than 6.5 million. Why is that important? Because when you think about the economic development of ethnic groups, you have to consider what access that ethnic group has to the resources that enable social mobility. By "social mobility" we mean having the ability to change your family's social status over time. In this context, we are referring to moving out of poverty into the middle class.

For example, education is an important vehicle for social mobility because it opens up opportunities for better jobs and economic standing. But if you don't have access to it because of poverty, poor schools, or discrimination, social mobility is very difficult. So, if you want to impact an entire community, you have to figure out what the key mechanisms of social mobility are and how your community is going to gain or create access to them.

The Jewish community of the late 1800s and early 1900s faced significant discrimination and harassment, and many of the new immigrants were impoverished. Their strategy was for the well-established members of the Jewish community to create a parallel set of institutions that would assist new Jewish immigrants and their children. Stanley Lieberson, in a book entitled *A Piece of the Pie: Blacks & White Immigrants Since 1880* (University of California Press, 1980), documents that within a few generations, the vast majority of Jewish immigrant families were doing well. Italian, German, and Polish immigrants followed this same pattern. Some of these organizations, church auxiliaries, and social clubs (among them, Knights of Columbus and the Polish American Club) remain to this day.

But this is where the numbers are very important. As noted previously, in 1865, there were 4.5 million Africans in America, 4 million of which were former slaves and living in poverty. They had varying levels of skills and talents (human capital). The social question of that day was: How do you address the social issues and economic development of these 4 million people representing almost 90 percent of the African-American community? We know that some fraction of these former slaves went on to take full advantage of the opportunities of being free, but most were illiterate and had limited opportunities to succeed beyond the kind of work they did as slaves.

One way to look at the challenges of the African-American community during this period is that no other ethnic group had to train, educate, and absorb as many people as the African-American community post-slavery. Within twenty years of the end of the Civil War, new laws were being established to further constrain opportunities for social mobility. From 1877 until 1965, there were laws on the books of many states that prohibited the access of African Americans to the most important vehicles of social mobility—education, homeownership, political power, and capital.

During this period, W.E.B. DuBois and others promoted the idea of "The Talented Tenth," referring to the 10 percent of the African-American population that would organize to help the other 90 percent. His idea that only the college educated will be the leaders of social change has proved not to be accurate. It would have taken more than 10 percent to put together the kinds of institutions needed to help the rest of the African-American community. By 1920, there were 10 million African Americans and the issues in the community were becoming more pronounced.

We argue that a significant part of the challenge of transforming the African-American community is fundamentally a challenge of proportions. If the number of people doing "well" in our community was equal to the number of people "not doing well," it would simply be a matter of each person taking responsibility for one other person and mentoring that person toward good citizenship, education, and wealth building. But, in actuality, the combined number of Black people in poverty or near poverty, who attend poorly performing schools, who live in crumbling neighborhoods, and whose movements are monitored by the state (in jail or probation or paroled) is larger than the number in college, in entrepreneurship, in homeownership, or without a criminal record. We are not here to debate all of the reasons for this (there are many), but the situation is what it is.

To redefine the game and reshape America, we must create systems that address our social and economic concerns in scalable ways. We must organize ourselves. We must be willing to take on the fight. Since the proportion of people who want to and can do this difficult work is small, we have to work smarter to get to more people and affect more lives. And that means understanding the concepts of synergy and scale, and revisiting the idea of institution building.

INSTITUTION BUILDING REVISITED

As we discussed in Strategy 8, *institutions are organizations that stand the test of time.* They will exist long after we have left this world and, in doing so, will continue to uphold their governing ideas of mission, vision, and values over time. Institutions can make sure that the social change you are advocating takes place for years to come.

In essence, Strategy 7 challenged today's intrapreneurs to urge their institutions to be more responsive to the needs of African Americans. Why? Because by changing their institutions for the better, the changes they've made become lasting changes. But remember that our definition of institution doesn't just apply to businesses. It equally applies to community, educational, philanthropic, and faith-based organizations, too. Strategy 8 essentially challenged African-American entrepreneurs to work together strategically to build institutions for a profit and for a purpose. Why? Because by creating institutions, the positive effort of the institution leads to *lasting* change. Scale and scope are the mechanisms that empower people to build institutions in ways that create *lasting* change.

In fact, effecting lasting change and leaving a positive legacy are the essence of our final chapter: Strategy 10: Give Back Generously.

Give Back Generously

For those to whom much is given, much is expected. —Luke 12:48

EACH AND EVERY one of us represents the continuation of a legacy, or, in fact, a countless number of legacies. Our family members who have passed away have left a treasured and timeless legacy that lives on within us.

The Founding Fathers of the United States left a tremendous and, at times, tumultuous legacy that dates back to the days of Plymouth Rock. Our Black ancestors have left a triumphant and trailblazing legacy that dates back to Ancient Africa. One cannot help but acknowledge that we are the fruit of the labor of generations and generations that came before us and left their legacy.

African Americans can be proud that the descendants of today are billionaires, Fortune 500 executives, military leaders, politicians, scientists, historians, clergy, authors, and educators. And now we can even look to the White House and see a Black person serving as President of the United States.

....
Life is temporary; legacy is eternal.
....

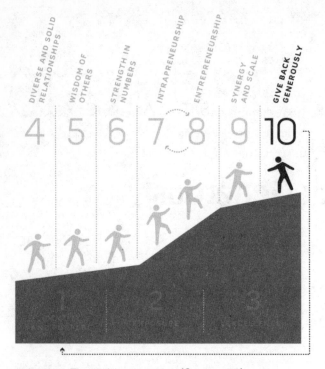

Figure 10–1. The path to greatness (Strategy 10).

Generations of African Americans who came before us made it possible for these dreams to become our reality. We owe it to them to leave a positive legacy that makes it easier for the next generation to reach these milestones and even exceed them.

Leaving a Positive Legacy

People who leave a legacy blaze a trail that others can follow. Throughout this chapter, we will share our favorite maxims about leaving a positive legacy. The first one, which Randal often cites in speeches, is by Albert Pike: "What we have done for ourselves alone dies with us; what we have done for others and the world remains and is immortal." This is the essence of the kind of legacy everyone should strive for: a positive one of helping others. (It is ironic that Pike, an attorney, writer, and military solider, left a legacy of having fought with the Confederate Army and supported slavery.)

We all inevitably leave a legacy, but we must ask ourselves: What kind of legacy am I leaving? What am I passing on to the next generation? What trails am I blazing for others to follow?

We encourage you to seriously consider your answers to these questions. Strategy 10 is about leaving a positive legacy, defined by a lifetime of service to others. This is the key to reshaping America for generations to come.

There are three ways to leave a positive legacy and make a lasting imprint on society—through your *light*, your *love*, and your *life*.

LIGHT

You leave a legacy of light through your example to others. Much like light radiates from the sun, a legacy of light radiates from your spirit, not your physical being. It can transcend your time on earth. You need not have direct contact with someone for your legacy of light to affect them.

For example, when we say someone has left "a legacy of excellence"—like Michael Jordan in athletics, Oprah Winfrey in media, Michael Jackson in music, and Michelle and Barack Obama in public service—we are referring to their legacy of light. As symbols, they have inspired millions of people through their example.

The light of Madam C. J. Walker's legacy of excellence in entrepreneurship motivated Jeffrey to think about the power of entrepreneurship to transform families, communities, and nations. Randal never met the first African-American billionaire, Reginald Lewis, but he read his book, *Why Should White Guys Have All the Fun?* (John Wiley & Sons, 1995), in a single day. Lewis's light—his legacy of excellence in business—continues to inspire Randal to this day.

Part I of this book spoke directly to the self-determination and excellence that can propel you to leave a positive legacy through your light. As you exude a strong identity and sense of purpose, your light can instill a sense of pride in those struggling to find themselves. By following your passion, cultivating your gifts, and becoming among the best in your field, you can inspire others to do the same. Your persona can emit positive energy and a positive "vibe" that rubs off on people in powerful ways. When you break down doors, overcome obstacles, and maximize your potential, you can influence others to follow in your footsteps.

The famous poem by Marianne Williamson, recited by Nelson Mandela in his inauguration speech in South Africa, perhaps best summarized a legacy of light: "We are all meant to shine, as children do. We were born to make manifest the glory of God that is within us. It is not just in some of us; it is in everyone. And as we let our own light shine, we unconsciously give other people permission to do the same."

LOVE

A legacy of love is one of service to others. A legacy of love is predicated on three basic principles:

- "Do unto others as you would have others do unto you." (Luke 6:31)

- "For those to whom much is given much is expected." (Luke 12:48)

- "I am my brother's keeper [and my sister's keeper]." (Genesis 4:9)

Accordingly, we believe that we are blessed to be a blessing to others. In Part II, we identified *unconditional love* as the highest level of love known to humanity. It is a sacrificial love that is unconditionally committed to the well-being of another. It is a supportive love that leads us to care for people regardless of their circumstances. And it is a selfless love that considers the needs of others ahead of our own. Therefore, a legacy of love is rooted in unconditional love. To embrace this type of love is to understand that we are all part of the same race—the human race—and we believe we are all part of the same family—God's family. And we believe that we have a responsibility to love each other as brothers and sisters. Personally, we strive to follow God's word, which states, "As I have loved you, so you must love one another." (John 13:34)

You can leave a legacy of love in several ways. It can be reflected through your personal interactions with family, friends, and those less fortunate than you. It can manifest itself through the comfort, the care, and the concern you show toward others. It can also be shown through the clubs, the causes, and the charities you support.

The impact of a life can be measured by people; the impact of a legacy can be measured by generations.

Timeless examples of a legacy of love can be found in the nonviolent movement of Indian spiritual and political leader, Mahatma Gandhi, which spawned India's independence; the unwavering commitment of the abolitionist and humanitarian, Harriet Tubman, which led to the formation of the Underground Railroad and the subsequent freedom of many slaves; the nonviolent protests led by the religious leader, Rev. Dr. Martin Luther King Jr., which changed the landscape of racial injustice in America; the activist efforts against apartheid of the former leader of the African National Congress, Nelson Mandela, which completely transformed the balance of power in South Africa. These men and women sacrificed themselves on behalf of others, many of whom they would never know.

A legacy of love is best summarized through the words of Marian Wright Edelman: "Service is the rent you pay for being."

LIFE

The impact you make in society is the legacy of your life's work. When you make a lasting difference in any context—a company, an organization, an industry, a community, a nation, or the entire globe—you leave the legacy of your life's work. It is the impact resulting from your own initiative. The central components of Parts III and IV—intrapreneurship, entrepreneurship, synergy, and scale—are the critical strategies for leaving this kind of legacy.

Shine light, show love, share life.

The contributions you've made to society become a part of your life's legacy. In this context, the possibilities are truly endless: creating a socially responsible product, discovering a life-saving treatment, authoring an empowering book, discovering a scientific breakthrough, or implementing a community service project, are just a few examples.

You may experience a tragedy in your life, such as losing a loved one to a disease or accident. As a result, you may dedicate your life thereafter to raising awareness of the disease or helping to prevent similar accidents from happening in the future. Your legacy may include legislation that gets passed or lives that have been saved through your efforts. In doing so, your tribute to the lost becomes your contribution to the living.

Creating an institution or transforming an institution can also be a powerful by-product of your life's legacy. The power lies in the fact that institutions can continue to carry out the work of their founders and members long after those individuals have moved on.

For example, consider the ongoing impact on the restaurant and hospitality industries resulting from Don Thompson's executive leadership at McDonald's; or the current and future impact on human lives made possible by Dr. Treena Arinzeh's trailblazing stem cell research at the New Jersey Institute of Technology; or the impact in Newark, New Jersey, and American politics resulting from Cory Booker's public service as mayor; or the impact in Chicago and the larger faith-based community that Rev. Otis Moss III has brought to fruition since taking the helm at Trinity United Church of Christ. We see the ongoing impact of Gabriella Morris's efforts at Prudential to challenge the corporation to continuously improve its philanthropic efforts; or the impact of Lisa Price's efforts to establish Carol's Daughter and transform the beauty company into an engine for wealth building, job creation, and economic opportunity for others. Whenever these individuals inevitably decide to move on to pursue new or different challenges, their legacies will continue to have life through the work of their respective institutions and the people they have inspired.

It is a waste of your precious time on earth to do everything you do—personally and professionally—and not leave something behind that makes the world a better place.

Our legacy does not always have to include lofty accomplishments. It could be as simple as creating an emergency fund at your church for low-income families or as elaborate as implementing a corporate-sponsored, government-supported matched savings program that helps low-income residents to create wealth across the globe.

From the moment you begin making a difference, your life's legacy—your impact on society—begins to take on a life of its own. And as Figure 10–2 shows, when you touch the life of one person, it touches the life of another person. It creates a ripple effect that expands across generations and time for all eternity. Winston Churchill best summarized the importance of

Figure 10–2. The ripple effect of a life's legacy.

leaving a legacy of your life's work when he said: "We make a living by what we do, we make a life by what we give."

America's Shape and Reshaping America

O, yes,
I say it plain,
America never was America to me,
And yet I swear this oath—
America will be!
            —Langston Hughes, "Let America Be America Again"

We are very proud to be Americans. We absolutely love this country. Despite America's imperfect past, it is a country that continues to take incremental strides toward a more perfect future. Like potters, African Americans have helped mold the shape of America and its values for centuries. At times, this has meant challenging America to live up to its ideals despite devastating and inherent contradictions such as slavery. In certain instances, this has meant standing side by side with fellow Americans to defend this country in times of war. And on other occasions, this has meant nonviolent boycotts, protests, sit-ins, and marches to draw attention to injustices such as separate but unequal.

We can be honest about America's past yet proud of America's progress. And because America still has a long way to go to fulfill its promise, we believe African Americans, like all Americans, have a responsibility to reshape America for the better. Reshaping America simply means helping others. It means giving back generously, which is Strategy 10.

....

The genius of our founders is that they designed a system of government that can be changed. And we should take heart, because we've changed this country before. . . . Each of us, in our own lives, will have to accept responsibility—for instilling an ethic of achievement in our children, for adapting to a more competitive economy, for strengthening our communities, and sharing some measure of sacrifice. So let us begin. Let us begin this hard work together. Let us transform this nation.

—President Barack Obama

....

The African-American Tradition of Giving

African Americans have a long-standing tradition of *philanthropy*, or giving back to improve the human quality of life. It is rooted in the African concept of family, which formed the basis for social life and social values in Africa. When Africans were kidnapped, enslaved, and brought to America between the sixteenth and nineteenth centuries as part of the Maafa (Swahili for "holocaust" or "great disaster"), entire families were torn apart. Those relationships were replaced by extended kinship networks that fostered an even stronger spirit of mutual support, cooperation, and reliance on one another. The new familial structures that developed served as a mechanism for survival when society completely ignored or provided grossly inadequate support for the needs of our people.

The Black church emerged as the cornerstone of African-American spiritual, social, cultural, and educational life, as well as philanthropic giving. First established during the eighteenth century, the church was the first Black-owned and -operated institution in America. Beginning in South Carolina in 1773 and Virginia in 1776, a major development for the Black church was when Richard Allen broke away from the European church community to form the African Methodist Episcopal (AME) church. These and other African-American denominational churches would play a central role in the creation of secondary schools and colleges and the provision of care for children, seniors, and the sick.

During the nineteenth century, several mutual aid societies, secret societies, and benevolent societies grew out of the African-American church. The first mutual aid society, the Free African Society, was founded in 1878 in Philadelphia by the African Methodist Episcopal and the African Protestant Episcopal churches. These societies offered social and communal welfare programs, including medical benefits, death benefits, and educational and job training.

A number of prominent African-American Civil Rights organizations, fraternities, and sororities were founded during the early part of the twentieth century, such as Alpha Phi Alpha Fraternity, Inc. (1906), Alpha Kappa Alpha Sorority, Inc. (1908), the National Association for the Advancement of Colored People (1909), the National Urban League (1910), and the National Council for Negro Women (1935), among others. To this day, these organizations continue to incorporate community service as central components of their programs and activities. These and many other organizations, including the Southern Christian Leadership Conference, were also at the forefront of the Civil Rights Movement of the 1960s and 1970s that involved scores of African Americans (along with other groups) in the fight to gain equal rights. It is because of their efforts that we enjoy many of the legal rights in housing, education, and voting that we do today.

In the twenty-first century, giving by African Americans reflects many of the traditions that have been established over the years. Modern African-American giving has distinct underlying philosophies and characteristics, namely:

▸ A broad conceptualization of family and kinship ties that include not only blood relatives but also distant relatives, friends, neighbors, and long-time acquaintances. This is embodied by references to other African Americans—even when they are not related to us—as "brothers," "sisters," "cousins," and the like.

▸ A relative preference for giving directly to individuals as opposed to nonprofit organizations.

‣ A higher value for contributions of time than money. The church is the single greatest beneficiary of African-American monetary donations. More than two-thirds of African-American charitable dollars are contributed to churches.[1]

‣ A deep feeling of obligation to help members of the Black community and others in need or crisis as a result of being helped by others. To the extent that someone is known or perceived to have abandoned this obligation they may be labeled as a "sellout" or an "Uncle Tom."

‣ A sense of responsibility to not leave anyone behind, and that success alone is insufficient without helping others to also be successful. Helping any part of the community is interpreted as helping the entire community.

Today, African-American giving is no longer only about survival or even helping each other; it is about empowerment and collective self-determination. Much like the concepts of *individual* identity and *individual* purpose introduced in Strategy 1, our giving is often rooted in our *collective* identity and guided by a semblance of *collective* purpose. It is through our giving that we are able to solve the problems we deem most important; address the issues that disproportionately affect our people; and advance the causes that uplift our community and our country.

We therefore encourage you to not just give back but to give back *generously*. Why? The case for giving back is based on an appeal to your spirituality, humanity, and sense of responsibility; it is based on the same arguments that were made in Strategy 9 concerning the critical importance of synergy and scale to African Americans.

As Reverend Otis Moss III impressed upon us, "You have an obligation to give back. It's not a choice. I don't believe it's a choice. When you have been blessed by God, the blessing is never for you. The true blessing is for you to pass what has been poured into you for someone else. For if you keep what has been given to you, it ceases to be a blessing...."

There are many challenges in our community. To address them, we must leverage our combined efforts through organizations and businesses to reach as many people as possible. This is vitally important because the need is great. How many Black children have to live in poverty? How many poorly performing schools must our children attend? How many Black men have to be unemployed before we act? How many Black children have to die because of violence in our communities? How many Black families will not be able to achieve the American dream? Our combined efforts to address these social problems should have some framework so that our efforts are not in vain. In this chapter, we talk about how giving back generously is an associated imperative for African Americans to redefine the game and reshape America.

Let's be clear: Giving back generously requires a great deal of sacrifice. It requires that we give up something now, so that others can reap the benefit later. But suppose our enslaved ancestors simply threw in the towel? What if Harriet Tubman felt like she was too tired to organize the Underground Railroad? What if Rosa Parks was not "sick and tired of being sick and tired" and took a seat in the back of the bus? Our community and our country would not be where they are today. So, while we cannot say giving back generously is easy, we can say that it is among the most fulfilling and rewarding of life's endeavors.

Giving back generously has such a powerful effect on your spirit that the giver often benefits as much as the recipient.

"You say giving back, I say empowering yourself," said Newark Mayor Cory Booker in an interview with us. "I think human beings are lifted, intellectually, spiritually, morally when we are giving of ourselves. And you actually, I believe, expand yourself when you give, when you do for others; you actually are a larger being. So to me it's not really about giving back, it's about being a better person, creating a better country." Booker T. Washington summarized this sentiment when he said, "If you want to lift yourself up, lift up someone else."

The second greatest challenge facing African Americans "is leveraging our might," Earl Graves writes in *How to Succeed in Business Without Being White* (according to Graves, the greatest challenge is racism). He writes, "If we don't leverage our collective economic, political, spiritual, and cultural power, we can never expect to control our own destiny in this country." It is through giving back generously and reshaping America that we move closer to controlling our collective destiny.

The ceiling of what the last generation thought to be possible must become the floor of what the next generation knows is possible.

The Four Foundations of Giving

One of the major challenges you'll face as a successful and busy individual is making decisions about the approach you'll take toward your giving. What is your strategy for giving? "Strategic giving" is a phrase we use to describe *giving in the right way at the right time for the right reason, cause, or issue.*

We believe the four foundations of giving are *time, talent, treasure,* and something we refer to as *touch* (see Figure 10–3). It is our personal responsibility to find ways to give back generously in each of these areas. It's been said that we should all donate 10 percent of our time, talent, and treasure to worthy activities and organizations that make the world a better place. The basic principle here is an ancient one called *tithing*—a concept that both of

Figure 10–3. Foundations of giving.

us wholeheartedly endorse. The idea of tithing has biblical origins. The people of God were required to give 10 percent of their earnings back to God. The priests received the tithe on God's behalf, and their responsibility was to distribute this money, as well as other goods and in many cases livestock and crops, to widows, the fatherless, strangers, and the homeless and destitute, and keep some for the operation of the house of God—the temple or the church. Clearly, this had positive effects throughout the community.

The principle of tithing is important because it sets some parameters around the idea of "giving back generously." It helps us answer the question, How much should we give by offering a target for our time, talent, treasure, or touch? We'll define these aspects of giving in the next sections.

TIME AND TALENT

Giving of your *time* and *talent* means giving of yourself. It includes volunteer service, ministry, coaching sports teams, assisting community organizations, mentoring, and many other activities.

The idea of giving 10 percent of your time and talent is one that has enormous potential. In 2008, *Time* magazine looked at volunteer service. It reported that in 2006, 61 million Americans donated 8.1 million hours of service. That sounds like a lot of service, but how does that stack up to our 10 percent principle?

Imagine if everyone donated 10 percent of their waking hours to service. That would be about twelve hours per week (assuming we all slept eight hours a night). That would mean twelve hours per week mentoring young people, volunteering at the church, visiting the elderly, working at soup kitchens, or other forms of service. If half of the people in the United States did that every week for a year, it would exceed 93 billion hours of service. So obviously, we aren't even close to donating 10 percent of our time in service to others. If half of the population were prepared to donate three hours per week that would be over 23 billion hours, and that is still three times the estimate cited by *Time* for the entire country. If you follow the math, it is obvious that some people are not pulling their weight!

Along the way in this book, we have pointed out many different ways you can give back generously through your time and talent, such as volunteering with community organizations (Strategy 6), using your expertise for the greater good, or mentoring younger people (Strategy 5). When you use your talent, you use your time in a particular way that is related to something you do well. The area where you have built up excellence (Strategy 3) can be used to help others also. There are undoubtedly many needs in your community or region that donating your time or your talent can help to address.

What does all of this mean? There are a lot of ways to spend your time but, honestly, we all waste a lot of time doing activities that aren't important, urgent, meaningful, or impactful. Volunteer service—the donation of our time—has meaning and makes an impact.

Ask yourself: When is the last time I really evaluated how I spend my time? We recommend evaluating whether your activities are in alignment with your personal vision for your life. Spending time in service to others is an important aspect of life itself. Being explicit about it helps to highlight its importance in our lives.

For activist Kevin Powell, giving back generously stretches through both his work and personal life. "I'm a full-time activist. This is what I do," Powell said in an interview with us. "This is my life. This is what I'm going to be doing for the rest of my life, and so there's not a day that goes by that I'm not helping folks around affordable housing, or around someone's son coming home from jail or trying to keep them from going to jail. You know I make my living doing college lectures and corporate lectures, but when I go into the schools, prisons, foster care, [and] religious institutions here in New York, all of that is for free. That is my way of giving back."

The same goes for biomedical engineer Dr. Treena Arinzeh. In her private life she does community service with Jack and Jill of America, a service organization focused on creating future leaders. Her work also gives her an opportunity to give back.

"A lot of my community service is embedded in what I do professionally, again at the university," Dr. Arinzeh said to us during an interview. "We have high school students come in the summer and we do mentoring. These are underrepresented minority students from Newark or the surrounding area. We generally take about two students a summer and try to get them motivated to pursue engineering undergraduate degrees."

Volunteering your talent will also give you a chance to use your expertise in a different context. The best situation is to find alignment between your gifts and abilities and the existing need. In this sense, finding alignment is finding the greatest leverage of time. It is also how we personally use our gifts to benefit others. For example, if you are a tax expert, it would be great if you could volunteer to assist low-income families with their taxes. Since you have skills in this arena, you can do the work faster and more efficiently than most other volunteers. You might even consider training other people how to assist low-income families with their taxes;

in doing so, you are further leveraging your expertise to help others. Other examples of giving your talent could be building a website for a nonprofit organization, working a political campaign, or providing repairs (e.g., computer repair or home repair) to people who need assistance. If you are a medical professional, you might consider organizing free health clinics for a community in need.

Giving your time and talent to organizations, individuals, communities, and institutions takes the attention off of yourself (which is our natural tendency) and forces us to think about the needs of others. In doing so, we make contributions back to society and learn about ourselves along the way.

TREASURE

Another way to give back generously is to donate your *treasure*—money, goods, and other resources—to worthy causes. In 1997, Oprah created Oprah's Angel Network, a campaign encouraging people to help others in need, which has already raised $12 million from viewer donations, sponsors, and celebrity contributions. The funds are used to grant scholarships and to build homes and schools in developing countries. As a result of Oprah's contributions to television, education, film, and music, and her efforts to raise social awareness, in 1998 she was named one of the 100 most influential people of the twentieth century by *Time* magazine.

In the United States, we have a long established tradition of giving treasure. Here are some statistics from the National Philanthropic Trust:

▸ 89 percent of households give monetary contributions.

▸ In 2007, American giving reached a record high of $314 billion.

▸ In 2008, during severe recession, Americans still gave $308 billion.

That is a lot of treasure that is being donated to charities, foundations, religious institutions, and other nonprofit organizations. And many non-profit organizations rely upon these types of individual donations.

Why do people give? Many do it because they believe in the purpose of the organizations. Some do it to lower their tax burden. As we discussed earlier in this chapter, the African-American community is generous in giving to churches—often an extension of the tithing principle.

There are many reasons people give their treasure. The very existence of nonprofit (or nongovernmental) organizations in the United States is a testament to the idea that giving is important for communities and for our nation. Charitable organizations can operate with tax-exempt status that allows them to operate without paying corporate taxes. It also allows charitable donations made to nonprofits to be itemized and deducted from an individual's tax burden each year. Therefore, the tax system encourages—in fact, incentivizes—all of us to give back generously.

Touch the life of one person and it touches the life of another.

TOUCH

There is a Liberty Mutual Insurance Company commercial that starts by showing a person doing good deeds. That good deed is observed by another person who proceeds to do a good deed of their own. The commercial shows five or six people following this pattern. The last person does a good deed for the very first person we saw in the commercial.

Giving through *touch* is a bit like the scenario played out in the commercial—you influence the lives of other people in a positive way even though you may never know what the ramifications are. Touching the everyday lives of others is an important aspect of living because, just as Aesop said, "No act of kindness, no matter how small, is ever wasted." When you show appreciation to people who don't normally receive that kind of acknowledgment, or when you do something for someone anonymously, or when you give an encouraging word to someone who needs it, or even when you offer someone a welcoming smile, you are practicing giving back through touch.

Developing a habit of giving through touch can make a big difference. These random acts of kindness generate goodwill that keeps on giving. Touch is a special way of giving time, talent, or treasure.

"Pay it forward." This expression means that if someone has done a good deed for you, you repay it by doing a good deed for someone else. In this regard, Strategy 10 could also be called "Pay it forward generously" instead of "Give back generously."

Strategy 10 to Strategy 1: Identity and Purpose Revisited

Perhaps not surprisingly, Strategy 10 brings us back to where we started: Strategy 1. Any final discussion about giving back generously and leaving a positive legacy is directly connected to our opening discussion in this book about establishing a strong identity and purpose. According to Paula P. Brownlee, former President of the American Association of Colleges & Universities, "To do good things in the world, first you must know who you are and what gives meaning to your life." Moreover, *your strategy for giving should honor your identity and fulfill your purpose.*

Strategy 1 talked about identity negotiation as the reconciliation of how you define yourself in relation to society. If you identify as an African American and an American, then you not only subscribe to the values of these groups, you also shape the values of these groups. Much like African-American history shapes American history, African-American culture shapes American culture. Mahatma Gandhi captured the connection between identity and philanthropy when he said, "The best way to find yourself is to lose yourself in the service of others." Emmett D. Carson, PhD, has challenged African Americans to examine the relationship between our identity and our philanthropy. In his chapter, "African American Philanthropy at the Crossroads," which appeared in *The Proceedings of the First National Conference on Black Philanthropy,* he wrote:

> Are we African Americans who share a common culture and values, one of which is a belief in an intertwined destiny that forces us to engage in activities to protect and celebrate our culture, or are we "Americanized Africans" who subscribe to a belief in individualism and, just coincidentally, happen to be of African descent? African-American philanthropy today reflects this growing identity crisis.

Table 10–1 maps how the seven principles of Kwanzaa, the *Nguzo Saba,* have flowed throughout this book. These principles connect us to our origins in the Mother Land while capturing cultural aspects of the African-American experience. We encourage you to reinforce these principles as part of African-American culture, infuse them into the larger American culture, and mold them in ways that maintain their relevance in the

Book Part	Kwanzaa Principle(s)
Part I: Learning the Game	**Nia** (Purpose) **Kujichagulia** (Self-Determination) **Imani** (Faith)
Part II: Playing the Game	**Umoja** (Unity)
Part III: Mastering the Game	**Ujamaa** (Cooperative Economics)
Part IV: Redefining the Game	**Ujima** (Collective Work and Responsibility) **Kuumba** (Creativity)

Table 10–1. Kwanzaa principles reinforcing Parts I through IV.

twenty-first century. Above all, remember that the expression of your identity through the providence of your philanthropy can shape our legacy as African Americans, and as Americans, for generations to come.

As we also stated in Strategy 1, any person serves multiple purposes. Your purpose could be to act as a loving and responsible parent; to uplift and inspire others through music as a composer; and to mentor young people in your immediate neighborhood—all at the same time. But, in each instance, *your purpose is to serve others.* In this context, *your purpose is your ministry.*

Each of the preceding nine strategies implies a way of giving back. When you expose others to new possibilities within themselves (Strategy 2), demonstrate excellence that inspires others or use your God-given gifts to benefit others (Strategy 3), step in to help others with whom you have a relationship (Strategy 4), impart wisdom that is of benefit to others (Strategy 5), work with others to contribute to the efforts of a group or organization (Strategy 6), direct others to be more civically responsible in an intrapreneurial (Strategy 7) or entrepreneurial (Strategy 8) context, or synergize with others to make a social or economic impact that reaches scale (Strategy 9), you may be fulfilling your purpose and pursuing your ministry (Strategy 1), but you are certainly giving back generously (Strategy 10).

Final Quotations and Final Questions on Giving Back

Here are another three of our favorite quotations on giving back:

The purpose of life is a life with a purpose. —Robert Byrne

We are not meant to see through each other, but to see each other through.
—Unknown

Life is God's gift to you; what you do with your life is your gift back to God.
—Unknown

In some ways, all three quotes suggest the same thing: Give back generously and leave a positive legacy. And, in some ways, they also give rise to the same three questions: What impact are you making in society? What kind of example are you setting for others? And, finally, the question identified by the Rev. Dr. Martin Luther Jr. as life's most urgent question: What are you doing for others?

What Does Redefining the Game and Reshaping America Mean to You?

Look back on Strategies 1 through 10 and you will begin to clearly see that redefining the game and reshaping America are not about excellence for the sake of excellence. They are not about relationship building for the sake of relationship building. They are not about climbing the corporate ladder for the sake of climbing the ladder. They're not about creating entrepreneurial wealth for the sake of wealth. And they're not even about giving for the sake of giving. Redefining the game and reshaping America are about all of these things for a much greater reason.

Your efforts to redefine the game and reshape America must be for a purpose. If there is no purpose, there is no point. Consequently, this book concludes by revisiting the same discussion we had at the beginning, about living a purpose-driven life. Your guiding light in determining what redefining the game and reshaping America means to you, and the kind of impact that can and should be made in this world by you, is your purpose. Or, as stated by Rick Warren in *The Purpose-Driven Life*, "If you want your life to have impact, focus it."

What is the underlying reason for doing everything we have suggested that you do throughout this book? Our answer: to fulfull the individual and collective purpose outlined for us; reach our highest potential given the blessings bestowed upon us; and, above all, to help others do the same.

Each of us has a responsibility to make an impact—to chip away at the walls of injustice so that others can more easily climb over those walls in the future. What kind of impact do you envision for yourself? What is your "end game"? The answer could be establishing a charter school, or manufacturing an environmental product that reduces carbon emissions, or creating wealth-building and health care social programs for low-income families. Your answer speaks directly to the core of what redefining the game and reshaping America means to you.

Ultimately, redefining the game and reshaping America means making it easier for the Black Faces in White Places who follow in your footsteps to realize their dreams and pursue their purpose. It means creating a United States of America that is not *post-racial,* but rather, *post-racism.* Above all, it means creating a society such that every organization at every level reflects the diversity of our society and a level playing field for those who compete in the ever-changing game.

Is Success the Standard or Is Greatness the Goal?

Whoever wants to be great must become a servant. —Mark 10:43

WE'VE COVERED A lot of territory in this book. Fortunately, the core of the book—the four parts and ten strategies—can be summarized in five simple concepts, which are summarized in Table 11–1.

> **Visit the website www.redefinethegame.com** *to access additional resources related to this book, learn more about our follow-up projects, and take action by joining the campaign to "redefine the game."*

Our path began in Part I with *self-determination*. Self-determination is a state of being that is achieved when you have accepted who you are and embraced why you were placed on earth (Strategy 1). It is *internally and spiritually centered*; that is, you must look within and look above to embody self-determination and establish a strong identity with a well-defined purpose. When you have reached this state of being and seek to obtain the broadest possible exposure (Strategy 2), you are able to forge ahead into the world with a sense of grounding, direction, and limitless possibilities.

The next major concept—*excellence*—is a personal quality that can be applied to any undertaking. Strategy 3 focused on personal and professional excellence. In this context, the standard for excellence is defined by you and your profession. In other words, excellence is *objective-centered*—it is determined based on objective measures for what it means for you to be the best that you can be and among the very best in your field or industry.

In Part II, our path continued on to *connectedness:* building meaningful relationships in a global society. Strategies 4, 5, and 6 foster connectedness. Connectedness is a quality in relation to others; it is *relationship-centered.* Whether or not you are "connected" is wholly dependent on the quality of your relationships with others.

The next-to-last stop along our path is *success.* We've discussed self-determination, excellence, and connectedness at length throughout this book, but we have not discussed success. We are asked quite often for our definition of success. By contrast, we are asked far less frequently for our definition of the fifth and final stop: *greatness.*

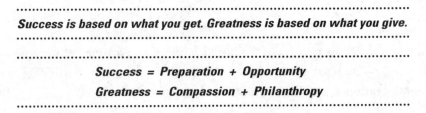

Success is based on what you get. Greatness is based on what you give.

Success = Preparation + Opportunity

Greatness = Compassion + Philanthropy

Success vs. Greatness

As a society, we don't talk about greatness nearly as much as we talk about success. Which raises the question: Is success your standard or is greatness your goal? To begin to answer that question, we must make a distinction between the two. From our vantage point, that distinction is described as follows:

▸ Success reflects what you accomplish for yourself, whereas greatness reflects what you accomplish for others.

▸ Success is making a difference in your life; greatness is making a difference in other lives.

▶ Success is about where you are; greatness is about how far you've traveled.

▶ Success is *self-centered;* greatness is *other-centered* and *spiritually centered.*

Success is finite, it is momentary, and it is discrete. It is a determination that is made at a particular point in time. For example, you can be successful in graduating from college, or successful in getting a job, or successful in launching a business. Greatness, on the other hand, is infinite. It is lasting, and it is limitless.

What makes the great "great"? They lead lives that have *significance* for the people around them and many others. They make a positive impact on the people, processes, organizations, and the systems they operate within and around. Therefore, the bridge between success and greatness is significance. Prominent figures like Oprah Winfrey or David Steward or Michelle and Barack Obama are successful because of their pedigrees, their positions, and their power. But they are not great just because they are successful. They are great because of the lives of significance they lead—the people they are trying to help and the ways in which they use their time, talent, treasure, and touch to impact others.

We see these people as we interact with them in our work and as we travel around the country. They make a difference. They make the world we live in better. And they are great because of it. The great figures among us have and will always maintain that distinction until the end of time.

Stated differently, *success is a destination* (or a series of destinations), whereas *greatness is a journey.* When people think of the markers of success, many times they think of things such as money, power, influence, fame, and fortune. When we think of the markers of greatness, we think of things such as service, compassion, consideration, benevolence, and humanity. In fact, you'll find a roadmap for becoming successful (i.e., reaching the C-suite, launching a business, establishing a nonprofit, etc.) in Strategies 7 and 8, while Strategies 9 and 10 provide a roadmap for becoming great (i.e., having an impact, making a difference, giving back to others, etc.).

	Part I: Learning the Game		Part II: Playing the Game	Part III: Mastering the Game	Part IV: Redefining the Game
	Self- Determination	Excellence	Connectedness	Success	Greatness
How is it defined?	To know who you are and where you are going	To be very good or superior	To build meaningful relationships in a global society	To make a difference in your life	To make a difference in the lives of others
What is it?	A state of being	A quality (in relation to self)	A quality (in relation to others)	A series of destinations	A journey
When is it achieved?	When you have revealed who you are and what you are called to do	When you are among the very best	When you have built quality relationships	When you have done something good for yourself (at a moment)	When you have done something good for others (over your lifetime)
Who sets the standard?	You and God (internal and spiritual standard)	You and your field or industry (objective standard)	People or network (social or relational standard)	Society (societal standard)	Universe and God (universal and spiritual standard)
Where is it centered?	Internally and spiritually centered	Objective-centered	Relationship-centered	Self-centered	Other- and spiritually-centered

Table 11–1. Five key concepts for Black Faces in White Places

We make the distinction between success and greatness because when you understand the difference between them, two things automatically happen. First, you never confuse *who you are* with *what you do*. Engineering and journalism and medicine are things that you do. Jobs, titles, and positions don't define us; and they certainly don't make us better than anyone else. Having more money, a nicer car, or a bigger home than another person doesn't make you better than anyone else, and it certainly does not define who you are.

Speaking personally, first and foremost, we see ourselves as children of God. That is who Randal Pinkett and Jeffrey Robinson are. Perhaps you are a son, a daughter, a brother, a sister, a husband, a wife, a mother, or a father. That is also who you are. You are blessed to be a blessing to others.

It is therefore what you do as an engineer or journalist or medical doctor to help others that further defines who you are.

When you understand the difference between success and greatness, the second thing that happens is that you come to know the answer to the question we raised earlier: Is success your standard, or is greatness your goal? As it relates to our tremendous legacy as African Americans and as Americans, success is *not* our standard, but rather, greatness is our goal! As we stated at the outset, in the introduction, being a "Black Face in a White Place," as the book is titled, is about pursuing *greatness* in ways that leverage your culture and ethnicity as assets and not as liabilities.

The ultimate goal is not to win the game; the ultimate goal is to redefine the game sufficiently to end the game itself. So, until the playing field is completely level, don't hate the player, hate the game!

The great figures among us have been ordinary people who have achieved extraordinary things. Honoring the legacy of the great African-American and American trailblazers who came before us means remembering that just as they walked along their path and did great things, you must walk along your path, knowing that you can also do great things. If you put anyone too high on a pedestal, or if you allow someone else's accomplishments to seem unattainable or unachievable, then not only do you do a disservice to their legacy, but you also diminish your capacity as an ordinary person to do extraordinary things.

William Jennings Bryan once said, "Destiny is no matter of chance. It is a matter of choice." We are all destined for greatness and, therefore, we want everyone to have the choice. The tragedy is when people are simply denied the opportunity because the playing field is uneven. How many Oprahs never had a chance to become Oprah Winfrey? How many David Stewards never had a chance to become David Steward? And how many Michelle and Barack Obamas never had a chance to become, well, Michelle and Barack Obama?

Redefining the game and reshaping America calls upon all of us to strive for greatness. And for those of us blessed with the opportunity to fulfill such a destiny, we must pave the way for others to be able to do the same, such that the ceiling, or upper limits, of what the last generation thought to be possible becomes the floor, the minimal expectation, of what the next generation knows is possible. It is then, and only then, that we not only move beyond the glass ceiling, but we also transcend the ever-changing game.

It is then, and only then, that those of us who've got game can make sure that if there is a young person with incredible game, nobody tries to run game on them. We must be able to ensure that those coming after us will have an equal opportunity to learn the game, play the game, master the game, and win the game, because we redefined the game and reshaped America.

Then, when that young man or woman grows older and somebody says to them, "You got game?" they can look them in the eye and confidently reply, "Don't try to game me. Not only do I have game, but I am a descendant of a people that have had game since the beginning of time. In fact, because of them, I don't even need to play the game anymore."

At that moment, we'll all be able to thank God that the game is over.

N O T E S

INTRODUCTION

1. Gay Bryant wrote an *Adweek* article containing the first documented use of the term *glass ceiling* in 1984. The term became a permanent part of the American lexicon with a subsequent article by Carol Hymowitz and Timothy Schellhardt, which appeared in the *Wall Street Journal* on March 24, 1986.

2. *Us Weekly* magazine, 566, December 18, 2005, p. 87.

STRATEGY 1: ESTABLISH A STRONG IDENTITY AND PURPOSE

1. Excerpted from Riesman, Freedman, Workman, and Cooley, *New Work for the Head, Heart and Hand.*

STRATEGY 3: DEMONSTRATE EXCELLENCE

1. *New York Times,* Sept. 9, 2009. "In Lawmaker's Outburst, a Rare Breach of Protocol," by Carl Hulse, http://www.nytimes.com/2009/09/10/us/politics/10wilson.html?_r=1

2. *New York Times,* Nov. 30, 2009. "In Job Hunt, College Degree Can't Close Racial Gap," by Michael Luo, http://www.nytimes.com/2009/12/01/us/01race.html

3. From *7 Kinds of Smart,* revised and updated edition, by Thomas Armstrong, copyright © 1993, 1999 by Thomas Armstrong. Used by persmission of Plume, an imprint of Penguin Group (USA) Inc.

STRATEGY 6: FIND STRENGTH IN NUMBERS

1. At the time of the April 4, 2007, Imus incident, CBS Radio managed Westwood One, which syndicated *Imus in the Morning* nationwide. A private equity firm, which began investing in the company in 2008, bought the remaining shares of Westwood One in early 2009.

2. Liberal watchdog organization Media Matters for America posted a video and this transcript of the incident on its website.

3. The November 20, 2001, *Newsday* quote was reported by Media Matters (http://media-matters.org/mmtv/200703280001) and also appeared in the *Jet Magazine* article "Fired White Sportscaster Apologizes for Remarks About Venus and Serena Williams; Gets Rehired", July 9, 2001, p. 32.

STRATEGY 7: THINK AND ACT INTRAPRENEURIALLY

1. Finding is from a 2008 study of the 119-school NCAA Football Bowl Subdivision: The Institute for Diversity and Ethics in Sport, "2008 Racial and Gender Report Card for College Sport," news release, Feb. 19, 2009, www.tidesport.org/RGRC/2008/2008CollegRGRC.pdf.

STRATEGY 8: THINK AND ACT ENTREPRENEURIALLY

1. Tom Lewis, "The Growing Gap Between Rich and Poor," *The Socialist Worker,* Aug. 1, 2003, http://www.globalpolicy.org/socecon/inequal/income/2003/0801gap.htm.

2. From Melvin Oliver and Thomas Shapiro, *Black Wealth/White Wealth* (New York: Routledge), 1995.

3. The collective buying power of African Americans, Asian Americans, Latinos, and American Indians is according to the U.S. Department of Labor and the U.S. Census Bureau.

4. United for a Fair Economy, "The State of the Dream 2004: Enduring Disparities in Black and White," http://www.racialwealthdivide.org/documents/StateoftheDream2004.pdf.

5. Associated Press, "Study Says White Families' Wealth Advantage Has Grown," Oct. 18, 2004, http://www.uwm.edu/~gjay/Whiteness/whitewealthgrows.html.

6. 1997 Economic Census data, cited in Boston Consulting Group, *The New Agenda for Minority Business Development,* June 2005.

7. Dennis Kimbro, http://knowledge.emory.edu/article.cfm?articleid=1086.<< must contact Kimbro to get full reference>>

8. U.S. Bureau of the Census, "Black-Owned Firms, 2002 Economic Census, Survey of Business Owners," issued Aug. 2006 . . .

9. Reynold et al, 2002 "The Entrepreneur Next Door" Kauffman Foundation http://www.kauffman.org/uploadedFiles/psed_brochure.pdf

10. Robinson, J., Mair, J., and Hockert, K. 2009 *International Perspectives on Social Entrepreneurship. London: Palgrave.*

STRATEGY 10

1. "African American Giving Comes of Age," *Business Week,* Nov. 29, 2004, http://www.businessweek.com/magazine/content/04_48/b3910417.htm.

INDEX

Abbott, Wayne, 53, 54
Adams, Alonzo, 74
affinity group, 167–168, 172
African-American leaders, xiii–xiv
African Americans
  churches, 240–241
  culture, 38–41
  vs. immigrant groups, 229
  professionals, 14
  progress in U.S., 8
African Diaspora, 52
Allen, Richard, 240
America, shape of, 239–240
American dream, 13
American Marketing Association, 172, 177
Amnesty International, 225–226
Apprentice (TV show), 1–3, 5, 11–12, 61–62
Arinzeh, Treena, 246
Armstrong, Thomas, 64
assimilation, 35
authors
  background, 25–27, 41–43
  gifts, 69–70
  mentors, 118
  relationships, 95–96
  on teams, 138
  website, 28

Bailey, Simon T., *Release Your Brilliance*, 75
barriers to advancement, overcoming, 14
BCT Partners, 142, 179
beliefs, 64, 75–77
Black business owners, 53–54

Black Data Processing Association (BDPA), 151
Black History Month, 40, 42
Black people, identity, 31
Black Wall Street, 53
Blackwell, Angela Glover, 204, 228
Blackwell, Marissa, 196–197
bodily-kinesthetic intelligence, 66
bonding social capital, 101, 132–133
Booker, Cory, 243
borrowed networks, 106–107, 109
bottom lines, double and triple, 159–160
Breaking Through (Thomas and Gabarro), 81–82, 84, 108, 121–122
Brownlee, Paula P., 249
Bryan, William Jennings, 256
Burt, Ronald, 103
business enterprise development, 199–200
business owner, 185, 193
Byrne, Robert, 251

Canada, Geoffrey, 227, 228
capacity building, 208–209
capitalism, 200
career aspirations, 9
career planning, 85, 174–175
  case study, 170–174
Carol's Daughter Holdings LLC, 183–185
Carson, Emmett D., 249
Carter, Majora, 224–225, 228
Carver, George Washington, 58
CASHFLOW Quadrant, 185–186
CBS Radio, 127, 259n
changing game, vs. redefining, 216–217

church, 240–241
citizenship, 55
civic ventures, 203–206
Civil Rights Act of 1964, 25
Civil Rights Era, 22
Civil Rights organizations, 241
civil society organizations (CSO), 205
Click: Ten Truths for Building Extraordinary Relationships (Fraser), 97
code switch, 96
Coleman, James, 100
collaborations, 154–155, 221
collaborative organizations, 144–146, 148
Comfort Zone, 48, 50–54
commitment, to excellence, 85
community investment, 178–182
community ventures, 203–206
competence, 73
conflict, between self-image and public image, 34
connectedness, 89–91, 254
cooperation, and synergy, 221
courage, 158
Covey, Stephen R., *The 7 Habits of Highly Effective People*, 89–91, 96, 217
craft mastery, 161
creativity, 55, 157, 220
C-suite, 7
Cuban Missile Crisis, 138–139
cultural background, 39
cultural capital, 52
cultural identity, 32
cultural reciprocity, 96
culture, 22

Davis, Shani, 4
decision makers, 83
dense networks, 105–106, 107, 132
destiny, 256
developmental relationships, 114–117
discipline, 64, 72–77
discomfort, 48, 49
discrimination, 60
disparities, progress in, 13
diversity, 93–96, 136, 138–139, 221
Dodd, Chris, 126
double bottom line, 159–160, 179, 200
double-consciousness, 35

DuBois, W.E.B., 35, 230

economies of scope, 224
Eden Organix, 207–208
Edmond, Alfred, 61
education, vs. wisdom, 110
Einstein, Albert, 87
Eliot, T.S., 48
emotional bank account, 96
employees, entrepreneurial mindset for, 193
End Racial Profiling Act (ERPA), 226
entrepreneurial mindset, 157–158, 160–161, 183, 191–193
entrepreneurship, 141, 159, 163, 186
    need for African-American, 188–191
    social, 200–203
    strategies for, 194–200
ethnic identity, 35
ethnic organizations, 177
evaluation criteria, 82
ever-changing game, 6–8
excellence, 58–86, 254
    congruence and, 78
    defining, 62–63
    facets, 63–75
    need for, 79–80
    strategies for demonstrating, 80–85
Executive Leadership Council, 173
existential intelligence, 68
experience, diversity of, 54–56
expertise, profiting from, 195
exposure to world, obtaining broad, 47, 48–57
Eyes on the Prize (PBS documentary), 43

failure, or success, 113
Fairchild, Greg, 190
faith, 77
family, 133
financial capital, 186–187
formal groups, 134
for-profit companies, social benefit of, 208
Fraser, George, *Click: Ten Truths for Building Extraordinary Relationships*, 97
Free African Society, 241
friends, 101, 133
funding, 208–209

Gabarro, John, *Breaking Through*, 81–82, 84, 108, 121–122
game, 6–7
 learning what it is about, 23–25
 mastering, 161–162, 214
 need to redefine, 8–9
 playing, 89, 214, 217
 two sets of rules, 59–62
 ultimate goal, 256
game redefinition, 14–16, 215–216
 approach to, 163–164
 meaning of, 251–252
 prerequisites for, 213–214
Gandhi, Mahatma, 214, 237, 249
gatekeepers, 83
gender identity, 32
Generation Y, 23
gifts, 36–37, 63, 64, 69
giving, 233–248, 251
Gladwell, Malcolm, Outliers, 73
glass ceiling, 5–6, 259n
globalization, 88–89
God, 37, 124–125
Goodwin, Doris Kearns, 138
Gordon, Bruce, 21
Granovetter, Mark, 101
Graves, Earl, 97, 190, 213
 How to Succeed in Business Without Being White, 85, 243
greatness, xiv, 253–258
Green Worker Cooperatives, 207
Greyston Bakery, 207
group mentoring, 119
group relationships, 131–134
groupthink, 138
growth and development, visual depiction, 48
growth paradigm, 209
growth ventures, 197–199
Growth Zone, 48, 50–51, 56
Grundy, Dallas, 179

Harlem Children's Zone, 227–228
Harper, Hill, 136
Harpo Productions, 211, 226–227
Hewlin, Patricia, 9–10
Hibbert, Lawrence, 179
Hill, Lauryn, 1

Hinton, Mel, 54
Hockerts, Kai, 201
home ownership, 8
Housing Act of 1968, 25
How to Succeed in Business Without Being White (Graves), 85, 243
Hughes, Cathy, 4
Hughes, Langston, 239
human capital, 64
Hunt, Rodney, 198
Huxley, Aldous, 57

identity, 9–10, 15, 25, 28–35, 37–41, 242, 249–250
identity negotiation, 30, 33–35
Imani (faith), 23, 39
immigrant groups, vs. African Americans, 229
Imus, Don, 4, 126
income streams, 192
influencers, 83
informal groups, 133
informal mentoring, 120
information sharing, 99
inner circles, 134–136, 142
innovation, 55, 202
instincts, 112
institution building, 210–212, 231–232, 238
intellectual capital, 137
intelligences, theory of multiple, 64–68, 80
interconnectedness, trends, 87–89
interdependence, 86
interpersonal intelligence, 66
intrapersonal intelligence, 67–68
intrapreneurship, 158–159, 163, 166–177, 178–182
investor, 186, 208–209

Jacobs, Jeff, 226–227
Jarvis, Rebecca, 1–3, 11
Jealous, Benjamin, 225–226, 228
Jewish community, 230
job applicants, 60–61
job assignment, 85
Johnson, Bob, 189
Johnson, Jeff, 79–80
Johnson, John H., 190
judgment, and wisdom, 111

Karenga, Maulana, 38
Kavanaugh, James, 225
Kelly, Gwen, 180
King, Martin Luther, Jr., 117, 237
Kiyosaki, Robert, *Rich Dad, Poor Dad*, 185
knowledge, 110, 195
Kujichagulia (self-determination), 23, 39
Kuumba (creativity), 39, 217
Kwanzaa, 23, 31, 38, 249–250

language, 32
leaders, xiii
leadership, 55, 140
learning your game, 82–84
legacy, 234–239
Lemelle, Zack, 82–83
Lewis, Reginald, 190
    Why Should White Guys Have All the Fun?, 235
Liberty Mutual Insurance Company, 248
Lieberson, Stanley, *A Piece of the Pie*, 230
life, legacy of, 237–239
lifestyle ventures, 194–197
light, legacy of, 235–236
linguistic intelligence, 64–65
logical-mathematical intelligence, 65
love, legacy of, 236–237

Maafa, 240
Mair, Joanna, 201
Majora Carter Group, LLC, 225
managing, vs. mentoring, 120–121
Mandela, Nelson, 236
Martin, Roland, 79, 132–133
mastering the game, 161–162
Media Matters for America, 259n
melting pot, 22
mentors, 109, 114, 116, 117–123, 171, 176–177
Merck & Co., 95
mergers, 200
meritocracy, 10–12, 15, 61–62
merits, or race, 59
The Millionaire Next Door (Stanley), 188
Mind, Body & Soul Enterprises (MBS), 141
"moment", 3–5
Monroe, Bryan, 128
morality, and discipline, 75–77

Morris, Gabriella, 181, 228
Moss, Otis, 242
MSNBC, 127
multiculturalism movement, 22
musical intelligence, 65–66

National Association of Black Journalists (NABJ), 128, 131
National Association of Hispanic Journalists (NAHJ), 129, 131
national identity, 32
National Philanthropic Trust, 247
National Society of Black Engineers (NSBE), 32–33, 44
naturalist intelligence, 67
nature and nurture, 37, 40
negotiation, 35
net worth, 12–13, 188
networks, 97, 98, 100
    bridging gaps, 102–107
    game-changing strategies, 107–109
    overcoming obstacles, 122
    strategic, 175–176
    types, 105–107
Nguzo Saba, 38
Nia (Purpose), 23, 39
nonprofit organizations, 203, 205–206

Obama, Barack, 4, 58–59, 228, 240, 255
One Economy, 207
openness, 25
opportunity, 13–14, 15, 217
organizational diversity, 93
organizations, 144–150
    broker collaborations among, 154–155
    identifying to address needs, 151–152
    identity-driven and issue-driven agendas, 152–154
    institutions as, 211
    strategies for involvement, 150–155, 177
Outliers (Gladwell), 73

Page, Clarence, 128
parents, role in identity development, 31
partnership, 141–143
passion, 36–37, 63, 70–72, 84–85, 157, 175, 203–205
"pay it forward", 248

peer mentoring, 119
peers, 31, 114
personal diversity, 93–96
personal identity, 30, 31–32
personal objectives, in strength in numbers, 149
A Piece of the Pie (Lieberson), 230
Pike, Albert, 234
playing field, 7
pluralist society, 22
Porter, Aldwyn, 179
"post-racial", 23
poverty rate, Black vs. white, 8
Powell, Kevin, 246
power, social identifiers and, 34
prejudice, reducing, 55
Price, Lisa, 195
    Success Never Smelled So Sweet, 183–185
pricing services, 139
pride, 40
privilege, social identifiers and, 34
pro-Black, 40
process and product of discipline, 73
professional identity, 32
professional landscape, 161
professions, African American under-representation, 165
protègè, 116, 117–121
Prudential Financial Inc., 181
purpose, 35–37, 45–46, 249–250, 251
    for African Americans, 37–41
    individual and collective, 242
The Purpose-Driven Life (Warren), 37, 46

race, 10, 21–23, 123–124
racial identity, 35
racial profiling, 225–226
Ramsey, Rey, 207
RealityTV.com, 12
redefining game, 213–214, 216–217
registered business, 186
relationships, 89–91, 92, 254
    building, 96–98, 161
    developmental, 114–117
    game-changing strategies for building, 107–109
    group, 131–134
    importance, 13

strength of, 99–101
Release Your Brilliance (Bailey), 75
religious identity, 32
resilience, 158
resourcefulness, 158
reverse mentoring, 119
Rheedlen Centers for Children and Families, 227
Riboud, Jean, 51
Rich Dad, Poor Dad (Kiyosaki), 185
roadmap for "ten strategies," 17
Robbins, Anthony, 76–77
role model, 115
Rosenberg, Sid, 126–128
rules of the game, xiii, 7, 15–16, 83–84
Russell, Herman J., 198
Rutgers University women's basketball team, 4, 126–128

Salk, Jonas, 38
Sankofa, 113–114
scale, 215, 216, 222–224, 228
scope, reaching, 222–224
seeing color in society, 92
self-determination, 45–46, 253
self-employed, 185, 193
self-mastery, 78, 161
services, pricing, 139
The 7 Habits of Highly Effective People (Covey), 89–91, 96, 217
small businesses, failure risk, 199
Smalls, Anthony Jerome, 180
social capital, 100–101
social enterprise, 209
social entrepreneurs, 159, 200–203
social identity, 30, 32–33
social intrapreneurs, 159, 178–182
social mobility, 229
social ventures, creating, 206–208
society, 12–13, 15, 92, 229–231
Southern Christian Leadership Conference, 241
sparse networks, 106, 108
spatial intelligence, 65
spiritual foundation, 41
spiritual identity, 32
spirituality, 124–125
sponsors, 109

Stanley, Thomas, *The Millionaire Next Door*, 188
stereotypes, 40–41
Steward, David, 225, 228, 255
strategic career management, 174–175
strategic mentoring, 121, 176–177
strategic networking, 175–176
strategic organizational involvement, 177
strategies
    for entrepreneurship, 194–200, 203–209
    for game changing, 16–19
    for giving, 244
    interdependence, 47
    for intrapreneurship, 168–177
    for organizational involvement, 150–155
    relationships, 56–57
strength in numbers, 126–131, 143, 149
Stringer, C. Vivian, 4, 129
success, xiii, 202, 253–258
Success Never Smelled So Sweet (Price), 183–185
sustainability, 202, 209
Sustainable South Bronx (SSBX), 224–225
Sweet Beginnings, 208
synergy, 215, 216, 219–222, 228

talents, 245–247
Tao Te Ching, 112
team mentoring, 119
teams, 137–140
technology growth, 88
theory of change, 202
Thomas, David, *Breaking Through*, 81–82, 84, 108, 121–122
Thompson, Don, 84–85, 228
time, giving, 245–247
tithing, 244
TJX Companies, 180

Todd, Thomas N., 165
touch, giving through, 248
transition mentoring, 119
treasure, donating, 247–248
triple bottom line, 159–160
Trump, Donald, 1–3, 5, 11–12, 61–62
trust, 94, 96, 102
Tubman, Harriet, 237

Ujamaa (cooperative economics), 39
Ujima (Collective work and responsibility), 39, 217
Umoja (unity), 39
United States
    population, 87–88
    and race, 21–23

volunteer service, 245–247

Walker, C.J., 183, 189, 235
Wal-Mart Stores Inc., 180
Warren, Rick, *The Purpose-Driven Life*, 37, 46, 251
Washington, Booker T., 243
weak ties, 99–101
wealth, 185–191
website, 19, 28
Westwood One, 259n
Why Should White Guys Have All the Fun? (Lewis), 235
Williamson, Marianne, 236
Wilson, Joe, 59
Wilson, Tod, 196, 197
Winfrey, Oprah, 189, 190, 211, 226–227, 228, 247, 255
wisdom, 110–113, 124
women, networks of, 109
work environment, inclusiveness, 94
World Wide Technology, 13, 225
worldview, 25

ABOUT THE AUTHORS

Randal Pinkett, Ph.D., MBA, was the winner of season four of *The Apprentice* and the show's first and only minority winner. He is the co-founder, chairman, and CEO of BCT Partners, a management consulting, information technology, and data analytics firm. Dr. Pinkett is based in Newark, New Jersey.

A sought-after speaker for corporate, government, and community groups, he has appeared on CNN, Fox, The *TODAY* Show, and *Nightline*. In 2009, he was named to NJ Governor Jon Corzine's official shortlist as a potential running mate for Lt. Governor. He is the author of *Campus CEO: The Student Entrepreneur's Guide to Launching a Multimillion-Dollar Business* and *No-Money Down CEO: How to Start Your Dream Business with Little or No Cash.*

Dr. Pinkett is a proud member of Alpha Phi Alpha Fraternity Incorporated, the National Society of Black Engineers, the National Black MBA Association, the Information Technology Senior Management Forum, and Black Data Processing Associates, and has served on the board of directors for the NJ Economic Development Authority, the NJ Public Policy Research Institute, the Nonprofit Technology Enterprise Network, and the National Visionary Leadership Project. He is also a national spokesperson for Autism Speaks, NJ Reads, Junior Achievement of NY, and the Minority Information Technology Consortium.

Dr. Pinkett holds five degrees, including a B.S. in Electrical Engineering from Rutgers University (where he competed on the track and field team as a high jumper and long jumper); an M.S. in Computer Science from the University of Oxford in England; and M.S. in Electrical Engineering, MBA, and Ph.D. degrees from MIT. He also received an honorary doctorate from NJIT. Most notably, he was the first and only African American at Rutgers to receive a Rhodes Scholarship and was the winner of NBC's hit reality television show, *The Apprentice*.

Born in Philadelphia and raised in New Jersey, Dr. Pinkett attends First Baptist Church. He is happily married to his wife, Zahara, and they are both proud parents of their daughter, Amira. Dr. Pinkett firmly believes that "for those to whom much is given, much is expected," so throughout his endeavors, he places great emphasis on his desire to give back to the community.

For more information visit: *www.randalpinkett.com* and ***www.redefinethegame.com***

Jeffrey A. Robinson, Ph.D., is an award-winning business school professor, international speaker, and entrepreneur. Since 2008 he has been a leading faculty member at Rutgers Business School, where he is an assistant professor of management and entrepreneurship and the founding Assistant Director of The Center for Urban Entrepreneurship & Economic Development. The Center is a unique interdisciplinary venue for innovative thinking and research on entrepreneurial activity and economic development in urban environments.

Dr. Robinson's research describes how business practices and entrepreneurship can be used to impact societal issues. He is particularly concerned about community and economic development issues for urban metropolitan areas in the United States and abroad. He is the author of books and articles on such topics as social entrepreneurship, African-American women in entrepreneurship, and Black unemployment. In 2007, he received the Aspen Institute's Social Impact Faculty Pioneer Award for his research, service, and teaching activities at the intersection of business and society.

Dr. Robinson is a sought-after speaker, author, and media commentator, appearing on *Dateline NBC* and *NBC Nightly News*, PBS, NJN News, NJBIZ, and in *The Star-Ledger* and *The New York Times*. He has been the keynote speaker at international events and conferences in China, Nigeria, and Endland and has been invited to present his work on six continents.

Dr. Robinson is co-founder and member of the Advisory Board of BCT Partners, based in Newark, NJ, a firm that provides management, technology, and policy consulting to non-profits, foundations, corporations, and various government entities as they plan and implement change strategies and improve organizational effectiveness. In 2008, Dr. Robinson and his wife Valerie Mason-Robinson opened Eden Organix, a day spa and retailer of organic skin and beauty products, in Highland Park, NJ, which was recognized by *New Jersey Magazine* as "one of the 10 best spas in the New Jersey."

Dr. Robinson has completed five academic degrees in the areas of engineering, urban studies, and management, including a Ph.D. in Management and Organizations from Columbia Business School. He lives in Piscataway, NJ, with his wife and their three children.